CHILD SEXUAL ABUSE AND

Child Sexual Abuse and the Churches

Patrick Parkinson

Hodder & Stoughton
LONDON SYDNEY AUCKLAND

British Library Cataloguing in Publication Data
A record for this book is available from the British Library
ISBN 0 340 63015 9

Printed and bound in Great Britain by
Clays Ltd, St Ives plc

Hodder and Stoughton Ltd
A Division of Hodder Headline PLC
338 Euston Road
London NW1 3BH

Contents

v

CONTENTS

CONTENTS

CONTENTS

Foreword

It is becoming clear that the sexual abuse of children is, sadly, neither new nor simply confined to Western countries. In view of the terrible damage it can inflict on people's lives, so vividly described in the many stories Professor Parkinson includes, the raised public awareness is welcome, if long overdue.

Public discussion is not without its dangers of course; particularly for those survivors of abuse who, in recounting their experiences, must necessarily recall their abuse and, to some extent, relive its trauma. What may make the pain of reopening old wounds worthwhile is the promise it holds for proper accountability and potential healing, not just for individuals but for wider society.

Sharing experiences which disclose one's vulnerability is strength, not weakness, and requires a courage which should be acknowledged. Part of its strength is to set in motion a process of disclosure and openness which makes public acknowledgment of abuse possible, indeed unavoidable. It is this which begins to dissolve 'the conspiracy of silence' previously surrounding child abuse and which was its strongest support. Prevention begins where denial (or plain ignorance) ends. Prevention is infinitely preferable to the acutely painful and damaging alternatives.

The discovery that much abuse takes place within the family has been a shock for many. A further shock has been the existence of abuse within the churches. Patrick Parkinson not only challenges us Christians to recognise this but provides very helpful, practical and balanced suggestions for both action and prevention. He also considers carefully the arguments for and against some of the controversial matters such as recovered memories, false memories, ritual abuse, and the relationship between forgiveness and repentance. I welcomed too his reference to the frequently neglected area of children abused by other children, often teenagers.

While he acknowledges that the official church responses are changing for the better, especially in Britain, he makes the chilling comment that 'in my experience of child protection in Australia, children are less likely to be protected in churches than in almost any other group in society'. If this is true it must cease, and his book will be a valuable contribution to those working for improvement.

In 1995, the House of Bishops of the Church of England produced a Policy on Child Abuse and new procedures for child protection, aiming to maintain the highest professional standards among clergy and laity who work for the church. The Policy carries the assurance that allegations of abuse will be taken seriously and specifies procedures; it requires disclosure of criminal, civil and other offences by clergy, lay staff and volunteers working with children, and accepts the intention of the Children Act 1989 that the welfare of the child is paramount. Training sessions are also available, in order to make this policy an effective measure for the protection of children.

Not surprisingly, this is an area where feelings run high, and it is hard for all of us to take a right, compassionate, just and healing action. This book is notable for its calm and measured analyses and guides to practical action, by one who cares and is informed. For this reason it is a valuable addition to the resources we have available for prevention and Christian response to one of the most serious wounds to people in our international society.

Jim Thompson
Bishop of Bath and Wells
Chairperson of the Church of England's
Board of Social Responsibility

Preface

Sexual abuse is a deeply hidden aspect of the lives of many church members. For some, it is a very unpleasant event from long ago which does not impact significantly upon their present experience. But for others, it is too painful to talk about in a fellowship group or prayer meeting even though the history of sexual abuse profoundly affects the person's life and faith. Because it is so hidden, many of us may be entirely unaware of the extent to which church members are affected by sexual abuse. Even more hidden in churches is the fact that so many practising Christians are perpetrators of sexual abuse.

My task, in writing this book, has been to take what is so deeply hidden in church congregations and to try to make it better known and understood. It has been an uncomfortable book to write, and it may well be an uncomfortable book to read. It brings into the spotlight a very dark side of human nature. It deals with issues which are painful. It is a book about children, but it is most certainly not a book for children. I have related a number of personal accounts of abuse at length. In so doing, I have not spared the reader from painful details where it was necessary to convey the dreadful reality of the victim's experience. If Christian books were given the same classifications as films, then this would definitely be in the adults-only category.

It is a book which I pray will be helpful to many, but which may also be disturbing, particularly for victims of sexual abuse. If you find that the book evokes very powerful emotions and traumatic memories of your childhood which you have not dealt with before, it is worth seeking assistance from a professional psychologist or counsellor who has experience in helping sexual abuse victims. Healing is possible, and God is gracious in bringing us to wholeness. But the first stage in the process of healing is to acknowledge the past rather than trying to bury it. If this book does bring back the past in a powerful way, then you may want to consider putting the book down for the time being. There is a right time and a wrong time to read this kind of book.

In telling individual stories of abuse, I have used pseudonyms in almost every instance to protect the privacy of the individuals. One asked me to use his real first name. The stories have been told largely without reference to place or time. Most, but not all the events happened in Australia, and the Australian events happened in many different parts of the country. Some of the stories relate to events which happened quite recently. Others happened as far back as fifty years ago. The stories which are told about churches come from a range of different denominations. All the names of perpetrators used are pseudonyms, and as far as possible, I have tried to omit all details which would give any indication as to their identity. The purpose of this book is not to accuse individuals, but to increase understanding of the issues. I have deliberately refrained from mentioning a number of cases in which the disclosure of sexual abuse by clergy has been very recent, as I do not want to comment on contemporary events which might be the subject of criminal proceedings or disciplinary hearings within denominations.

It is possible that readers may think that they recognise one person or another, but please do not jump to conclusions. Sadly, the story of sexual violence, exploitation and betrayal of trust has been repeated on countless occasions all over the world through the ages. The chances are that the story which is told may sound familiar, but has no connection whatsoever with people you know. If you think you recognise an individual account in this book, please respect the privacy of the people involved.

I owe a great debt of gratitude to many people who have helped me to write this book. In a general sense, I am indebted to the many professional colleagues with whom I have worked in Australia as part of an interdisciplinary group, and who have taught me so much. Working closely with social workers, child psychologists, therapists, paediatricians, police and prosecutors through the NSW Child Protection Council (and in other contexts) has been a great privilege. I have also benefited greatly from discussions with experts from many parts of the world who have visited Australia to speak at seminars and conferences.

I am also grateful to the many people who have shared with me their personal experience of sexual abuse. Because of my professional involvement in child protection, many friends, students and professional colleagues have entrusted me with their stories – stories which sometimes their close friends and even husbands or wives would be very surprised to hear. This knowledge has deepened my understanding greatly, and strengthened my conviction that we must do everything possible to prevent sexual abuse in the future and to respond more appropriately when it occurs.

In particular, I am grateful to the people who have allowed me to include their stories at length in this book. Their courage and honesty was refreshing, as was their openness in answering questions on matters which were very private. These stories convey so much that could not have been conveyed in any other way.

A number of people assisted me in particular ways in the course of writing the book. Helen Last and Neil and Thea Ormerod have been tireless advocates for those who have been sexually abused by clergy, and introduced me first to some of the people whose stories are told here. Rev. Dr Peter Horsfield's work on the issue of forgiveness and sexual assault was particularly helpful to me in writing the chapter on forgiveness. Bill Andersen, Sue Foley, Martin Goodwin, Elizabeth Jones, Neil Ormerod and Dale Tolliday were kind enough to read chapters of the book. Dale's knowledge and experience of running a treatment programme for perpetrators was an especially valuable resource. My wife Mimi helped in numerous ways, typing interviews, taking telephone calls, and coping for many months with an untidy study strewn with books and articles on sexual abuse. I am also grateful to the Faculty of Law at the University of Sydney which has facilitated my research and community involvement with the issue of child sexual abuse in numerous ways.

My particular thanks go to June Glanville, a wise and experienced professional counsellor, who read through the manuscript in its entirety and made many valuable suggestions from a therapeutic perspective. Any deficiencies in the manuscript are my responsibility alone. There would have been many more but for June's careful reading and thoughtful advice.

There are many others who have encouraged me and supported me along the way when I would rather have been writing about almost any other subject in the world. Sexual abuse is not a topic which can bring any joy to the heart. But it exists. It is widespread. It is happening in Christian families and in local churches. And a large number of survivors of abuse are in our churches. It is therefore an issue which no one who is in a position of Christian leadership can ignore.

Patrick Parkinson
Sydney, 1996

Chapter 1

Breaking the Silence

A Very Private Grief

Sexual abuse is a difficult topic to talk about. For some readers of this book, it will be difficult because child sexual abuse has been all too real and painful in their own experience, either because they were abused themselves or because someone close to them was sexually abused while growing up. For others, it may be a difficult subject because they have never known someone who was sexually abused, and cannot imagine how anyone could do such a thing to an innocent child.

Precisely because it is so difficult to talk about, sexual abuse has been a dark secret for a long time. For its victims, child sexual abuse tends to be a very private grief, and it is unlike any other. When we lose someone very close to us through death, people generally understand our grief and try to support us, even if sometimes they may not know quite what to say. But many survivors of child sexual abuse suffer in the loneliness of silence, grieving for the time when they first lost their belief that the world is a safe place and that adults will protect them from harm. For them, the experience of being molested as a child may be too shameful to talk about openly. It can be hard to explain even to close friends why these childhood experiences are still so distressing many years after the abuse has ended.

1

Yet in recent years, people have begun to speak out, and it is because of this that we have become aware of just how widespread child sexual abuse is, and how it occurs. People are now giving voice much more freely than before to a subject that has hitherto been taboo. Child sexual abuse is no longer a crime in which the conspiracy of silence continues to the grave. Now there are countless books on the subject of child sexual abuse – books to help people deal with their own history of abuse, books to help those who support them, books for professionals working in child protection, books for therapists helping the survivors of abuse. The topic is frequently discussed on talk shows and in magazines. The silence has been broken.

Everywhere, perhaps, except in our churches. For while things are changing, it is not an issue that is addressed very often in Christian circles. When I look back on twenty years as a committed Christian, being involved in well-known evangelical churches and Christian organisations both in Britain and Australia, I can scarcely recall any mention of the subject as an issue for Christians. Adultery, perhaps, premarital sex, certainly. But the sexual abuse of children? If it is part of our consciousness at all now, it is probably because of the attention that the issue has received in secular society. There is a tendency to treat it as a problem 'out there', and not one which deeply affects Christians. Yet in every church there will probably be people who carry this private grief, and there may be many others who are not in our churches because they find that the church, by failing to address the issue, is remote and irrelevant to their needs.

Because child sexual abuse is not often discussed in Christian circles, many adult survivors of abuse find that the church is not a safe enough place for them to be able to talk about their experiences. There is thus a zone of silence within which many Christians hide this aspect of their lives, despite the profound effect the abuse has had upon them. There are survivors of sexual abuse in our churches – many of them. And unless we understand something of their pain, and the struggle of faith which so many experience, we will not be able to minister to them with the love and grace of Christ, and to be sensitive to their needs as members of the church family.

Perpetrators in the Churches

Are there also perpetrators in our churches? This question is a very threatening one. For if it is hard for us to understand how any human being could sexually exploit a child, it is even harder for us to believe that a Christian could do so. How could a follower of Jesus sin so grievously? And how could God allow it? Facing up to these questions requires us to face up to some difficult questions about our faith. It also requires us to face up to the possibility that children might be sexually abused in our churches – in Sunday schools, in youth groups and on church camps, and even in the minister's office.

In recent years, the newspapers have been full of stories of ministers and priests who have been charged with sexual offences against children, often involving multiple victims over a number of years. A very large number of the court cases have involved priests within the Catholic Church. There are many reasons why the Catholic Church should have had so many cases of child sexual abuse in the past. That Church has long played a prominent role in running schools and orphanages. Certain religious orders have been particularly involved in the care and education of children, and these Orders are a natural gravitation point for men with paedophilic tendencies. The tradition in Catholic churches of having altar boys who are left alone with the priest, combined with the particular authority and trust that the priest enjoys in the life of the congregation, have also created the conditions in which numerous opportunities for sexual abuse can occur.

It would be foolish to believe, however, that child sexual abuse is a problem peculiar to Catholicism or that it is a consequence of the Catholic tradition of celibacy, even if this is a contributing factor.[1] The reality is that child sexual abuse occurs in all Christian traditions, and there is nothing in Scripture which should lead us to believe that, because a

3

person has made a public profession of faith in Christ, he or she is not capable of abusing children. Thus far, the problem of child sexual abuse among evangelical Christians has not attracted much media or public attention. Many cases have been dealt with very quietly. The head of a missionary society resigns 'for personal reasons' after being convicted of sexually abusing a teenage boy, and goes into Christian work in another part of the country where his past will not be known. A popular minister with extensive involvement in youth ministry first goes from parish to parish sexually abusing young women, and then, after being forced to resign from his denomination, becomes actively involved in youth ministry as a layman in another denomination. A revered minister with a strong reputation as an evangelist retires early from ministry after secret deals are done with the police. The Church muffles the screams of the children in order to avoid damage to its reputation.

The Churches' Responsibility

We need to face this issue of child sexual abuse which has been hidden from us for too long. Under God, we have a responsibility to the survivors of sexual abuse in our churches. The Spirit of Jesus is the Spirit that commissions God's servants to bind up the broken-hearted, to comfort all who mourn, and to bestow upon those who grieve a crown of beauty instead of ashes, the oil of gladness instead of mourning, and a garment of praise instead of a spirit of despair.[2] The Church could have an important ministry to women and men who have been sexually abused if ministers and other leaders were better able to understand what it is that they have been through and the ways in which it has affected their life and faith. Conversely, Christians may be Job's comforters to those who have been abused – or worse – if they are insensitive to victims' needs and experiences.

We also have a responsibility to the children in our churches today. We have a responsibility to try to prevent it from happening and also to respond appropriately if a child discloses sexual abuse to us. It is very hard for children to break the silence about sexual abuse; and when they entrust us with that knowledge, we need to take action.

And yes, we also have a responsibility to the offenders; for the message of the gospel is that even the worst of sins can be forgiven. Christ did not die to save us only from little sins.

PART I

UNDERSTANDING CHILD
SEXUAL ABUSE

Chapter 2

The Nature and Prevalence of Child Sexual Abuse

What Is Child Sexual Abuse?

Child sexual abuse is the involvement of dependent, developmentally immature children and adolescents in sexual
activities with any person older or bigger, which they do
not fully comprehend, and to which they are unable to give
an informed consent. This definition emphasises a number of
things. First, sexual abuse may be committed not only by
adults. Often the perpetrators of sexual abuse are teenagers
who take advantage of the vulnerability of much younger
children. Sexual abuse is an abuse of the power and authority
that come from being older and bigger than the child victim.
Second, the 'consent' of the victim is irrelevant. For that
reason, many people speak in terms of 'child sexual assault'
to emphasise the criminality and the non-consensual nature
of the offence. Not all sexual abuse of children is the result of
coercion. Often, sex offenders prey upon needy and vulnerable children who come from difficult home situations and
who crave love and attention. Sex with such children is a
form of exploitation. Their consent is not a mature and
informed consent, and it does not provide a defence to
criminal charges.

Sexual abuse takes a number of different forms. Often it is
talked about as if all the victims of child sexual abuse have

similar experiences and suffer similar effects. The reality, however, is quite different. Abusive behaviour includes a range of activities, such as exposing oneself to a child, engaging in voyeuristic activity, showing the child pornographic pictures, fondling a child's genitalia, getting the child to fondle the adult's genitalia, oral-genital contact, masturbation, penetration of a girl's vagina with a finger or object, vaginal intercourse and anal intercourse. For some children, the sexual abuse occurs just once, and the perpetrator is an acquaintance or a stranger. For others, the abuse continues regularly for years and the perpetrator is a parent or other trusted adult. For some children, the sexual abuse is accompanied by violence; for others it is coerced by threats; others still are enticed into sexual activity, and may become willing and active participants in the sexual relationship. For some, the sexual abuse begins before they are of school age. For others, it begins when they are about nine or ten years old, and for others still after puberty.

As the nature of sexual abuse varies from one case to another, so does the harm it causes. For some children, the most traumatic aspect of the abuse is not the sexual abuse but the violence that accompanies it. Children who are the victims of violent sexual attacks are often threatened with serious harm if they ever tell a living soul. For other children, the worst aspect of the pain is the impairment of their self-esteem as they blame themselves for what has happened or are persuaded by the perpetrator that they are bad or worthless. For others still, the pain derives from a sense of betrayal – that a parent, teacher or youth leader who was in a position of trust and was meant to protect them betrayed that trust and used them for his sexual gratification. This sense of betrayal can be both deep and debilitating even if the child rejected the perpetrator's sexual advances and no physical contact occurred. For other children again, the greatest harm comes from the turmoil of emotions, as fear and sexual pleasure, shame and gratification are intermingled. Children who are sexually abused sometimes experience sexual feelings, since this is a physiological response to sexual stimulation; but that

10

tends to be coupled with shame and confusion in both the short and long term.

For other children still, some of the greatest long-term damage is caused by being introduced to sexual relations when they are far too young to be able to cope with sexual feelings and experiences. In the Song of Solomon, the wise advice is given: 'Do not arouse or awaken love until it so desires.'[1] Many abused children have sexual love awakened much too early; they may find it difficult to cope with their awakened sexuality, and, sometimes, to have a caring relationship with another person which does not involve sexual intercourse. Thus it is not uncommon for child victims of sexual abuse to become promiscuous as adults and to have difficulty in establishing stable relationships with the opposite sex. Others respond to the sexual abuse in the opposite way, and cannot readily include sex in a loving relationship because they associate sex with being used.

Although not all children are adversely affected by episodes of sexual victimisation, many victims find that it affects their whole lives. Sexual abuse is frequently associated with severe depression, mental illness and marital problems twenty, thirty, even forty years after the abuse has ended. Sexual abuse robs some children of their childhood, and it can never be restored to them.

Incest

Some of the worst effects of sexual abuse occur when children are the victims of incest. The Bible condemns it in the strongest of terms. The Lord is recorded in Leviticus 18:6 as giving the instruction through Moses: 'No-one is to approach any close relative to have sexual relations. I am the Lord.' The command is amplified and explained through the rest of that chapter. The proportion of girls who have sexual intercourse in childhood with a father or stepfather is probably about 1.5 per cent of the female population, and many more girls are the victims of sexual molestation by a parent figure in a way that does not involve penetration.[2] Children who are sexually abused within the family experience not only the invasiveness, shame and confusion of the sexual abuse itself, but also a nurturing environment that is seriously toxic to their emotional well-being. Roles within the family become utterly confused. Daughters are seduced into becoming lovers, or coerced into being unwilling sexual partners for their father. Other distortions within family life occur from the secrecy surrounding the abuse. The child is often emotionally isolated both from the mother and from brothers and sisters. Children's experience of incest is not only an experience of sexual exploitation, but of an utterly defective pattern of nurture.

When a parent or a step-parent is the abuser, it is particularly difficult to find ways of avoiding the abuse. The perpetrator is a constant presence in the household, and can usually find myriad different ways of molesting the child without being detected. The child may also find it very difficult to speak out. It is sometimes the case that children who are being sexually abused by their father or stepfather try to tell the mother or another trusted adult, but for various reasons they are not heard.

Sarah's Story: Abuse at Bedtime

Sarah grew up in a working-class family. Her parents were pillars of their local Anglican church. Her father was at various times a church-warden, Sunday school superintendent and leader in a boys' association. Her mother was also active in the church, a member of numerous committees and of organisations such as the Rotary Club. It was a respected family. Women in the church would tell Sarah that she was lucky to have such a nice Christian family.

The reality was very different. From the time she was eleven until she was sixteen, Sarah was sexually abused almost every night by her father. Typically, he would come into her bedroom as she went to bed and undress her, fondling her breasts and genitals while he did so. The sexual abuse did not occur only in the bedroom. Sometimes he would come into the bathroom as well, since there was no lock on the door to keep him out. He would fondle her while she was bathing, and after she got out of the bath. Sometimes he would have an erection and press himself against her body or pull her body against his.

Sarah coped with the abuse in a number of ways. While the abuse was happening, she would sometimes dissociate, looking down on herself as if it was happening to her body, but not to 'her'. After the nightly ritual was over, she would often bang her head until she fell asleep.

She tried to get him to stop the abuse, but he threatened that the whole family would break up if he were to stop, and if that happened, she would be responsible. The abuse ended when she was sixteen only because by this time she had found ways of avoiding him. When she was seventeen she left home.

Sarah told her mother what was happening about a year after the abuse started. The mother said that she would tell her husband never to do it again, but he continued with the abuse. When Sarah asked her mother for a lock on the bathroom door, her request was refused.

There was only one person outside the family whom Sarah ever told about the abuse while it was happening, and that was her minister, an Anglican clergyman. He did not believe her. After all, he knew the family. The father was a respected leader of the congregation. He told her that 'things like that don't happen in families like yours', and walked away. It was a comment he remembered for the rest of his life, and regretted. Years later, when he was in hospital dying of cancer, he asked to see Sarah. He told her he should have listened to her when she told him about the abuse. He asked for her forgiveness.

The abuse has had a marked effect on Sarah's life. From the ages of eighteen to thirty-one, she was on antidepressants. She has been in and out of therapy. Despite all that she has been through, Sarah remains a convinced Christian, but it has not been an easy path for her.

Sarah's story is typical of so many daughters who are sexually abused by their fathers. It was a household in which the father ruled the roost. He was a jealous man. He did not like Sarah to have friends, and was especially hostile to the idea of her having boyfriends. Despite his own involvement in the life of the church, he was not keen even on her going to the youth fellowship. Not only was Sarah kept isolated from her peers, she was also unable to turn to her brother and sister for friendship and support. Theirs was not a close family.

This pattern of isolation is quite common in families where sexual abuse is occurring. The father maintains the secret of the abuse by ensuring that the daughter is kept isolated from her peers and does not form strong emotional attachments to others with whom she can talk about what is happening. Sarah's father tried to lock up his daughter, not for her protection, but for his.

Is Child Sexual Abuse a Recent Phenomenon?

Child sexual abuse is not a new problem. Sadly, the sexual exploitation of children has a very long history. For example, we can read about the sexual abuse of boys in the classical literature of the Greeks and Romans, where young boys were often spoken of as a source of sexual pleasure. In the Roman Empire, boy brothels were popular in a number of cities. Anal intercourse with young boys was also quite common.[3] The Didache, a commentary on the Gospels from the early second century, indicates its awareness of the problem when it provides a trilogy of prohibitions concerning the sins of the flesh: 'Thou shalt not commit adultery; thou shalt not commit fornication; thou shalt not seduce young boys.'[4]

Sexual abuse of girls also has a long history. In the Bible we read of numerous incidents of sexual violence against young women. In 2 Samuel 13, we are told of the rape of Tamar by her half-brother Amnon. Both of them were children of King David. Tamar was a virgin, and probably just a young teenager, since girls married at a much younger age then than they do now. Amnon took the advice of his friend and uncle about how to make sure he was alone with Tamar. He then seized her and raped her. The Bible records that after he did so, he 'hated her more than he had loved her'. Amnon had believed that he loved Tamar, but he loved her only with his eyes, and his feelings towards her after he had raped her showed his real contempt for her. Before the rape, he had gone to great lengths in order to be alone with her. After the rape, he wanted to get her out of his presence as quickly as possible. Although most translations record that Amnon told his servant, 'Get this woman out of here', in fact the word 'woman' does not appear in the Hebrew.[5] She is just 'this', a thing to be used and then discarded. Amnon's sexual gratification lasted a moment, but Tamar's shame lasted a lifetime. It is a story which has repeated itself for countless other young women throughout history.

This is not the only incident of child sexual abuse in Scripture. Twice in the Old Testament, in Genesis 19:8 and Judges 19:24, we read of fathers offering their virgin daughters to violent men because it was better for them to rape a daughter than to rape the male guests under the father's roof. Lot offered his virgin daughters to the men of Sodom for sex. In Judges 19, a similar story is told of an old man in Gibeah who welcomed a Levite and his concubine into his home. When some men pounded on the door of the house and demanded that he bring out the guest so that they could have sex with him, the old man offered instead his virgin daughter and the guest's concubine. It was a 'disgraceful thing' to rape an honoured male guest, but a teenage daughter or the man's concubine was fair game (vv. 22–4). In some ancient cultures, daughters were loaned to guests as an act of hospitality,[6] and the Old Testament stories may reflect these cultural practices in the Middle East during this period.

The sexual exploitation of children has also been a feature of society in more recent times. In Britain, child prostitution was common in the eighteenth and nineteenth centuries and often chloroform was used to stifle the children during intercourse. Demand for young girls was motivated in particular by fear of sexually transmitted diseases such as syphilis. Experienced prostitutes were more likely to be diseased. It was only the persistent campaigning of reformers, including Bramwell Booth of the Salvation Army, that led to measures being taken, towards the end of the nineteenth century, to stamp out the practice of sex with children.[7]

Child sexual abuse is also known to be a feature of many other societies. In India, for example, the early sexualisation of children has historically been a common practice of the culture. An old Indian proverb stated: 'For a girl to be a virgin at ten years old, she must have neither brothers nor cousin nor father.' Girls were often married to much older males well before the age of twelve in order to protect them from the advances of other males around the home. These marriages were consummated when the girls were still very young.[8] Child prostitution has been common in Asian societies for centuries, and temple prostitution of both boys and girls was institutionalised in many societies. Child prostitution continues to be a major problem in Asia, the trade in children being made more lucrative by the numbers of child sex tourists visiting from Western countries.

How Widespread Is Child Sexual Abuse?

Despite its prevalence throughout history, it is only in the last few years that we have become aware of how widespread the sexual abuse of children is. The most reliable indications of the extent of sexual abuse in our society come from studies of adults who have been asked about their experiences as children. Necessarily this means that they are describing the extent of sexual abuse many years ago, but there is little reason to believe that the present generation of children is more or less in danger of abuse than previous generations.

These surveys of adults about their childhood experiences of sexual abuse all indicate that the number of children having such experiences is very high indeed. Nonetheless, the surveys have produced varying estimates of the extent of sexual abuse, depending on how the survey defined sexual abuse, the age limit taken, the way the survey was conducted and many other factors.[9] A common pattern is that the more in-depth the interview is, the higher the rates of sexual abuse that are revealed. Child sexual abuse is not easy to talk about to strangers. Interviewers cannot conduct such surveys in quite

16

the same way as pollsters can ask about voting intentions or preferences for fast food.

In defining sexual abuse for the purposes of such surveys, it is important to distinguish between sexual abuse and childhood sexual exploration. At the same time, one cannot focus only on unwanted or coerced sexual experiences. The fact that a child was a willing participant in the sexual activity with an adult does not make it all right. A common way of defining sexual abuse for the purposes of these surveys therefore is to define it as sexual contact between a child and an adult or a minor who is at least five years older, whether the child was a willing participant in the activity or not.

The Sexual Abuse of Girls

Almost all surveys have indicated that the sexual abuse of girls is very common. One of the best-known surveys done of sexual abuse in childhood was the landmark research conducted by David Finkelhor in the United States towards the end of the 1970s.[10] Finkelhor interviewed about 800 students about their experiences of sexual molestation as children. He defined sexual abuse as a sexual incident involving a child under thirteen and a perpetrator who was at least five years older, or involving a young person between thirteen and sixteen years old and another person who was at least ten years older.

Finkelhor asked questions about all forms of sexual experience in childhood including situations where men exposed themselves, or made sexual advances which the child rejected. He found that 19 per cent of the women reported some such experience in which the perpetrator was an adult or a much older adolescent. When Ronald and Juliette Goldman conducted a similar survey of nearly a thousand students in Australia, they discovered even higher rates of abuse.[11] Nearly 28 per cent of the women responding to the survey reported some sort of abusive sexual experience before the age of sixteen.

SEXUAL ABUSE OF GIRLS: AUSTRALIA

Child under 13, partner over 18	14.8 per cent
Child under 13, partner under 19 but at least 5 years older	8.3 per cent
Child 13–16, partner at least 10 years older	4.5 per cent
Total	27.6 per cent

Source: Goldman and Goldman, 1988.[12] Sample 603 females.

Although these were both surveys of college students, the results are broadly consistent with surveys which have been conducted of the general population. In a major study of 930 women in San Francisco with whom in-depth interviews were conducted, Diana Russell found that 28 per cent of all women reported some kind of experience of sexual exploitation or abuse before the age of fourteen, and 38 per cent by the age of eighteen.[13] This included unwanted sexual contact involving other children of the same age. A similar study in the Netherlands found that 33 per cent of the women interviewed had been victims of sexual abuse involving genital contact before the age of sixteen.[14] In another national survey conducted by an in-depth telephone interview in the United States, researchers found that 27 per cent of the women reported some experience before the age of eighteen which they regarded as sexually abusive.[15]

The levels of sexual abuse in Britain might perhaps be a little lower. One large survey of the general population, conducted in Britain by a market research agency, found that 12 per cent of women reported a sexually abusive experience before the age of sixteen. The researchers had reason to conclude, however that these figures were probably an underestimate.[16] Other studies in Britain, while not using a nationally representative sample, have discovered levels of child sexual abuse comparable to the surveys in the United States and Australia.[17]

RELATIVES WHO ABUSE GIRLS: UNITED STATES OF AMERICA

	No.	Per cent
Uncle	48	25.8
Biological father	27	14.5
Brother	26	14
First cousin	26	14
Stepfather	15	8
Grandfather	8	4.3
Other male relative	28	15
Female relative	8	4.3

Source: Adapted from Russell, 1983.[18] 186 cases.

About 90 per cent of all sexual abuse of girls is by men. There are some cases where both a male and a female abuse girls together. Sexual abuse of girls by other females acting alone is uncommon, although it does happen.

Only a minority of abusers are relatives, although most victims know the perpetrator. Diana Russell's study of 930 women in San Francisco found that a total of 29 per cent of the perpetrators of abuse were relatives, 60 per cent were known to the victims but unrelated to them and 11 per cent were total strangers. The amount of sexual abuse by uncles and stepfathers is particularly high. More fathers abuse their daughters than stepfathers, but fewer children grow up with a stepfather. In Russell's study, one sixth of girls who had grown up with a stepfather were sexually abused by him. In contrast, one in forty girls was abused by her natural father.[19] Similar results have emerged from other studies.[20] The lack of a biological relationship is significant. There is such a thing as an incest taboo. Men who bond with their biological children from birth are much less likely to look on them sexually than men who come into the household at a later stage and who have no such attachments to the child. Furthermore, stepfathers often have difficulty finding what their role should be within the family, where they do not have the same authority as natural parents. It is more likely therefore that they will look on a child within the household as an object of sexual gratification than if they were well-established in a parental role towards the child.

It is clear from these surveys, then, that the level of sexual abuse of girls is quite horrifying. However, these surveys need to be put into perspective. The majority of the experiences reported on by adults were isolated incidents. While single instances of sexual abuse (such as rape) can cause the most severe trauma, a single instance of sexual contact by an adult without coercion may not have particularly negative effects. Children can be very resilient. In particular, children with high self-esteem and good family support are able to deal with a great range of unpleasant and distressing experiences in childhood. Nor did all respondents in these surveys view their sexual experiences negatively. Some even had a positive view of their experience, although this is a more common reaction for boys than girls. Of course, the fact that a person does not perceive the experience as negative does not necessarily mean that the sexual contact was harmless. Sometimes, the extent of the harm resulting from sexual abuse is apparent only many years later. Such delayed harmful effects are most likely where there was no therapeutic intervention in the immediate aftermath of the abuse.

These statistics demonstrate how great is the social problem of sexual abuse of girls by males. One thing that differentiates the churches from many other sectors of society is their clear teaching on sexual morality. Most churches are uncompromising in their message that premarital sex and adultery are contrary to God's law, and the message is often repeated in talks on sexuality in youth groups and high school Bible study groups. But little tends to be said in churches on the issue of sexual molestation. Perhaps boys don't need to be told that it is morally wrong to make lewd sexual remarks to girls, to force a girl to undress, to grope at her breasts or to coerce her into engaging in sexual acts. But all the evidence suggests that this form of sex education is sorely needed in the churches. At the heart of the Ten Commandments is the notion of respect – respect for God, respect for parents, respect for life, for marriage, for property, for truth. Jesus modelled in his life the importance of respect for women, and Paul's instruction to Timothy was to 'treat . . . younger women as sisters, with absolute purity' (1 Tim. 5:1–2). To the Thessalonians, Paul wrote that 'you should avoid sexual immorality . . . each of you should learn to control his own body in a way that is holy and honourable, not in passionate lust like the heathen, who do not know God' (1 Thess. 4:3–5). Perhaps our lack of teaching on sexual purity in relations with girls and women reflects our lack of awareness of the extent of the problem.

Sexual Abuse of Boys

Although the majority of victims of child sexual abuse are girls, a substantial number of boys are abused as well. Indeed, where young children are abused, there are almost equal numbers of boy and girl victims.

From all the evidence available, it is a reasonable estimate that about one tenth of boys are sexually abused in childhood. David Finkelhor's survey of students in the United States, and Ronald and Juliette Goldman's similar survey of students in Australia, both found that 9 per cent of boys had been sexually abused in childhood, a significant proportion of them by adolescents at least five years older.[21] The national survey conducted in Britain by a market research organisation found that 8 per cent of males reported being abused.[22] Other surveys have reported figures as high as 16 per cent.[23] Although boys are abused less frequently than girls, a greater percentage of boys experience on-going molestation. The Goldmans' survey in Australia, for example, found that 48 per cent of the boys reported that their abuse lasted more than a week, in contrast to 28 per cent of the girls.

SEXUAL ABUSE OF BOYS: AUSTRALIA

Child under 13, partner over 18	3.1 per cent
Child under 13, partner under 19 but at least 5 years older	5.4 per cent
Child 13–16, partner at least 10 years older	0.5 per cent
Total	9 per cent

Source: Goldman and Goldman, 1988.[24] Sample 388 males.

In the past, the sexual abuse of boys has been well known, but its seriousness and criminality have not been adequately understood. The priest engaging altar boys in sexual activities, the dirty choirmaster and the perverted scout leader all were part of our consciousness a generation ago, but these things were not seen as particularly harmful. They were just quirks of adult sexuality, and, for boys, a rite of passage. Few people thought much more of it. Like homosexual relations between senior boys and junior boys in boarding schools, it was something that many people were aware of, but few talked about. If complaints were made about priests abusing altar boys, the priest was quietly moved to another parish.

The attitude that the sexual abuse of boys does not matter, and the idea that men should be macho, confident and comfortable with their sexuality have made it especially hard for many men to acknowledge openly the abuse they experienced as children. Boys tend to grow up with an ethic of self-reliance. Admitting to pain, weakness and vulnerability does not come easily. When boys are abused by men, as mostly they are, they often have to struggle with the stigma of homosexuality. If they talk about an experience of molestation, they run the risk of being labelled 'queer'. Many boys come to think that there must be something wrong with them to have attracted the attentions of a paedophile, and the experience of sexual abuse generates considerable self-doubt. Acknowledging sexual abuse by men is difficult, but talking about sexual abuse by women is almost impossible. Who would believe them? In our culture, we tend to assume that men are in control of sexual encounters. Sexual abuse is thus particularly difficult for boys to speak about.

In recent years, the scandal of the sexual abuse of boys has particularly affected the Catholic Church. A considerable number of priests have been jailed for sexual molestation in the United States and elsewhere.[25] There are some indications that the numbers of priests in the Catholic Church who abuse boys is out of proportion to the numbers of paedophiles targeting boys (rather than girls) in the community. This emerges from a major study conducted in the United States. A questionnaire was sent to more than seven thousand adults who were randomly selected from the mailing list of a religious publishing house which had a mainly Catholic readership.[26] 25 per cent responded. Most of the people who completed the questionnaire were priests, nuns or actively involved in lay ministry within the Catholic Church. Of the men in this sample 3.3 per cent said that they had been sexually abused by a priest before the age of eighteen. The corresponding figure for females reporting abuse by priests was 1.7 per cent. Nearly twice as many men as women reported abuse, whereas in the general population girls are at least twice as likely to be sexually abused as boys, even if incestuous sexual abuse is excluded. This finding is supported by another study, which compared child molesters who were Roman Catholic clergy with non-clerical child molesters, and found that the clergy were more likely to abuse boys, and the boys tended to be older than was the case with the non-clerical child molesters.[27]

The problem is as great with members of religious orders. In numerous countries around the world, stories have been emerging of the most horrific sexual abuse occurring in Catholic orphanages and boarding schools run by religious orders, the same few brothers apparently molesting large numbers of boys in their care, generation after generation. In Western Australia there have been numerous accounts of physical and sexual abuse in the boys' homes run by the

Christian Brothers. Many of the children who were physically and sexually abused in these homes were child migrants from British orphanages who had been sent to Western Australia in the belief that they would have a better life there.[28]

While it is only in recent years that men who grew up in the homes have spoken extensively about the sexual abuse they experienced, many allegations did surface at the time. The sexual molestation of boys was regarded as a serious matter. Nonetheless, in some instances, those responsible felt that they had to be satisfied with a brother's categorical denial, and on other occasions the boys simply were not believed.[29]

If the stories about the Christian Brothers have attracted the most public attention, it is clear that the sexual abuse of children did not occur in one religious order only. There are many such cases involving institutions run by other religious congregations.

Bob's Story: Humiliation in the Dormitory

When Bob was nine years old, he was sent away to a boarding school run by a very respected religious congregation. His family lived in a remote part of Australia, and the only education he had received before that time was from the School of the Air, a classroom run through radio communications. Education was very important to his parents, and they sacrificed much to send Bob to this school.

Boys in those days were housed in very large dormitories. In Bob's dormitory, there were fifty boys. The man in charge of this dormitory was Brother John, a young brother in his early twenties. A few months after he first came to the school, Bob began to realise that he was being singled out by Brother John for special attention. Until then, another boy had been Brother John's favourite, but curiously, when the attention turned to Bob, the other boy showed no signs of jealousy or ill-will.

For three or four years, Brother John sexually abused Bob in this dormitory. Once the lights were turned out each night, he would sit on the chair beside Bob's bed, and put his hands beneath the bedclothes in the darkness. He would rub and fondle Bob all over his upper body. After a while, he began to fondle Bob's genitals as well. Each period of molestation lasted some ten to twenty minutes, after which Brother John left. The abuse happened in the darkness, but the other boys were aware of it. This was confirmed to Bob by another member of his dormitory with whom he discussed it some twenty-five years later.

The worst aspect of Bob's experience was not what happened under the bedclothes, but what happened in front of all the other boys. After the boys had gone into the washroom each night, Brother John would sit on a chair waiting for them to come out. Often, he would grab Bob and make him sit on his lap and cuddle him. Bob was utterly humiliated by this, since he was singled out. Only occasionally did Brother John do this with any other boys. Sometimes the boys would help Bob by telling him when to leave the washroom to avoid having to walk past this man.

Brother John also loved shower duty. It was a rotated duty, but he ensured that he was assigned to it very regularly. While other brothers would just wait outside the shower room and read, intervening only if there was a lot of noise, Brother John would stay in the shower room, watching the boys while they were naked.

In all the years that Bob was abused, he never told an adult what was happening. He did not tell his parents because it would have broken their hearts. His mother had never been to school herself, and was very keen indeed to see him go to the school despite the difficulties of transport from such a remote outback location. Brother John also enforced the silence. Regularly, he would ask whether Bob intended to tell anyone. Bob answered 'no'. On one occasion, when he said 'I don't think so', Brother John was enraged. He dragged Bob out of bed, put him in the washroom and pinned him against the wall, shouting at him that the abuse was Bob's fault. Bob was rescued by another boy who came into the washroom to go to the toilet, and defied Brother John's attempts to get rid of him. That interlude was sufficient to calm Brother John down. The other boys found it difficult to say anything to Bob about the abuse, but in their own quiet ways they did what little they could to protect him.

When Bob was thirteen an incident occurred that must have made Brother John realise that Bob was not going to keep quiet much longer. He stopped abusing Bob and instead turned his attentions to another young boy.

In the long term, Bob's sexual abuse has had some serious effects. For years, he would have something of a nervous breakdown at about the same time each year. He would wake up in the middle of the night with a nightmare about a brother standing over him. For about a week afterwards he would be very depressed, even suicidal. Therapy has helped to diminish the severity of his reactions, but they still continue. To this day he says that the worst aspect of the abuse was the humiliation arising from the fact that all the other boys knew what Brother John was doing. In his adult life, Bob has found it very hard to trust people. As he put it: 'When the world is full of people pretending to be virtuous who aren't, you start to believe that no one is moral. The message you are given is that if you are bigger and stronger you can do whatever you like.'

Bob has also found it hard to have intimate relationships because of the difficulty in taking the final step of trusting people. He has been active in the gay community for many years, and has had one long-term relationship, but he prefers sex without love and love without sex, since it is difficult for him to put sex and love together.

Child Sexual Abuse as a Sin

The sexual abuse of children is a violation of Scripture's general commands about the misuse of the gift of sexuality. It is not merely a sexual sin, however. It is not wrong just because the Bible condemns both adultery and fornication. It is not wrong merely because the perpetrator has acted upon feelings of lust. To abuse children sexually, perpetrators have

THE NATURE OF CHILD SEXUAL ABUSE

to violate many other commandments. There is the sin of covetousness, of wanting something that cannot be yours. There is the sin of deceit, since sexual abuse is an activity that can thrive only in squalid secrecy. There is the sin of violence, since in many cases, perpetrators use force to make children do what they want.

Child sexual abuse is also an abuse of power. While normal adult sexual relations are based on mutual affection and agreement, child sexual abuse involves a great differential in power between the offender and the victim. That power may be used to gain sexual gratification through coercion, or it may be used in a more subtle way. Children tend to be brought up to obey what adults tell them. They may have been taught to be suspicious of strangers, but not of fathers, uncles, school-teachers or scout leaders. The perpetrator uses the power, authority and status of adulthood to entrap children in sexual activities which they are too young fully to comprehend.

Above all, child sexual abuse is a sin because of its devastating effects on children. Jesus had a special concern for children. When the disciples considered him too busy to attend to them, he said: 'Let the little children come to me, and do not hinder them, for the kingdom of heaven belongs to such as these' (Matt. 19:14). One of the many effects of sexual abuse is that it hinders some children from entering the kingdom of God. Children who have seen love distorted and abused can find it harder to believe in a God of love. Children who have had trust betrayed may find it harder to trust again. Child sexual abuse is a sin against the soul of children as well as the body.

On another occasion, Jesus called a little child to him and said: 'Whoever welcomes a little child like this in my name welcomes me. But if anyone causes one of these little ones who believe in me to sin, it would be better for him to have a large millstone hung around his neck and to be drowned in the depths of the sea' (Matt. 18:5–6). The word 'sin' in this translation is literally 'stumble'. The Living Bible, appropriately perhaps, paraphrases it as causing 'one of these little ones who trust in me to lose their faith'. What can have caused

Jesus to issue such a dire warning? Perhaps in that moment, knowing the secrets of men's hearts, and being able to see what was so deeply hidden from the view of others, Jesus was thinking of all the children who would be caused to stumble and to lose their faith by the sexual exploitation of adults.

Jesus took the protection of children seriously. And so should all those who follow him.

Chapter 3

The Perpetrators of Sexual Abuse

How could someone sexually abuse a child? Why would they want to do so? And can Christians abuse children? These are important questions for an understanding of the nature of sexual abuse and in determining how to respond to perpetrators within the churches.

What Sort of People Abuse Children?

Those who sexually abuse children come from all walks of life and socio-economic backgrounds. Although many years ago there were experts who used to talk about the profile of a sex offender against children, it is now accepted that no such profiles are reliable. There are no clear identifying characteristics of abusers[1] other than that the great majority are male. Nor is there much substance to the idea that child molesters tend to be dirty old men hiding in the bushes of a public park. Most perpetrators of sexual abuse are under fifty and know both their victims and their families. Many abusers are related to their victims, and outside the family circle the danger of sexual abuse is more likely to come from a neighbour, teacher or youth leader than it is from an unknown assailant.

It would, of course, be much easier for us to recognise perpetrators of sexual abuse if they had horns and tails. But perpetrators are not thinly disguised devils. We could not pick them out in a crowd. They are human beings like all of us. They marry and have children, they work with us in our places of employment, they are our neighbours and friends. We meet them on social occasions and they come to dinner. They may even be members of our family. 'They' are 'us'.

And they are in our churches. They sing with us in the church choir or music group. They offer themselves as candidates for the ministry or they volunteer to run the youth group and they do so with a complex mixture of motivations. They may of course be wolves in sheep's clothing, but it may equally be the case that their belief in God is genuine and their faith in Christ is a real one, even though there is an area of their lives – their sexuality – which is assuredly not under the lordship of Christ. The reasons why they sexually exploit children are complex, sometimes the product of circumstances both in the past and the present; but they are not merely victims of circumstance. Acknowledging all the factors which may lead people to abuse children should not distract us from holding people accountable for their actions – as God does.

The Dark World of the Sex Offender

A major factor which has led churches in the past to minimise the seriousness of child sexual abuse has been our lack of knowledge about why some people abuse children. There are a great many myths which have thus grown up about perpetrators. Recent research on the dynamics of sex offending against children has given us far more information than we had in the past about deviant sexual behaviour, and indicates that it is a grave mistake to minimise the seriousness of any form of sex offending.

One myth that seems to have been widely believed in some church circles is that the sexual abuse of children is just an inappropriate response to stress, which can be resolved by sending the offender away for a period of quiet prayer and contemplation. This assumes that the offending behaviour was just a temporary aberration, and that the offender is not habitually engaged in the sexual molestation of children. All the evidence now suggests, however, that the number of offences that come to light could well be a small fraction of the number actually committed by each perpetrator and that, for a large percentage of sex offenders against children, offending is a deeply ingrained and habitual behaviour which they will find very difficult to change.

Sex Offending as Habitual Behaviour

In the past one barrier to our learning more about sex offending behaviour was the problem of obtaining reliable information. Most of the early research was done on convicted sex offenders in prisons, and while these studies revealed that most offenders would admit to more offences than they had been charged with, there are good reasons why they should understate their degree of dangerousness. Even if confidentiality was offered, there was a risk that information would be recorded on prison files and could be used against them in an application for parole.

Consequently, the most reliable information is likely to come from offenders who are not under coercion, and who have less incentive to minimise their admissions. One such study was done in the United States in the mid-1980s using voluntary clients at clinics seeking help for a range of 'paraphilias'.[2] A paraphilia is a generic term for any form of deviant sexual behaviour. Abel and his colleagues interviewed 561 men in the study including men who were primarily seeking treatment as child molesters, rapists, exhibitionists, voyeurs and others. The researchers took elaborate precautions to ensure that the men were certain of absolute confidentiality. Their records were completely protected from being seized by any law enforcement agency in the United States. The interviewees were also promised that the information gained would assist the researchers to treat the patients. The men were thus able to be much more honest about their sexual proclivities.

This research demonstrated that many sex offenders commit a very large number of offences. The researchers examined the numbers of offences and the number of victims per offender for incest offences and non-incest offences separately. Some offenders committed both incest and non-incest offences so, as will be discussed further below, these are not two distinct groups of offenders.

Men who abused their own children or grandchildren generally admitted to doing so on a very large number of occasions.

INCEST OFFENDERS:
NUMBERS OF VICTIMS AND OFFENCES

	No. of offenders	Mean no. of victims	Mean no. of offences per offender
Abuse of girls	159	1.8	81.3
Abuse of boys	44	1.7	62.3

Source: Abel et al., 1987.[3]

Men who abused children outside of the family were likely to have multiple victims, some having hundreds of victims. Men who abuse boys are especially likely to have large numbers of victims if their offending careers are not interrupted and if they are not treated successfully.

Of course, not all offenders have this number of victims. These figures are an average of all the participants in the survey. It is probable that the sample of men who abused boys included some very long-term and hard-core offenders. Other researchers have likewise found that men who abuse children often have multiple victims, even if the figures are not as high as in Abel's study. For example, another study of sixty-seven child molesters found that they admitted to more than 8,000 sexual contacts with 959 children, a mean of fourteen victims each.[5] In this group, the number of victims per offender ranged from one to 200.

NON-INCEST OFFENDERS: NUMBERS OF VICTIMS AND OFFENCES

	No. of offenders	Mean no. of victims	Mean no. of offences per offender
Abuse of girls	224	19.8	23.2
Abuse of boys	153	150.2	281.7

Source: Abel et al., 1987.[4]

It is clear, then, that men who have a lot of access to children without attracting suspicion over a long time have the potential to wreak havoc in the lives of hundreds of victims. In the United States, the Catholic priest James Porter was one such man. As a priest in the 1960s and early 1970s, it was normal for him to be a visitor at the local Catholic school, to be alone with altar boys and to have countless other opportunities to spend time with children. Families trusted him because he was a priest. They taught the children that priests were handpicked by God. It was only in the early 1990s that the story of his predations was made public. About two hundred people made complaints. As has been the case with so many other abusing priests, James Porter's superiors were aware of some complaints of sexual abuse at the time.[6]

Incest Offenders and Child Molesters

Are all people who abuse children capable of committing multiple offences with numerous victims? Years ago, the answer would have been given that a distinction should be drawn between a compulsive child molester such as Father Porter and incest offenders. It was thought that, unlike child molesters who abuse children outside the home, incest offenders weren't likely to be a danger to other children. Incest offending was considered to be the consequence of certain family dynamics. Most attention was paid to father-daughter incest. The father was assumed to have used his daughter to meet his sexual needs because they were not being met by the mother. The mother might be chronically sick, or just uninterested in having sex with her husband. The daughter thus became the substitute sexual partner for a father who wanted heterosexual adult relations and the mother went along with this incestuous relationship because it was better for that to occur than to see the whole family break up. In this sense, the mother was regarded as a co-conspirator with the father and often the siblings also were assumed to be aware of what was happening and for the same reason were parties to the secrecy.

It has now become clear that while this explanation of incest offending might partially explain the dynamics of abuse in some families, it is not an accurate explanation for most cases of sexual abuse within the family. While in some cases mothers do know what is going on and allow it to continue, in the great majority of cases the mother has no idea of what is happening until the abuse comes out into the open. As will be seen in the next chapter, offenders are usually very careful in the way that they operate, and have numerous means of ensuring children's silence. In cases where the mother is told by the daughter, the fact that she does nothing to prevent it may well be because she feels powerless to prevent it rather than because the daughter is being sacrificed for the sake of marital stability. Homes where sexual abuse occurs are frequently characterised by very dominant fathers who enforce their rule firmly – and, if necessary, by violence.

Furthermore, while there are times when only one child in the family is abused by the father, and that child is the oldest daughter, it is more common for fathers and stepfathers to abuse more than one child. They may indeed abuse every child, male and female, and, years later, offend against the grandchildren as well. In a sample of sixty-five cases of incest involving biological fathers, one researcher reported that about four-fifths of the men molested more than one child, and in a third of the cases, the man also had victims outside of the home.[7]

This is not at all unusual. Abel and his colleagues, in their interviews with 561 men, found that while some offenders engage in incestuous abuse only and others offend against children outside their family only, many men do both.[8] In their research, they found that 49 per cent of the men who engaged in the incestuous abuse of girls also targeted girls outside the family, and 12 per cent also abused boys both inside and outside the family. Thus the fact that a man has been known to offend against his own children only does not mean that he is safe to be around children outside the family. An incest offender may well abuse other children.

Child Sexual Abuse and Other Sex Offences

Men who sexually abuse children may also commit other sex offences. For example, Abel and his colleagues found that 25 per cent of the men who targeted girls outside the family also committed rape. Of the sample, 29 per cent were exhibitionists and 14 per cent were voyeurs. Similarly, the fact that a man is arrested for a sex offence against an adult does not mean that he is not also a danger to children. Of the 126 rapists in their study, 44 per cent had engaged in the extrafamilial sexual abuse of girls, 14 per cent in the extrafamilial abuse of boys, and 28 per cent in exhibitionism. Many rapists were also incest offenders. Similar results have been found in other studies.[9]

It follows that if a man is caught offending in other ways, for example as a flasher or a peeping Tom, there must at least be some concern that he is capable of more serious sex offences. The offence for which a sex offender is caught is unlikely to be the only offence he has committed. It may not even be the only *type* of sex offence which he has committed.

Christians Who Abuse

Being a Christian, or even a minister or priest, does not automatically take away the desire to molest children any more than it automatically relieves men of homosexual tendencies or the temptation to commit adultery. All the evidence suggests that there are a lot of offenders who have strong religious convictions. Indeed, the number of perpetrators with criminal convictions for child sexual abuse who have some church involvement is alarming. In one secular treatment programme in Australia which takes offenders who have abused their own children or stepchildren, more than half of all those referred to the programme had themselves, or were married to someone who had, some active involvement in a church.

One expert on sexual abuse in the Catholic Church, himself a priest and a psychotherapist, has estimated that 2 per cent of the population of priests in North America are paedophiles abusing pre-pubescent children. About three-quarters of them have a preference for abusing boys. A further 4 per cent become sexually involved with adolescents, the gender preference being more evenly distributed among this group.[10] Similar estimates are not available for Protestant churches. It is noteworthy, however, that in a survey of 643 adult members of the Christian Reformed Church in the United States, 3 per cent admitted to some form of sexual abuse of others (including of adults).[11]

From all the evidence, it is clear that sex offenders are found in all denominations and in people of many different theological persuasions. The indwelling grace of Christ may act as a brake on a Christian's tendency to sin by enlivening his or her conscience. But ultimately Christ does not take away our free will, and Christians, as well as others in the community, suffer from deviant sexual urges, and choose to act on them.

Roseanne's Story: The Bible-believing Minister

Roseanne grew up in a devout Christian family. All her family were members of a small Christian denomination which had its origins in the Holiness Movement. The church held strictly to its belief that the Bible was the divinely inspired and infallible Word of God. Family devotions, Bible reading and Christian music were part of normal family life. Sunday was always a strict Sabbath day. It was a day for sitting quietly and reading the Bible, rather than a day of leisure. If the children wanted to make a noise they had to go outside. It was also a close-knit church. Marriage outside the church was strongly discouraged.

Roseanne's family migrated to Australia in the 1950s. At first, they were temporarily housed in a migrant camp. As soon as Roseanne's father could earn enough money, he bought his own block of land and put a tent on it. He began working there to build a double garage in which the family could live while he built a house for them. He asked for his eldest daughter to come and live with him in the tent in order to be his 'cook and bottle-washer'. She was approaching thirteen at the time.

Once the double garage was built, the rest of the family came to live there. There were three girls and one boy in the family. Roseanne was the second youngest. The boy slept in a separate alcove, while the three girls were together in one 'room' of the garage separated from the parents only by wardrobes. The two younger ones were in bunk beds and the eldest girl had her own bed. Almost every night, in the middle of the night, the father came to where the girls slept. The main focus of his attentions was the oldest daughter. He used to get into bed with her, and Roseanne would hear them making noises.

When Roseanne was seven or eight years old, she also became the subject of her father's attentions. He would fondle her and put his finger in various body parts. He would also guide her hand to caress him. Her mother was often at shift work during odd hours and he would carry Roseanne into his bed. He said it was a 'game', and he was checking on her proper physical development. Roseanne had no framework for knowing whether the sort of contact in which her father engaged was right or wrong. However, she was often frozen with fear when she heard his footsteps in the night. She was sworn to secrecy by his threats and by her own sense of guilt and shame. Her father's behaviour made her feel dirty and used, but it was the only form of affection she knew. Her mother seemed to her to be emotionally and physically distant, and rarely touched the children.

While all this was going on, the father started his own church. Church members in this denomination believed that if there was no congregation in a place to which they moved, then it was their duty to start one. In this way, Roseanne's father became a founding minister. It was a small congregation. Eventually they built their own church building. Roseanne's father was highly respected in the church and community. He continued to work in a full-time secular job as well. Roseanne worshipped and loved her father. He was a very hard worker and a hypnotic preacher.

When Roseanne was about twelve, her sister was sent away from home after she told her boyfriend about the sexual abuse. The older sister was in her late teens by this time. The boyfriend, a young man in his early twenties who had dedicated himself to Christian ministry, had the courage to confront the father about the abuse. His stand was in vain. The father denounced the boyfriend for telling such wicked lies about him and had him thrown out of the church. He sent his oldest daughter off to live with relatives overseas, and she remained there. Roseanne listened to many bitter fights, tears and arguments because her sister did not want to leave, but both parents had decided that she must go. The reason given to the church members for her sudden departure was that she was to study at the Christian college for their church overseas, as there was no such opportunity in Australia.

This left Roseanne as the oldest child living at home, and she became the main object of her father's sexual attentions. One day, he told her that they needed to go over to the church building to get something. Alone with his daughter in the back of the church, he violently raped her. She was only twelve or thirteen years old, and was seriously damaged by the rape, both physically and emotionally. She remembers running from the church, torn and bleeding, to the nearby toilet and locking herself in for some time. Her father dragged her out and drove back home, telling her to 'stop snivelling' and behave like a good girl, or else.

The father tried to silence her, threatening her that she would be treated the same way as her older sister if she told anyone. He also assured her that no one would believe her. His prediction proved to be true. Roseanne did try to tell her mother. Her response was to say, 'How dare you say such a thing about your father, who is a Man of God and a minister!' She called Roseanne a liar and a prostitute, which appeared to be a way of telling her simultaneously both that it wasn't true and that, if it was, it was her fault for being a slut. The mother finished by giving Roseanne a severe hiding. The pain was such that she was unable to attend school for several days. Violent punishment was common in their family where the parents firmly believed that to 'spare the rod was to spoil the child'. Her mother made her ask her father and God for forgiveness for telling vicious lies and making up stories. Roseanne got the message that she was to blame for the rape. It was a guilt that she carried with her for many years. She was also haunted by a recurring nightmare of the tall shadow of a man standing at the foot of her bed, coming to molest her.

With all these experiences, it was very difficult for Roseanne to listen to her father preaching twice every Sunday about holiness, sexual purity and forgiveness. He taught that children should honour their father and mother, and that they should be loving and obedient. He taught that girls had to be virgins until marriage. The hypocrisy was very difficult to take.

Roseanne did, however, manage to stand up to her father. She knew she had to do something to prevent the abuse occurring again. She prepared her speech in advance, trembling with fear inside because she believed that he might kill her if she confronted him. She told him that what he was doing was not right – it was not in the Bible. She threatened to tell another church member. This violent and oppressive man started crying and begged her not to tell anyone. He never touched her again.

The burden of guilt and shame weighed heavily upon Roseanne during her teenage years and beyond. She felt the only right and proper course of action to atone for her terrible sins was to go into full-time Christian service. For years, she tried to block the horrific experience of the rape out of her mind, but she could not forget it entirely. Indeed, when she had a gynaecological examination in her early twenties, the doctor remarked, 'My God, who did this to you!' However, it was not until she was in her thirties that the word 'incest' began to have any meaning for her, and even then she still blamed herself for what had happened. She was careful not to let anyone get too close to her, whether it was her sisters or girlfriends. No one must know the awful truth. Not even her husband knew. A lesson she had learned early in life was to trust no one (especially not in the family or the church). It was only after the death of both parents and her own divorce that she was finally able to confront the traumatic childhood experiences, and with professional help to begin the difficult journey towards inner healing.

Women Who Abuse

Another of the myths that have been challenged by recent research is the idea that females are rarely guilty of sexual abuse. While the great majority of offenders are male, it is clear now that many women also abuse children. It has been estimated that about 20 per cent of the abuse of boys and about 5 per cent of the abuse of girls is by females.[17] There remains some debate about the numbers of female offenders. Certainly, very few cases of sexual abuse by females are reported. Of sex offenders who appear in British courts 3 per cent are women and of these, half are charged together with a male co-defendant.[13]

One reason why so few cases are reported may be that it is easier for women to cover up sexually abusive activities in a camouflage of nurture. Bathing and dressing children, comforting them by allowing them to sleep in the mother's bed, hugging them and kissing them are all natural maternal activities. Although fathers do all these things as well, inappropriate behaviour by mothers is less likely to be noticed, or to be interpreted as sexual. Another reason why sexual abuse by women is likely to have been under-reported in the past is a reluctance to believe that it could be true, or even a denial that it does occur.

This has been so even with child protection workers. It was after all the women's movement that played such an important role in raising consciousness about the problem of child sexual abuse in the first place. Child sexual abuse was thought to be inherently tied up with male sexuality and male power.

Although experts in the field have acknowledged the problem of sexual abuse by women, the explanation often given is that these women were accomplices to men, and were under their power and control. In some cases women who abuse are certainly the submissive collaborators of male perpetrators, but this accounts for some female offenders only. While it is rare indeed for women to be solitary sexual predators, befriending children and luring them into sexual activity, it is not so uncommon for women and older girls to engage in the sexual abuse of family members and other children they know. A lot of sexual abuse by females is when teenage sisters use younger siblings or other close relatives for purposes that go far beyond normal sexual exploration. Female babysitters also may abuse the children in their care. Another context in which sexual abuse occurs is when young women in their late teens or early twenties coax pre-pubescent boys into having sexual intercourse. They may rationalise the sexual abuse as stemming from a wish to teach the boy about sex, or from 'love' for the boy.

Such abuse by women can have serious and long-lasting

effects. There are indications that the behaviour of some men convicted of rape and other forms of sexual assault on women may be linked to unresolved feelings of anger and rage at having been sexually molested as children by females. Studies of imprisoned adult rapists have demonstrated that of those who reported such childhood sexual molestation, a significant number were molested by women. In one study of 348 adult sex offenders, 31 per cent had been sexually molested as children, and in 41 per cent of these cases the perpetrator was female.[14] In another study of eighty-three men who were imprisoned for raping women, 59 per cent had been molested by women when they were children, and more than 82 per cent of the abuse involved intercourse.[15]

Women who abuse are very likely to have been abused themselves as children. In one study, more than 90 per cent of female perpetrators reported having been abused as children.[16] One woman who sought help after molesting her own sons has told the story of how she was sexually abused for years, often sadistically, by her own mother.[17] It was a devout Christian family, who attended church regularly. Both parents were respected professionals. The mother, according to her daughter, was the ring mistress of a sex circus, whipping her children into performing acts which they tried to resist, sometimes penetrating the daughter with objects, sometimes having sex with her oldest son, and at other times helping him to rape his sister. The mother claimed that her actions were normal – her own parents had done it to her.

Sex Offending in Childhood and Adolescence

About half of male offenders first begin sex offending against children when they are adolescents,[18] and it is significant that much reported sexual abuse is by older adolescents. In a study of reported child sexual abuse in Liverpool, England, about one-third of all cases of child sexual abuse involved a perpetrator of seventeen years or younger.[19] Adolescents between thirteen and seventeen years of age were more than twice as likely to be investigated for sexually abusing a child as any other age band. Because the onset of much sex offending is in adolescence, adolescent treatment programmes are a very important strategy for reducing the incidence of child sexual abuse in the community. If early intervention takes place successfully with young offenders then the long-term benefits to the community are enormous. Sex offending by adolescents which involves abuse of younger children should not be dismissed merely as teenage experimenting or as a behavioural problem. It is important to take it seriously in order to prevent much more serious problems later.

Some offenders begin their careers even before they reach adolescence. Bill Anderson's book *When Child Abuse Comes to Church* recounts the story of the havoc that was caused in his congregation by the discovery that many young children had been abused, many of them in the nursery at church and on other occasions on church premises. At least sixty-four children had been molested and physically abused. Both boys and girls had been raped, sodomised, beaten and forced to participate in oral sex. The perpetrator of this abuse was an eleven-year-old boy, Donald, who had often helped out in the nursery and, together with his older siblings, babysat free of charge for many of the church's young families.

It seems incredible to describe an eleven-year-old boy as a child molester. Many people have a deeply ingrained desire to want to explain this sort of behaviour away as some form of sex experimentation, or perhaps a passing phase of anti-social aggression. Bad behaviour, certainly, but not sexual abuse, and certainly not a matter for the criminal courts.

Nonetheless, Donald is not alone in violating so many young children. There are a small number of children who engage in seriously abusive behaviour towards other children before reaching puberty, and for whom expert therapeutic intervention is essential. Awareness of the nature and extent of this problem first developed in the late 1980s through work published in the United States. Toni Cavanagh Johnson reported on a study of forty-seven boys seen in a specialist treatment programme for children under thirteen. These were children who were engaging not in normal sexual exploration but in sexual molestation of other children. She also reported on thirteen cases of girls aged between four and twelve who were engaging in similar kinds of abuse. Sexual behaviours included penetration of the vagina and anus, oral copulation and simulated intercourse. She found in these studies that nearly 50 per cent of the boys were known to have been sexually abused themselves.[20] Every one of the girls had been sexually abused.[21] In one case, an eight-year-old girl who was highly sexualised had manipulated her eleven-year-old brother into engaging in intercourse. He didn't want to do so. She said, 'I like his penis so much 'cause it's small and doesn't hurt like my dad's.'[22] Subsequent research has demonstrated that all these children who engage in sexual molestation have either been abused sexually or come from chaotic and dysfunctional home situations in which there are physical abuse and other serious problems.[23]

Children, of course, often engage in a great deal of exploration both of their own bodies and the bodies of other children. This exploration is intermittent and balanced by curiosity about other aspects of their environment. Generally, this exploration is consensual. When children under the age of twelve start to become preoccupied with sexual arousal or involve other children in acts involving vaginal or anal penetration, there is cause for serious concern and professional assistance is needed. Expert assessment is needed to determine the reasons for the child's behaviour, and to engage the child in appropriate therapy. However, it is not appropriate to assume that pre-pubertal children are just very young 'offenders'. Many of the children who are molesting other children or engaging in inappropriate sex play are acting out the effects of the abuse on themselves. They are not motivated by a desire for sexual pleasure, but engage in sexual activity as a means of trying to alleviate feelings of anger, anxiety and confusion. In some cases, this takes the form of a re-enactment of previously distressing experiences.

A small number of pre-pubertal children who persistently engage in seriously abusive behaviour should be regarded as very young sex offenders. These are children whose sexual behaviours have a compulsive, impulsive and aggressive quality.[24] They use bribery and trickery or coercion to involve other children in the sexual behaviours. These are very damaged children for whom expert and intensive treatment is essential to prevent them from developing into long-term sex offenders.

Why Do People Sexually Abuse Children?

There is no one explanation for the causes of child sexual abuse.[25] Child molesters may or may not have a definite sexual orientation towards children rather than adults. It used to be very common to classify sex offenders into fixated and regressed offenders.[26] Fixated offenders are said to be those who have a primary sexual attraction towards pre-pubescent children, while regressed offenders have a primary sexual orientation towards adults, but also abuse children episodically. This clear division into two categories of offenders is falling into disuse now, since experts working with offenders have found that many offenders are somewhere in between the two groups.[27] Some offenders, indeed lack a clear sexual orientation to either children or adults, and are sexually abusive towards both.[28]

Many incest offenders have a primary heterosexual orientation towards adults, and are married men who have an active sexual relationship with their partners. Some men are prepared to use any female for sexual gratification, whether she is an adult or a child. Such men find it difficult to treat women as equal partners in a relationship, and use sex to fulfil their own sexual needs, not as part of a mutual commitment to pleasing each other. These men are as likely to pressure or force their wives into unwanted sexual intercourse as to coerce a daughter. They tend to dominate the household, and may well use violence to enforce their rule. Unfortunately, such ideas which men have about 'owning' their wives and children are reinforced by Christian teachings about headship which, if misunderstood, can give such men a biblical justification for dominating their families and requiring submission by other family members.

There are other sex offenders against children who are socially and sexually inadequate. These are men who are sexually attracted to adult women, but who lack the social skills to form adult relationships and abuse children as a nonthreatening substitute for sex with an adult. These men may be developmentally delayed, and have not learnt the social skills necessary to relate appropriately to their own age group. Their sexual experience with children is likely to be the only sexual experience that they have had.[29]

There are also other men who offend against children because of antisocial tendencies. Their sex offending, against both children and adults, is part of a broader pattern of criminal behaviour. Large numbers of both rapists and child molesters commit other non-sexual crimes as well.[30] These men may not be responding to a particular sexual orientation towards children, although they may be sexually aroused by violence generally. Their sex crimes may well be opportunistic acts committed while carrying out a burglary or some other offence.

Some offenders are episodic offenders only, while others habitually target children to abuse. Those who are episodic offenders only may turn to children at times of particular stress in their lives. A common excuse made for offending behaviour is that the man was experiencing stress at the time or had marital difficulties; but everyone experiences times of great stress, and many have marriage difficulties, including sexual difficulties. Most do not react to these pressures by sexually abusing children. Thus stress is not the cause of the problem nor the reason why abuse has occurred. It may, however, be a catalyst for the man to offend at a particular time.

Sexual Attraction to Children

While the sexual abuse of children is not linked solely with a sexual orientation towards children, a great many offenders do nonetheless have a primary sexual attraction to children.[31] They are sexually aroused by pictures of children. They use child pornography. They fantasise about sex with children, not only in masturbation but even while having intercourse with an adult woman. They gain an erotic enjoyment from having children as companions, and they have established a pattern of acting upon their sexual feelings.

It is not clear why some people develop a sexual attraction to children. Paedophilia is a diagnostic term for those who have such an attraction, and it is listed as a paraphilic disorder in the American Psychiatric Association's *Diagnostic and Statistical Manual of Mental Disorders*.[32] There it is said that paedophilia 'refers to the recurrent, intense sexual urges and arousing fantasies, of at least six months' duration, involving sexual activity with a pre-pubescent child.' There is some evidence that, for many paedophiles, the patterns of interest in children begin in early childhood, and that the sexual interests and tendencies of children who grow up to be paedophiles are different from those who grow up to have normal heterosexual patterns.[33] One theory about the development of sexual orientation is John Money's theory of the 'lovemap'. The lovemap is a picture or template in each person's brain of the idealised lover, and of what constitutes an erotic relationship with that person. Money believes that the lovemap usually forms in the first eight years of life. A paedophilic orientation may be the result of genetic factors or neurochemical factors as the brain develops in the womb. Alternatively, it may be that the development of the lovemap is affected at a critical stage by what the child learns, sees and experiences.[34]

Whatever the reasons for developing a sexual orientation towards children, the decision to act upon that orientation is a choice which the offender makes. As with all sexual desires, there is a difference between having feelings and acting on them. Sexual abuse of children may in many cases be the result of the perpetrator's sexual desires, which he or she finds very hard to control. This, however, is only an explanation, not an excuse.

When the Abused Become Abusers

Another of the myths surrounding child sexual abuse is that perpetrators abuse solely because they were sexually abused themselves as children. There are certainly many offenders who have themselves been victims of sexual abuse as children. In some prison populations, the majority of those imprisoned for abusing children report that they were sexually abused themselves. The most reliable estimates now are that no more than 30 per cent of perpetrators of sexual abuse were victims of sexual abuse themselves when they were children or adolescents.[35] It is sometimes the case that offenders abuse children who are much the same age as they were when they were abused, thus replicating their childhood experiences, but changing their role from victim to perpetrator.

There are many theories about the reasons why victims become offenders. One theory is that offenders are trying to overcome their own victimisation by taking on the powerful role of an offender, rather than the powerless role which they had experienced as victims. The offender in a sexual abuse situation is in a powerful and directing position, and this may alleviate intense feelings of inadequacy. Other explanations concern the way in which sexual arousal towards children may be 'transmitted' by experiences of victimisation. Being sexually abused introduces children to sexual relations and sexual feelings at a much younger age than is normal for children. Boys normally engage in a lot of sexual exploration, often with each other. But male victims of child sexual abuse experience much more than this. They are introduced to anal and oral sex, as well as sensual genital fondling, which is generally different to the kinds of experiences that boys have either alone or with their peers. It is possible that boy victims come to associate sexual arousal with child-adult sexual relations, and so, as adults, find themselves attracted to children. They become 'stuck' in an association between children and sexual pleasure.

Another explanation is that childhood sexual experiences, pleasant or unpleasant, provide the content for early masturbatory fantasies, and so the person becomes conditioned to sexual arousal in the context of child-adult relations. Children can become sexually stimulated even by distressing sexual experiences. For example, one man has told of being sexually abused first in a Catholic institution and later in a foster-home. In the Catholic institution run by an order of brothers, he was one of a number of victims of Brother X. Later, when he was placed in a foster-home, his foster-mother regularly abused him sexually while her husband was away. As a teenager, he was obsessed with sex and masturbated very frequently. To his horror, he found himself fantasising about sex with Brother X, even though he had been terrified of this man and hated the abuse. He also fantasised about sex with his foster-mother. Later, as an adult, he molested his young sister-in-law, his own daughter and an eleven-year-old boy.[36]

If some perpetrators of child sexual abuse were themselves sexually abused as children, there are equally a great many who were not. Furthermore, it is far from inevitable that if someone has been sexually abused as a child, he or she will grow up to be an abuser. There are comparatively few female offenders, but a very large number of girls who are victims. Even among male victims of sexual abuse, the great majority do not grow up to offend. Many victims of child sexual abuse have a strong commitment to child protection as adults. There is some link between being abused and then going on to abuse, but it is certainly not destiny.

Sex Offending and the Conscience

For people to abuse children, they must overcome the internal inhibitors to offending. For committed Christians, the power of conscience ought to be a particularly strong inhibitor. After all, those who have committed their lives to the service of Christ have the indwelling presence of the Holy Spirit. Paul wrote in his letter to the Romans: 'You however, are controlled not by the sinful nature but by the Spirit, if the Spirit of

God lives in you. And if anyone does not have the Spirit of Christ, he does not belong to Christ' (Rom. 8:9). If this is so, how can a Christian abuse children? Is not the Spirit of God within a powerful constraint? Perhaps our difficulty in believing that a Christian could abuse children is ultimately a theological difficulty.

There are many sex offenders, and not only religious ones, who engage in an intense struggle with their consciences before they offend. They may give in to their sexual feelings by abusing children, but sexual gratification brings with it self-loathing. It is likely that conscience does act as a strong restraint for Christians. Ultimately, however, the Holy Spirit does not prevent Christian believers from falling into sin. When we sin, we may sense that we are grieving the Holy Spirit, but the decision whether or not to sin is our own.

Even sex offenders who do struggle with their consciences when offending may find it very difficult to refrain from molesting children. Sometimes they describe their behaviour as 'compulsive' and something like an addiction. One minister, imprisoned for abusing his grandson, explained that he had a compulsion to abuse despite his knowledge, as a Christian, that it was wrong: 'I suppose that, being a devout religious person, if I had of believed with all of my mind and heart that the earth was going to open up and swallow me up in hell, I would have went ahead and done it anyway [sic].'[37]

One Catholic priest wrote about his abusing behaviour: 'It did seem like an addiction to me. I was out of control. As an addiction, it started off small. It was like what others say about taking cocaine: you start taking one hit, then you take two and three and four. I really had no control over it . . . God did not seem to be buying my prayer. I would confess, repent and no sooner feel clean when I'd sin again.'[38]

While offenders may describe themselves as having little control over their desires to molest children, in fact they often show an extraordinary degree of patience and control in creating the conditions in which they can abuse children without getting caught. Sexual abuse of children is rarely an impulsive act. As will be seen in the next chapter, it tends to be carefully planned.

If offenders feel that they are addicted to offending, it is often because they have trapped themselves in a vicious cycle of offending. One experienced therapist writes: 'Many men who experience their offending as somewhat compulsive in nature, describe cyclical patterns of behaviour in terms of an escalating experience of self-intoxication in which they become increasingly preoccupied with their own fantasies and feelings of excitement, arousal and urgency at the expense of other rational thoughts.'[39] The cycle often begins with masturbatory fantasies about having sex with children. It progresses eventually to the stage where the man acts on those fantasies and begins to target a particular child, perhaps befriending him or her and then setting the stage for the molestation. Afterwards there may be shame and guilt, but eventually the cycle begins again, with the previous incident of molestation forming the content of masturbatory fantasy.[40]

Rationalisations for Sexual Abuse

Perpetrators of child sexual abuse rationalise their abuse in a variety of ways. Some have convinced themselves that what they do is not morally wrong. It may be a criminal offence, but that is only because, as they see it, society does not understand childhood sexuality and persecutes them for acting on their natural desires towards 'consenting' children. Such views have gained some support from libertarians. One writer, who has been an influential senator in the Dutch parliament, believes that there is nothing wrong with any kind of sexual relations between adults and children as long as the intercourse is consensual and cannot be proven to have caused harm. He ascribes the current views on child sexual abuse to a belief that children are 'asexual', and argues that this is incorrect:

It is now known that children have sexual feelings from birth and that at a very young age they spontaneously begin sexual play. Thus they know very well whether they want a particular kind of sexual contact with a specific person and whether they want it here and now. In other words, the concept that below a certain age a child can have no will or desire of his own in these matters, or if he did that it would be judicially irrelevant is not based upon fact.[41]

This belief that children are sexual beings and desire sexual intercourse in some way has gained support from Freudian theory. Whatever Freud himself believed about his clients' reports of sexual molestation, many psychoanalysts within the Freudian tradition treated accounts of adult-child sexual interaction either as fantasies or as experiences which the child subconsciously wished for.[42] The psychiatric literature in the 1930s and 1940s gives an indication of this kind of view. Two researchers on incest, writing in 1942, stated that 'the child itself often unconsciously desires the sexual activity and becomes a more or less willing partner in it.' Two others, reporting on a study of children's reactions to sexual relations with adults, wrote that the children were 'bold, flaunting and even brazen' and often played 'an active or even initiating role.'[43]

Such beliefs feed the paedophile's rationalisations for acting upon his own sexual desires. He is simply showing love to the child. One medical practitioner with a strong interest in paediatric medicine has recounted his own long history of sexual relations with children, for which he was eventually imprisoned. He concluded with a strong defence of himself as a humanitarian:

I have never interfered with, injured or thwarted the growth and development of another human being. I have never hurt a child. On the contrary, I have loved children in a way that covered every aspect of the human-love spectrum . . . It is remarkable in my opinion that an individual can be imprisoned for such a long period . . .

and looted of life simply for trying to add to its full-ness.[44]

Of course, children are sexual beings. They may be aroused by sexual stimulation, and as part of the process of growing up they sometimes engage in sexual exploration with each other. This does not mean that they want sexual intercourse with adults. Offenders misread signals from children and interpret them as sexual; they also project their own sexual feelings on to the child, imagining the child to feel the same way as they do and to enjoy the sexual aspect of the relationship as much as they do. Certainly, many children are apparently willing to participate in sexual activity and return to the abuser again and again. But their search is a search for love and attention, not sex. Children may become sexualised, but only because the perpetrator has first aroused these sexual feelings and desires within them.

Another rationalisation is to see the child as the seducer. Those who specialise in treating sex offenders are only too familiar with the story of the child who seduced the reluctant male into sexual transgression. They have heard it many times before. The flirtatious four-year-old, the eight-year-old daughter who 'asked for it' in the way in which she looked at her father, the teenager who 'wanted to be raped' by the way in which she dressed. The story of the seductive child is a story which many sex offenders tell to explain and justify their behaviour even when their victims are very young indeed. Because they perceive the innocent behaviour of children as being both sexual and seductive, they convince themselves that the child flirted with them and wanted sex.

Cultural factors may also hinder an abusive man from taking responsibility for his actions. The belief that sex is an entitlement for the male in the household, a conjugal right which is to be demanded if necessary, may lead men to see it as their right to demand sexual favours from a daughter if the wife is unresponsive. Notions of possession of children may also influence the offender's behaviour.

It is a characteristic of sex offenders that they have an

extraordinary capacity for self-deception. Furthermore, whatever beliefs they may have about their 'love' for the children, they are characterised by a lack of consideration for the human needs of the victim. Part of the therapeutic process of treating sex offenders is to deal with the offender's level of denial and his sometimes bizarre distortions of reality. The offender also needs to come to understand things from the perspective of the victim.

LEVELS OF DENIAL

1. Denial of fact ('Nothing happened')
2. Denial of responsibility ('Something happened but it wasn't my idea')
3. Denial of sexual intent ('Something happened and it was my idea, but it wasn't sexual')
4. Denial of wrongfulness ('Something happened and it was my idea, and it was sexual, but it wasn't wrong')
5. Denial of self-determination ('Something happened and it was my idea, and it was sexual and it was wrong, but there were extenuating factors')

Source: Pollock and Hashmall, 1991.[45]

The Church and the Child Abuser

In the light of all that is now known about sex offenders, and why it is that people sexually abuse children, it must be clear that the past policies and practices of churches in dealing with perpetrators of child sexual abuse have been seriously mistaken. The church has been misled on countless occasions in the past into believing that sex offending is a short-term aberration or a forgivable lapse into temptation, rather than a most serious long-term problem in the lives of offenders. Because these men do not appear to be criminals in other respects, and perhaps because other forms of sexual temptation are only too real for many church leaders, there has been a strong tendency to minimise the nature of the offence and to accept the offender's assurance that this was a lapse of judgment of an otherwise godly man. It is because of this that, so often, ministers and priests who have abused children in the parish have been quietly moved on to another parish after some 'counselling'. Consequently, the church in the past has been a safe haven for those who want to abuse children. Even if detected, the church has so often covered up, forgiven and allowed the offender to continue unhindered in his predatory career.

Part of the problem concerning the church's complacency about child sexual abuse is that church leaders have tended to accept offenders' own explanations for their behaviour. This assumes both honesty and a capacity for insight on the part of the offender. There is no reason to expect either. Perpetrators of sexual abuse have a powerful motivation to minimise their offending behaviour and to explain it away as an aberration. They have much to lose once a child has disclosed the abuse, and for many offenders it may be a purely tactical decision whether to accuse the child of lying or to throw himself on the mercy of church leaders seeking their pity and forgiveness.

All the forgiveness in the world will not change a fixated child abuser's desire for children. Abusers can learn means of preventing themselves from re-offending, but the road is long and tough and full of pitfalls. Even those who do not offend because of a primary sexual attraction to children, but perhaps use children for sexual gratification in the same way that they use and abuse adults, find it very difficult to change. The path of treatment involves fundamental adjustments to their beliefs about sexuality and their attitudes to other adults and children.

For all sex offenders against children, the road towards change is a steep and difficult one, and there is a very strong likelihood that they will offend again unless they face up to their offending behaviour and take full responsibility for it. The path of Christian love, therefore, is not to minimise the offence but to realise how serious it is, the devastation it has caused to the victims and the difficulties of change for the offender. The church that just forgives and forgets, without more, loves neither the victim nor the offender.

Chapter 4

The Process of Victimisation

How is it that perpetrators manage to abuse children without attracting suspicion? Why it is that children sometimes seem to acquiesce in the abuse, or keep silent about it subsequently? It is, after all, very difficult for most parents to believe that their own children would allow an adult to molest them sexually. At least once children reach an age when they are not under constant parental supervision, they know better. And if, God forbid, they were the victim of a sexual approach or an attack, they would tell their parents immediately, wouldn't they?

Maybe. But perpetrators of sexual abuse are often very clever in the way in which they entice children into sexual activity and secure their silence. Many children who are sexually abused are like flies caught in the spider's web. Once they get entangled, it is very difficult for them to extricate themselves.

Choosing the Victim

Research with sex offenders against children has demonstrated that they target their victims carefully.[1] The starting point for this process is that the offender may be attracted towards a particular gender or age of child. Among those to whom he is attracted, he chooses those children who are most likely to be responsive and least likely to tell. Some children

57

are more likely to be abused than others. Young children may be targeted because they are less likely to perceive the sexual contact as inappropriate and are more easily induced not to reveal the secret than older children. Furthermore, they have limited language skills and so may not have the words with which to tell clearly what has been happening. It is also the case that good children make good victims. Children who are trusting and friendly are more likely to respond positively to the friendship and attention of the abuser than a child who is reserved and distrustful. A child who has been trained to obey adult authority without questioning is also less likely to resist abuse than a more strong-willed and disrespectful child.

While many victims of sexual abuse come from homes which are happy, and have parents who are deeply committed to their welfare, children who have been starved of affection are particularly vulnerable to abuse from someone who befriends them and shows them special attention. Children who are experiencing temporary strains in their relationship with parents and who are thus somewhat isolated from protective adults are also particularly vulnerable to abuse, as are children who are lonely and have very few friends. Children who are known to have been abused before may also be targeted. It is thus not uncommon to find children have been abused on different occasions by more than one adult.

The victimisation of children can occur in a number of ways. There are some offenders who make no attempt to secure the child's compliance. Some offenders ensure the acquiescence of the children by asserting raw power and instilling fear.

Such a perpetrator will make no pretence that what he does is for the child's good or that it is part of a game. However, that may be a risky path for the perpetrator. If the child is motivated to keep quiet only by fear of the consequences, then sooner or later he or she may find the courage to tell. Furthermore, the sexual arousal of many offenders is linked to the belief that the child enjoys the sexual activity, so coercing the child is not sexually arousing for them.

Thus while some offenders rely only on threats, many others

look for ways to secure the compliance of the child without relying entirely on force or the threat of it. This process of securing the compliance of the child is known as grooming.

Grooming the Child

The sexual abuse of children is usually carefully planned and stage-managed. It is usually premeditated. In the process of grooming, the perpetrator creates the conditions that will allow him to abuse the children while remaining undetected by others, and the child is prepared gradually for the time when the offender first engages in sexual molestation. It is a process which has been acknowledged frequently by offenders in treatment programmes, and it may take weeks or even months.

The grooming process takes many forms. The patterns by which perpetrators victimise children depend to a great extent on the relationship between them. If the offender has children of his own, or is living in a household with children, then he has ready access to them. The stage is set for abuse to occur if the perpetrator is motivated to target these children. If, on the other hand, the perpetrator is targeting a child outside the home, the first stage is to gain access to the child without attracting suspicion.

Intrafamilial Abuse

It can be very difficult for people to understand how a man can sexually abuse his children or stepchildren without his wife ever finding out, even by accident. There are ways in which this can occur. For example, one father who abused all his children made the bathtime his special time alone with them, away from the mother. This was his particular contribution to the child-rearing, and he used this natural situation to abuse the children. Another father made it his habit to be alone with his child, reading to her at bedtime, and it was at these times that he molested her.[2] At other times, the abuse may occur on regular occasions when the wife is out for an evening or engaged in some other activity. There are some perpetrators who are extraordinarily brazen about the abuse. They fondle the child (for example by moving their fingers underneath the child's pants) even when others are around.

The offender may groom the child through a variety of means. One means of grooming is by forming an alliance with the child. Typically, a father or stepfather will show special attention to a particular female child, giving her treats and in subtle ways isolating her from her mother. One offender acknowledged in interviews with researchers that he went along with anything his stepdaughter wanted. Another said he bought his daughter presents, let her stay at girlfriends' homes and showed her favours which he didn't show to any other of the children.[3] In this way, the offender forms a particular bond with the child. He develops a pattern of spending a lot of time alone with her. He may well treat her emotionally like an adult friend, sharing intimate details about his sex life and adult relationships.[4] The child thus, quite inappropriately, becomes the man's confidante.

Gradually, as she responds to his attention and affection, he initiates a degree of sexual contact which is explained as being a special way in which he shows his love to her. He may talk more to her about sex, and show her sexually explicit pictures. As time goes on, this sexual intimacy increases. Gradually, the relationship is transformed from that of father and daughter to that of father and lover. This transformation of the relationship can be very confusing and difficult for the child. On one level, she remains his daughter with all that means in terms of his power and authority over her. Yet in secret he relates to her quite differently, as sexual 'partner' and lover. The feelings of pleasure or of being special are usually mixed inextricably with feelings of guilt, shame and even a sense of betrayal that the father has abdicated his purely paternal role.

Another form of grooming takes the form of innocent touching that gradually develops into sexual touching. At bathtimes, for example, when it is natural for the child to be naked or scantily clothed, the perpetrator may begin getting the child used to the touching of the child's genitals, perhaps by a special washing routine or by playing games which involve 'accidental' contact with sexual organs. He may be partially undressed himself as they splash water together, or he may get into the bathtub with the child. Similar kinds of activities may occur at the child's bedtime or on occasions when the child gets into the bed of the parent.

Gradually, over a period of time, the sexual contact becomes more explicit and invasive, until it clearly crosses the line between appropriate and inappropriate contact. Because the grooming occurs gradually, the child may not realise that the boundary line of appropriate behaviour has been crossed, even though the sexual contact may make her feel very uncomfortable. By blurring the boundary lines between normal and abnormal parent-child interactions, the parent causes the child to be confused about what is appropriate behaviour and what is not, and the extent to which she ought to be able to have a realm of bodily privacy which her father or stepfather should not invade.

Sexual abuse can go on for years in some families before a child realises that other fathers don't behave in the same way with their children. Parents have the power and influence to define the child's reality, especially when the child is kept relatively isolated from other children and adults. The activity may feel wrong to the child, but if Daddy says it is okay, then it is okay. Understanding behaviour as a form of abuse requires a frame of reference which does not derive solely from the perpetrator's own explanations. Thus, the child may define the activity as being aversive without realising that it is abusive.[5] One of the aims of protective education programmes for children is to give them that alternative frame of reference.

Another feature of the grooming process is that often the child is alienated from the mother and other siblings. This can occur in many different ways. It is not uncommon, for example, for the father to claim that his wife's sexual unresponsiveness is a justification for the sexual relationship with the daughter, and the daughter may come to resent the mother for this. Another false message is that the mother knows what is happening and doesn't care, so there is no point in turning to her for comfort.[6] The special attention shown to the child, perhaps in the form of favours and privileges, may also alienate siblings. Child victims may also be alienated from their friends because the father dominates the child's life and discourages normal interactions with peers.[7]

The child's compliance may also be secured in other ways. The perpetrator may, for example, offer a plausible reason to the child for the abuse. The father may tell the daughter that he is giving her a bit of sex education, or preparing her for her future husband, or that this is the way all Daddies show love to their daughters. A grandfather may convince the child that it is his role to give her a special examination of the vagina to make sure she is medically 'all right'.

These various means of grooming the child and securing his or her acquiescence are not mutually exclusive. They can occur together in various combinations. Furthermore, such methods may have been learnt. The techniques of grooming may be passed on from one offender to another, or the offender may replicate his own experience as a child.

Abuse Outside the Family Setting

Where the perpetrator is not living in the same household as the victim, he does not have the same opportunities for natural intimacy with the children as parents do. Thus grooming will take different forms. He must find ways of gaining access to children without arousing undue suspicion, and endeavour to create an environment in which sexual abuse can occur. Even those who are in occupations which bring them into contact with children extensively tend to see children in groups. How then do they manage to abuse individual children and secure their co-operation or their silence?

Some perpetrators choose jobs that naturally bring them into contact with children and give them the opportunity to befriend individuals. They may be music teachers who see children individually, other teachers, scout leaders, sports coaches or youth workers, the people who readily volunteer for children's work in churches and in community groups. They may even marry or live with a woman who has children, primarily to gain access to the children. Others hang around amusement arcades and video game centres to get in contact with a lot of boys who are away from their parents and who may need love and attention. To the outside, these men present as people who love children and have an excellent rapport with them. It is their capacity for leading a double life that makes them so dangerous, especially when they get involved in church activities.

For these men, it is a very conscious decision to target children. These are the wolves in sheep's clothing who may, for example, pretend to be active Christians in order to gain the trust of parents and church leaders. They are skilled deceivers, who prey on the trust and naivety of parents. They may have so convinced the parents of their sincerity and trustworthiness that when a child discloses sexual abuse, the parents and other adults find it very difficult to believe the charge against them.

There are other perpetrators whose decision to engage in activities that will bring them into proximity with children takes place at a less conscious level, and they may not realise the significance of what they are doing. This is particularly the case with men who are troubled by their sexual proclivities. They feel a need to be around children, and may have convinced themselves that they love children and that children love them, so it is natural for them to gravitate towards activities which involve children. A sex offender may feel a genuine sense of vocation as a teacher or a youth worker. He may also be extremely good at it. But such vocations place these men in much the same situation as an alcoholic going into a pub to have an orange juice. In situations where they are close to children, the downward spiral of offending is all too likely to begin.

Grooming a child outside the family setting often requires the perpetrator to form a special friendship with the victim, which allows him the opportunity to be alone with the child. A sequence of events can be observed. For example, as preparation for the abuse of a pre-pubescent boy, the perpetrator may select a particularly open and trusting child, gradually befriending him and giving him treats so that the boy wants to come back to play with him again. The offender also needs to build trust with the parents. There must be a plausible reason why the offender should be spending so much time alone with the boy, and the parents must feel they can trust the offender absolutely and without the least suspicion.

The abuse may begin with games involving physical contact. In this process of grooming, offenders are generally careful to proceed gradually with the child. The offender will not only ensure that he has the child's trust, but may also try out the child's reactions to touching by hugging him or engaging in some other form of non-sexual contact. A child who responds negatively to such physical contact is highly likely to resist any sexual moves. By engaging in this form of non-sexual contact, the offender 'tests the waters' with the child.

If the offender does not receive a negative reaction, he may move on to touch various parts of the body affectionately, and will gradually move from non-sexual to sexual touching. Because he has an affectionate relationship with the man, and enjoys many of the games they play, the boy maintains the secret. Indeed, he may well experience sexual feelings as well, as his penis is rubbed and stimulated in a way which he had only experimented with previously on his own. By the time the relationship becomes sexual, the boy believes he has agreed to it, and he feels trapped in it.

Ray Wyre, a British expert on sex offenders, illustrates well the confusion of feelings which the molested child may have, in recounting how an eight-year-old girl felt about her abuse:

She put her hands sort of down below saying, 'It felt nice here'; she pointed to her tummy and said, 'I felt sick here'. She pointed to her heart and said, 'I feel guilty here', she pointed to her head and said, 'I don't understand it here'. That eight-year-old girl summed up what sexual abuse is about at the hands of a paedophile.[8]

Alison's Story: The Exploitation of Loneliness

While some offenders groom children to such an extent that there is no need either to use force or to threaten the child in order to carry out the sexual abuse, others groom children only sufficiently to get them to a place where the abuse can occur away from other adults. It is then that the child sees a more brutal side of the offender, and may be frightened into keeping silent. This was the situation for Alison.

Alison was eight or nine years old when she formed a friendship with a couple who lived two doors down from her house. The man, George, was in his fifties. His wife, Elizabeth, was quite sickly, and therefore Alison would tend to spend most time with George, who was more exciting to be with. She was a regular visitor to their house. Sometimes she would go down to his garage at the bottom of the garden, where George would be working on one thing or another. On other occasions, they would take her out on day trips.

Alison was a very lonely child. She had been adopted, and was never sure that she was loved unconditionally. Her mother had her own history of sexual abuse. Years after Alison was abused, she discovered that her mother had been sexually abused as a child by a Catholic priest. Her mother never allowed her children to play with Catholic children, and she also had a fetish about cleanliness. She would regularly wash Alison's genitals to make sure they were absolutely clean. Alison always had to behave well. She felt that she couldn't just be an ordinary child. Mum did not encourage her much, and Alison felt as if she was constantly being put down.

Alison was drawn to Elizabeth and George because they took an interest in her. George was not only active and interesting, he also made her feel important and listened to her. Alison was also vulnerable because she was not someone who stood up for herself. She was always told what to do. She did not know how to say 'no' to an adult. One day, she went down to the garage with him, as he said he wanted to show her something. When they were down there, he grabbed her and began to kiss her, putting his hands down her pants, rubbing her vaginal area and getting her to rub his penis. This seemed to her to last for an eternity. She felt trapped, and eventually began to cry. When she started crying, he stopped, and told her that it was to be their secret.

The following week, the couple invited Alison to go to the beach with them. When Alison had come out of the water, George wanted to help dry her. She became highly agitated, and refused to let George touch her.

After this, Alison kept on visiting this couple, partly out of fear that Elizabeth would suspect something was wrong if she stopped visiting, and partly out of fear that George would do something worse if she stopped coming. However, she wore more and more clothes as a means of protecting herself from his advances.

He attacked her once more when they were alone in the garage. He tied her up with rope, but before he could do anything more to her, Elizabeth came down to the garage. She saw Alison tied up, and told George to let her go. George explained it all as a game that they were playing.

After this, Alison told her mother what had happened, and the mother told the father. Both parents were furious with George, but they did nothing to comfort and support Alison. Her mother told her not to tell anyone else what had happened. If the parents reported the matter to the police, Alison was not made aware of it.

In Alison's case, George picked a lonely, vulnerable and isolated child who did not have the capacity to stand up for herself, and could be induced, for a while, to keep the abuse secret. He had cultivated her loyalty for months by befriending her and doing exciting things with her. He had won the trust of Alison's parents, and finally he made his move to molest her. It was no momentary aberration and nor was it an isolated incident. Years after these events happened, Alison's family doctor discovered that George had abused other children too, including his own grandchildren.

The Silence of the Lambs

People often ask why so many of the victims of sexual abuse never tell anyone. Generally, there are two reasons. Either they are trying to protect others or they are trying to protect themselves.

Protecting Others

Sometimes children do not tell their parents about sexual abuse, not because they are estranged from them, but out of a desire not to hurt them. Alison, for example, was very concerned that her father should not know about George's behaviour in the garage because he was a quadriplegic. She was told many times as a child that if she ever did anything to upset him, he might die. Therefore, when Alison told her mother, she urged her not to tell the father. The mother told him anyway, and Alison felt utterly betrayed.

Similarly, when Adam was abused for a couple of years by a Brother who was the principal of his day school, he did not tell his parents because he did not want to hurt them. His father was quite unwell and would be distraught if he had known. Adam knew that if he told his mother, she would tell his father. It was only after his father died when Adam was a young teenager that he told his mother the secret that he had been carrying alone for so long.

Some children's silence is the result of what the perpetrator has said. There may be direct threats against the safety of a loved one, or even a pet, if they tell. Alternatively, the perpetrator may secure the child's silence by warning that if the mother ever finds out she will have a nervous breakdown, or the family will break up, and thus the responsibility for protecting the mother or preventing the family break-up is placed upon the child who needs to maintain the secret. These warnings are designed to ensure that the child maintains silence out of loyalty to others, even the perpetrator. Children's feelings towards the perpetrator are often mixed. They want love and attention, and in many cases this is what they have received from the perpetrator. They may feel very uncomfortable, and even traumatised by the sexual activity, but this does not necessarily mean they have no affection whatsoever for the perpetrator. There is also sometimes a great reluctance to see him go to jail.

Protecting Themselves

Children also keep silent in order to protect themselves. Sometimes, perpetrators threaten them with serious harm if they tell anyone. They may also have been warned by an abusing father or stepfather that if they speak out they will be taken away from the family by the welfare department. However difficult things may be at home, there may be more security there than in contemplating the unknown world away from the parents. Of course, children who are sexually abused by a member of the household are not always removed from the family home. This occurs only if the mother is not able or willing to take the necessary action to protect the child – which usually means separating from the perpetrator, at least for a substantial period of time.

Other powerful influences in making children keep silent are shame and guilt. Many victims of sexual abuse feel a profound sense of shame about the sexual activity. Children are usually brought up to regard their genitals as private. Often, they get the message very early on that sex is 'dirty' and something to be ashamed of. Talking about anything to do with sexual touching can therefore be very embarrassing. The problem is compounded if, as is so often the case, the child feels a sense of responsibility for allowing the abuse to occur. This sense of guilt and shame about letting the abuse happen can be so deep that it keeps the victim silent well into her adult years. Many adults today quietly carry a burden of guilt concerning their childhood victimisation which operates as a cruel bondage, keeping them from seeking the help they need.

Why would children feel responsible for the abuse? The sense of guilt is seldom rational, but it can arise in a number of ways. The child may feel guilt at having accepted rewards for complying with the perpetrator's wishes, or for simply having failed to say 'no'. Often, the perpetrator's sexualisation of the relationship is a very gradual process. A male abuser may begin by talking to a girl victim about sexual matters, then showing her his penis and encouraging her to show him her private parts, all of which is disguised as an educational exercise or a game. His touching and caressing may first be non-sexual in nature, but then becomes sexual. In this process, the perpetrator confuses the child about which kinds of touching are acceptable and which are not. By the time the activity becomes overtly sexual and the child realises that what is going on is wrong, she has missed the moment when it would seem right to say 'no'. She has allowed him first to see, then to touch, and perhaps to go even further. It is too late for her to object. She has as much invested as he does in keeping what has happened a secret, because she is so ashamed about what she has 'let' him do. The child carries a burden of guilt and shame about her responsibility without realising how she has been manipulated by the perpetrator.

Children may also feel a sense of responsibility for allowing themselves to get into the situation where the abuse occurred, and this message may be reinforced by the perpetrator. One man has told the story of how, as a boy of primary-school age, he went with some friends to visit an industrial painter who paid them handsomely to masturbate each other while he watched. Subsequently, he went back to this man on his own, and the man raped him. He couldn't tell anyone because he thought he would be in big trouble if he did. The painter pointed out that he had come to the premises voluntarily, knowing what would happen. He had therefore 'asked for it'.

The boy grew up to become an offender. He befriended a great many boys while working as the manager of an amusement arcade. He was a father figure to them, a patient listener with whom they could talk about anything.

In those circumstances it was easy to introduce conversation about sex . . . When I finally reached the stage of enquiring whether I could touch a boy's penis, I was seldom rejected.

69

If there was a protest, it was easy to shift the blame . . . I told diffident boys that they only had themselves to blame when I introduced sex: they 'knew what I wanted' and they 'came voluntarily'. That silenced them just as effectively as it had silenced me.[9]

A Safe Enough Place to Tell

It is very difficult for children to tell of their abuse. Frequently, they will try to tell an adult just once, and if they are not believed or the adult does nothing to stop the abuse, they will not tell again. Their disclosure may initially be very cautious as they test the waters to see how the adult will react. The voice of the perpetrator may be ringing in their ears threatening the consequences of disclosure. But as we create a safe place for children, they may come to trust us enough to tell us about what is happening. Understanding the process of victimisation may help us to read the signals, and may help children to trust us sufficiently for them to tell us their secret.[10]

Chapter 5

Controversies About Child Sexual Abuse

When child sexual abuse first became an issue for widespread public discussion in the media in the 1970s and early 1980s, the public reaction was typically one of shock at the extent of child sexual abuse in families and sympathy for the victims of abuse. Women's magazines and talk shows were full of stories of adult survivors revealing for the first time the private horror of their childhoods, and if there was controversy about the topic, it concerned only the slowness of governments and the legal system to respond to the problem.

In recent years, however, certain issues concerning child sexual abuse have become contentious. One of the debates concerns adolescent sexuality. There are those who argue that consensual relations between adults and physically mature young teenagers should not be criminalised, and that prohibiting adolescents from engaging in sexual intercourse in the name of 'child protection' is a violation of their rights as sexual beings.

Another major controversy concerns recovered memory. There have been movements formed of people claiming that their children have wrongly accused them of sexual abuse as a result of 'false memories' of abuse which have been induced by therapists. For years, therapists working with troubled adults have believed that children, and even adults, who have suffered particularly traumatic experiences can block them out so that they have no conscious recollection of them until the memories surface again in adulthood. This view has been challenged not only by the people who claim to have been wrongly accused, but by some psychologists who believe either that there is no such thing as 'repressed memory' or that such occurrences are very uncommon.

A third area of controversy concerns 'ritual abuse'. Some people have reported the most serious abuse as children in satanic cults or in similar groups where the physical and sexual abuse were part of some form of ritual. These claims have given rise to significant controversy, particularly where they have been based upon a recovered memory.

Sexual Relations between Adults and Young Teenagers

The 'age of consent' is the age at which a young person is deemed capable of giving a valid consent to sexual relations. It varies from one jurisdiction to another, and depends to some extent on the relationship between the young person and the partner. In England and many other English-speaking countries, the 'age of consent' is sixteen years. Sexual intercourse with a minor below that age is a criminal offence, as is any other form of sexual contact, although these cases tend not to be prosecuted where a girl is fifteen and her partner just a little older. The law assumes not only that a girl under sixteen lacks the maturity to give valid consent to sexual intercourse, but also that such activity will be harmful to her. As one English judge put it, 'There are many things which a girl under sixteen needs to practise, but sex is not one of them'.[1] In most jurisdictions, the age of consent to homosexual relations tends to be higher than is the case with heterosexual relations.

The view that sexual relations between young teenagers and adults constitutes 'sexual abuse' has been challenged. What exactly is wrong with a consensual sexual relationship between a young teenager and an adult? If a fourteen-year-old girl has sex by consent with a thirty-year-old man, or if a schoolgirl exchanges love letters with her teacher and they end up in bed, is this sexual abuse? Of course, as Christians we may express our moral disapproval. Nonetheless, can it be said that one is victim and the other an offender? Should it be possible for a man to be sent to jail for such an offence? When prosecutions are brought against men who have had consensual sexual relations with a physically mature fourteen- or fifteen-year-old girl, there is often a great deal of sympathy shown to the offender. After all, men can be forgiven for being sexually attracted to a physically mature and good-looking adolescent.

The issue is an important one for considering the problem of child sexual abuse in church communities. Among ministers and priests, there is a much higher incidence of abuse of young adolescents than of abuse of pre-pubertal children. Should this make a difference in considering the suitability of that person to remain in ministry? That depends to some extent on whether we regard sexual relations with young adolescents as a less serious kind of offending.

The argument against criminalising consensual intercourse between adults and post-pubertal teenagers rests on a number of grounds. From a biological point of view, it may be regarded as natural for girls who have reached the age of child-bearing to engage in sexual relations.[2] Procreation is one of the most powerful of human instincts. There is also an argument from history. Throughout the ages, it has been very common for girls to be married as soon as they have reached puberty, or very shortly after, as indeed was the case in biblical times.[3]

This argument from history needs to be put into perspective. There is a world of difference between a marital relationship and sexual experience outside any context of permanent commitment. While in modern times few would say that marriage at a young age is a good idea, at least the sexual awakening of the young adolescent has a proper context for expression within a permanent relationship, and in cultures where adolescent marriage was or is common, the extended family plays an important role in supporting the young couple. In contrast, sexual relations between adults and adolescents outside marriage can be exploitative, the adult using the girl to meet his sexual needs for a little while before discarding her. For the girl in such situations, there are often strong feelings of betrayal.

Nonetheless, the arguments from biology and history are put forward as indications that it is quite natural for some young adolescents to engage in sexual activity. The reality is that many adolescents have had sexual intercourse by about the age of fifteen. If some of them choose to engage in sexual experimentation with older males, does this make a difference? If a fourteen-year-old girl has sex with a fifteen-year-old boy one Saturday night, and the following week has sex with his twenty-five-year old brother, is there such a difference between the two incidents that the first should be quietly overlooked while the second is regarded as a criminal offence? Why is one sexual experimentation and the other sexual abuse? If a teenage girl consents to intercourse, does it really matter how old her partner is as long as he wears a condom?

Together with the belief that there is nothing abnormal in adult-adolescent sexual relations is the view that to describe the adolescent as the victim is frequently to misread the dynamics of the relationship. Who seduces whom? Are all adolescent girls naive and sexually unaware innocents who are the victims of male predations? It is common to hear men who are accused of sexual relations with young adolescents defending their actions by saying that the girls flirted with them and led them on. This explanation by the offender often strikes a sympathetic chord in listeners. The teenager is seen as being substantially to blame for leading the adult into temptation. After all, it takes two to tango.

The arguments in favour of decriminalisation have also been presented as an issue of young people's rights to sexual freedom and privacy. For example, Terrence Sullivan, an influential social policy expert in Canada, has argued that law reforms aimed at protecting young adolescents from sexual exploitation are an interference with their rights to autonomy and deny their natural sexuality.[4] He questions the way in which adolescents are regarded as 'victims' by well-meaning social work and health professionals, when the adolescents themselves do not perceive the incidents as damaging. He goes on to argue that we should listen 'to young persons recounting their own versions of sexual experiences with each other and with adults' without trying to influence them to speak in ways 'consistent with our own moral rendering of adolescent sexual experience'.[5]

These are powerful arguments. But too much emphasis can be placed on the issues of consent and harm where young teenagers are concerned. It is not necessary to show that the teenager was entirely the unwilling victim of the adult's sexual predations in order to label the relationship as abusive. The issue is not whether the young person is consenting, but why. The bonding of a young adolescent to a much older adult may be the result of her emotional need to have a surrogate parent or charismatic leader rather than because she is sexually interested in him as a lover. Furthermore, if he is in a position of authority in relation to her, his assurances about what is morally right and wrong may overwhelm her doubts. In the early years of adolescence, young people are usually just beginning to work out for themselves whether they can accept the moral codes concerning sexual relations with which they have grown up. Their views about sexual morality may well be quite malleable, and pleasure may persuade more than the arguments for abstinence. The adult's gradual and deliberate sexual stimulation of the adolescent may be one powerful source of persuasion. The process of seduction is one in which the adult in the relationship is often very practised, in contrast to the naivety of the young person.

As the 'consent' of the adolescent needs to be examined critically, so too must his or her assertion that it did no harm. In many cases, adolescents' sexual experience does no harm. Sexual relations with peers at the age of fourteen and fifteen are not uncommon, and may have no lasting adverse effects. Adolescents who have sex with older partners sometimes look back on those experiences as beneficial and pleasurable, and harbour no regrets. Yet for others, the adverse effects can be profound, and may not be obvious for many years to come. It may be only with the hindsight of adulthood that a person comes to realise that a first affair was abusive and caused considerable emotional damage.

Anna's Story: Affair or Abuse?

When Anna was twelve years old, she began to attend a Catholic high school. It was an all-girls school. Mr Jones (as we shall call him) was the deputy principal. He was a maths teacher and had primary responsibility for Anna's form when she was in year seven. He was a married man aged about thirty-five, and had three children. It was clear to Anna from the beginning that Mr Jones had favourites, and she became one of those favourites.

It is difficult for her to say when their intimate relationship began. Over a period of time, Anna started to spend more and more time with Mr Jones in his office, helping him by doing odd jobs and filing. He took an interest in her well-being, and would ask her about her home and family. He even managed to persuade Anna's mother that she could do great things in maths with a little extra coaching. Anna was very responsive to the attention that he showed her. She came from a family which had experienced divorce, and she was quite an unhappy girl. More than anything else, Anna craved love and security.

One day, when she was about thirteen years old, Mr Jones's relationship with her took a new direction. He reached out and touched her knee, and then withdrew his hand again. It was over in an instant. Anna froze, not so much in fear as in surprise, and with interest – even a little excitement. Over a period of time, he increased the amount of physical contact he had with her. One day, he touched her on the shoulder as they were looking at a computer screen. On another occasion, he shut the door and held her for a long time by the hand. He asked her whether she had ever been in love with anyone and whether she had had sex. For reasons she cannot now explain, she responded to the question by telling a wild story about having had sex with a teacher at primary school. She was very creative at weaving this tale, but of course it lacked detail. All she could say was that they 'did it', but that they had done it in a different way – it was not proper sexual intercourse. Mr Jones was very interested in this. He pressed her for details, and she found it quite hard to maintain the lie. At one point she told him that the teacher had given her a gold ring as a pledge of affection. In fact, the ring had come from her grandmother.

A little while after this, Mr Jones organised a camp at his house, with twenty girls. While his wife was sleeping in the house, Anna shared a small tent with Mr Jones and his seven-year-old daughter. She woke up the following morning to find that he was tenderly rubbing her arm and staring lovingly into her eyes. He made her feel very special. The next day, when her mother came to pick her up, he touched her hand in a secretive way as a sign of affection.

Anna began to babysit for them during the holidays. This involved staying overnight with them. One night, after they came home from their time out, Anna recalls that she was crying about something. He held her hand, and said that he would kiss her tears away. He then kissed her on the mouth. Anna was shocked by this. It was naughty but nice. He then moved his hand over her chest and down to her vagina, and fondled her. She felt very embarrassed that he was touching that private part of her. The next day, while driving her home, he drove off the main road and parked in a secluded place. He fondled her again, trying to stimulate her sexually.

On another occasion, while they were going along in the car, Mr Jones asked her to take off the ring which she claimed the primary school teacher had given her. He took the ring from her, saying that it symbolised the previous relationship with that teacher. Telling her that his love would be much better than all that she had experienced before, he threw the ring into a creek and promised to replace it with a gift from him. Later, he gave her a gold bracelet.

They continued to see a great deal of each other, often spending time talking in his office or just gazing out of the window. They fantasised about escaping together. When she was about fourteen years old, they went on a school excursion which involved an overnight stay. Late in the night, after the other girls in Anna's room had gone to sleep, he sneaked into the room, put his hand down her pants and began to fondle her. Anna remembers saying that they should go out into the corridor. They kissed passionately. He pressed her against the wall and tried to penetrate her.

Soon after, Mr Jones introduced her to oral sex. It was something that Anna had read about in a women's magazine. When they were together one night, he undid his trousers, and Anna was drawn into fondling him so that he had an erection. He played with her hair while she began to perform oral sex on him. After this incident, oral sex became a feature of their relationship. From then on, Anna developed a compulsive habit of putting lanolin on her lips to stop them getting dry.

Their first act of intercourse occurred in his car. During a school fete, he drove her over to some sports fields that were isolated. There was a bench seat in the car, and somehow they both ended up completely naked. It was cold. For Anna the sexual intercourse was very painful. There was little foreplay. She was also embarrassed. This was the first time that she had been completely naked before him, and she was self-conscious about her small breasts. On this occasion, he asked her to promise him that however many babies she eventually had, the first one would be his.

After this time, they began to have sex regularly – sometimes more than once a week, at other times with longer intervals – whenever they could be alone together. Mr Jones organised the school timetable in such a way that Anna had a period off, and during this hour she was meant to be in the library working under the librarian's supervision. In fact, she was always with Mr Jones. They talked a great deal during these times. Mr Jones had become emotionally dependent on Anna. When his father died, he cried in front of her and looked to her for emotional support. He told her that he needed her. They never had sexual intercourse in his office, although he fondled her and penetrated her digitally.

They also arranged meetings at other times. For a while, Anna had an orchestra practice which began at 5 p.m., and thus the period from 3.30 to 5 p.m. was free. There were very few people around then, if anyone. On these occasions, they used to meet in a particular classroom and sometimes had sex on the floor. Anna was often the one who initiated sex on these occasions, because she believed that if they had sex it meant that he really loved her. Typically, his response was to say, 'no, no, no, yes'.

Anna had effectively become Mr Jones's mistress. She was extremely jealous of his wife since the wife had his company most of the time while Anna had to meet him secretly. The wife knew about the relationship. She had found Anna's love letters to him and also found Anna's belt in the back of the car. When she confronted Anna about this, Anna told her that they were having sex. The wife's response was to say that men had different needs from women.

In the course of year nine, when all this was going on, Anna told two teachers about it. One of them told her that he couldn't help her. It was just too difficult for him to deal with. The other teacher, a young woman, told her that she needed to find a younger boyfriend. Anna was very confused. To this day she doesn't know whether her motivation in telling them was a cry for help, or whether she was just showing off about having an 'adult relationship'.

It all ended a few months later when Anna was fifteen, at a time when she was sufficiently troubled by their relationship to want the truth to come out. It had lasted for about two years. She had received a Valentine's Day card from Mr Jones, and she showed it to one of the nuns who was teaching at the school. The nun showed it to the principal. The principal interviewed Anna, first alone and then together with Mr Jones. Even when it had reached this point, Anna was unable to tell the whole truth. The principal wanted to know how many times they had had intercourse. Signalling beneath the table, Mr Jones indicated four times, and that was the answer Anna gave. She lied for him because she still loved him. He resigned that day for 'personal reasons'. The incident was kept very quiet. The parents did not want to press charges for Anna's sake. It was also agreed that Mr Jones would not teach in the area. Eventually he gained another job at a well-known private school in a different part of the country.

Anna's parents were initially angry that she had not been able to talk to them about it, but after that the subject was never mentioned again. There was complete silence about it in the school as well. She received no pastoral care. Indeed, she felt as if she was blamed for what happened, and was shunned. In that school, girls were given the message that they were supposed to be the guardians of their moral virtue, because men had the raging hormones. Anna felt that Mr Jones was forgiven but she was not.

For years, Anna looked on this relationship as her first love affair. She had been passionate about Mr Jones, and, although at first she did not find the sex pleasurable, she had come to be excited about it. She was as active a participant in their secret trysts as he was. Indeed, she initiated some of their sexual encounters.

Anna went on to do very well at school and university. Eventually, she had other sexual partners. Later, she married and had children. Certainly she was young, but only as young as many other teenagers who have their first experience of sexual intercourse. Perhaps it was inappropriate that Mr Jones should have had an affair with one of his pupils. In a Catholic context, having a sexual relationship with anyone outside marriage would be regarded as unacceptable. However, allowing for all of that, was this really sexual abuse? Should it be a criminal offence?

Anna no longer sees this relationship with Mr Jones as just an 'affair'. Reviewing this story, it is possible to see so many of the techniques of seduction which were described in the previous chapter. Here was a troubled girl, one of the very few in that school from a divorced family, needing love and attention. Mr Jones began by first touching her knee – momentary, non-sexual, harmless, but also unnecessary and unprompted. Perhaps he was just trying to see how she would react to physical touch. Then he engaged in more touching and caressing, still non-sexual but increasingly intimate. He made her feel special. He related to her as he would to an adult friend. He treated her as an equal although she was just a junior member of the high school in which he held authority as the deputy principal. Eventually, he began to touch her genitals, and then graduated to full intercourse. By that time, her sexual feelings were fully awakened, and they became lovers. She came to him for love, he took advantage of her for sex. As an experienced adult male, he initiated her into sexual activities which she had only read about in magazines.

Was this merely a harmless affair for Anna? At the time that the relationship was disclosed, Anna was examined by a psychologist who pronounced her to be a normal and healthy adolescent. Anna would have said that the relationship had done her no harm at all, although she suffered from the moral condemnation after it came to light. The subsequent story, however, indicates that the real harm was latent. Anna's life began to fall apart after the birth of her first child, a son. She suffered severe post-natal depression, and was unable to cope with him. Ever since, she has been quite severely troubled. At times, she has been suicidal. A decade after she first began to put lanolin on her lips after beginning oral sex, she still applies this ointment, many times a day. It is a compulsive disorder. She now has other compulsive disorders as well, such as a fetish for hand-washing and cleanliness (including constant showering) and a need to change her underwear several times a day. She experienced a lot of self-loathing and guilt. If she finds herself alone with a middle-aged man in a room with the door shut, she is more likely than not to have a panic attack. When she was fourteen, she had long hair flowing down her back. Now she cuts it short because she cannot bear to look as she did then.

There have also been effects on her relationships with men. She views most men in a sexual way, and assumes that a close involvement with a man will have a sexual element. At university, she had a lot of sexual relationships, believing that if she had sex with men it would mean that they loved her. She has been in and out of psychiatric clinics, being treated for depression, narcotic abuse and the compulsive disorders. An important part of her treatment programme has been coming to terms with what happened between the ages of thirteen and fifteen with Mr Jones.

As a result of her problems, her marriage fell apart. Although she has a close relationship with her children, they live with her former husband. After she came to realise the effects on her of the sexual relationship, Anna decided to press charges. She did not want revenge. Her main concern at that stage was that he might be doing this to other young teenagers. Jones eventually pleaded guilty and was sentenced to three and a half years' imprisonment. Only now is Anna beginning to rebuild her life.

Sex with Adolescents and the Abuse of Power

Anna's first sexual experience was not mere high school experimentation but an affair with a married man more than twice her age, conducted at a time in her life when she ought to have been engaged in far more trivial pursuits. At an age when many girls try on their first make-up, Jones had involved her in a relationship as his lover and confidante. Many years later, she is still coming to terms with it.

Was Jones's offence any the less because he targeted an attractive, pubescent girl? Diagnostically, he would not have been said to be a paedophile. A distinction is sometimes drawn in this context between paedophilia, technically, a sexual attraction towards pre-pubescent children, and ephebophilia (or hebephilia), an attraction towards post-pubescent children. The argument offered for treating this distinction as significant is that paedophilia is listed in the *Diagnostic and Statistical Manual of Mental Disorders* (DSM-IV), used by psychiatrists, as a sexual disorder, whereas ephebophilia is not regarded as an abnormal pattern of arousal.[6] Relations with teenagers might be socially inappropriate but sexual attraction to teenagers is not regarded as a psychiatric condition.

While this may be a significant distinction for some diagnostic purposes, there are dangers in drawing the implication that in some way ephebophiles in positions of responsibility with children represent less of a danger than paedophiles. The patterns of predatory behaviour may well be the same whether the child is nine or fourteen, as may be the deleterious consequences for the child. The harm caused by sexual abuse may in part be a consequence of the betrayal of trust and the abuse of power, which a teenager may come to realise only some time after the sexual relationship has ended.

People who believe that there is nothing wrong with sex between adults and adolescents fail to understand that such relationships involve more than physical intimacy. The emotional dynamics of the relationship are very difficult for young teenagers to handle. Where the adult is in a position of trust and responsibility towards the child, the relationship inherently involves the most serious abuse of trust and power. Diagnostic criteria which emphasise a medical model distinguishing between psychologically normal and abnormal attractions are apt to ignore the common pattern of a betrayal of trust and an abuse of power involved whatever the age of the victim.

The Recovered Memory Controversy

Another major controversy concerns the issue of 'repressed' or 'recovered' memories. It has long been believed by therapists that memories of traumatic experiences may be repressed or blocked out from conscious memory. This is different from forgetting. We forget all sorts of things, perhaps because we are simply not very good at remembering or because they were transient or insignificant events, of insufficient importance to be stored in our long-term memory. Forgetting is a natural process, however much we might sometimes wish it to be otherwise. According to the theorists, however, repression is different from forgetting. The memory is not forgotten. It is stored in the subconscious, but it is blocked out from conscious recall as a coping mechanism because otherwise it would be too painful to deal with.

In adult life, when perhaps the person is more able to deal

with the pain than as a child, the person begins to recall the traumatic event. This can occur in numerous ways, for example in the form of flashbacks that are triggered by a smell or a location, or through memories that resurface at significant moments such as the beginnings of an adult sexual relationship, or when a child reaches the age at which the parent was abused. Some accounts of repressed memories that have apparently been recovered in adult life are very well known. In 1991, Roseanne Barr Arnold, the American comedy star, went public with her account of the memories she recovered in therapy. In the same year, a former Miss America spoke of the abuse by her father which she remembered again when she was twenty-four.[7]

Therapists report that in regard to sexual abuse the recovery of memories is a common occurrence. In a survey of 810 chartered psychologists conducted by the British Psychological Society, more than one in five had seen a client in the previous year who had recovered a memory of child sexual abuse, having previously been completely unaware of it. Over half had seen a client in the course of their professional career who had recovered a memory of some kind of traumatic experience. While it is commonly assumed that such memories surface only with the assistance of the therapist (and therefore may have been induced by the therapist), about a third of the respondents reported that the clients had recovered memories of child sexual abuse before having any therapy.[8]

In recent years, these beliefs about repression have been seriously challenged. The issue first received serious public attention as a result of the work of the False Memory Syndrome Foundation which was established in the United States in 1992. 'False memory syndrome' is not an accepted clinical syndrome with recognisable symptoms. Rather it is a name which was coined by those who claimed to have been wrongly accused of abusing their children. The movement spread to other countries. In England, the British False Memory Society was formed in 1993. While the main organisers of these groups were people who had been accused of abuse – or their spouses – they have received considerable professional support. In America, for example, the False Memory Syndrome Foundation attracted an advisory board which consisted of highly reputable psychologists who also had serious doubts about the validity of some alleged memories of abuse. A debate which had until then be conducted in scholarly journals and the corridors of university psychology departments became a major public issue. There have even been cases in the United States where therapists have been sued for allegedly implanting false memories of sexual abuse.

Typically, the argument of those who claim to be the victims of false accusations is that the memories of sexual abuse were false memories which had been induced by therapists using hypnotic suggestion and other such means. Particular controversy has surrounded some of the literature concerning child sexual abuse, and the therapeutic techniques for memory recovery which they recommend.[9] Some books on sexual abuse written in the 1980s went so far as to publish a list of symptoms which were said to be indicative of sexual abuse even if the person had no conscious recollection of them. If, for example, a woman displayed or herself identified a sufficient number of these symptoms, the chances were she had been sexually abused and should seek therapy to help her both to remember the abuse and to work through it so that the symptoms would abate. Most controversial has been *The Courage to Heal* by Ellen Bass and Laura Davis, which is one of the most widely read and highly regarded self-help books on child sexual abuse. The book lists a range of abusive experiences that people may remember, and goes on to say that even if you don't have such memories, but have a feeling that you may have been abused, you should treat those feelings as valid. The authors conclude by saying, 'If you think you were abused, and your life shows the symptoms, then you were.'[10] The symptoms are said to include low self-esteem, suicidal thoughts, depression and sexual problems. Child sexual abuse was thus seen by some counsellors and therapists as the number one suspect when a female client presented with serious emotional difficulties that did not seem to have an obvious cause. For very troubled people searching for answers to serious life problems, the possibility of sexual abuse as an explanation may have been readily grasped.

The Evidence for Recovered Memories

Is there any such thing as delayed and recovered memory? Some people argue that those who experience highly traumatic events in their lives suffer the opposite problem – they cannot forget the experiences they have had or the terrible scenes that they have witnessed. The images play over and over again in their minds. For such tormented souls, amnesia would be a blessed relief.

A few years ago, one of the arguments used against the idea of repressed memory was that there was no research evidence to support it.[11] More recently, however, it has been demonstrated very clearly that a significant number of victims of child sexual abuse do go through long periods of life with no conscious memory of abuse, and that this amnesia cannot be attributed to forgetting in the usual sense.

In the 1970s, a study was conducted of 206 girls and women who between 1973 and 1975 had been aged between ten months and twelve years and had been the victims of sexual assault. All had been seen at the same hospital in an American city, and interviews had been conducted with the child or caregiver (or both). In 1990–91, a researcher managed to trace most of the children. By this time, they were between eighteen and thirty-one years old. Exhaustive interviews were conducted with 129 women, most of them African-American, and although many questions were asked in different ways about the occurrence of sexual abuse in childhood, 38 per cent had absolutely no recollection of the events that had caused them to end up in hospital as victims of sexual assault.[12] Of the remainder who did recall the abuse, 16 per cent said that there was a time in the past when they had not remembered the abuse. There was no evidence that those who said they did not recall it were simply too shy to tell these details to the researchers. Many of them reported other incidents of sexual abuse later in childhood which were clearly unrelated to the event reported in the earlier study, and were prepared to talk openly about other sensitive issues such as drug abuse, abortion and prostitution.

In all of these cases, the abuse had been discovered and the child went to a hospital. It is possible that the percentages who do not remember abuse will be higher among those victims who suffered entirely in silence because the abuse was never discovered.

There are, of course, a variety of reasons why some individuals may have no memory of experiencing sexual abuse even though they were hospitalised and were the subjects of a research study. We do not record every event in our lives. An event not perceived as significant by a child may not be stored in the memory, or capable of being recalled, even though the same event would be very significant to an adult. Adults may realise that a certain kind of touching of a child is sexually abusive even if the child does not so perceive it. Another explanation is 'infantile amnesia'. It is very unusual for children to remember anything that happened to them before the age of three, and most of us do not recall very many incidents from the first five or six years of life. In the American study, the amnesia was greatest for the children who were youngest at the time of the abuse. Of those who were abused before the age of four 55 per cent had no recollection of it, and of those aged four to six 62 per cent had no recollection. Nonetheless, among older children, 31 per cent of seven- to ten-year-olds and 26 per cent of eleven- to twelve-year-olds did not recall the abuse.

Some of the victims who had no recollection of the abuse had experienced very traumatic events indeed. One girl was raped by her father at the age of twelve. Another, recorded in 1973, had been abused by her father at least six times, the last incident occurring when she was twelve.[13] Another was four and a half when she was abused by her uncle, although as an adult she reported that she had never met her uncle. Her account was that he had died before she was born after he had molested a little boy and was killed by the boy's mother. She had no recollection that she herself had been one of his victims and had even told her mother about it. Her mother told the mother of one of the uncle's other victims and that woman had stabbed the offender to death. The little girl had even attended his funeral.

That 38 per cent of the interviewees in this study had no recollection of their abuse, and that there were others who had forgotten it for a time puts into perspective the figures quoted in chapter 2 on the prevalence of child sexual abuse in our society. All the indications are that these figures could be an underestimate, particularly in the case of those samples of college students in their late teens or early twenties who may have completed the survey at a time when they were still unable to recall any incident of sexual abuse, but who may later in life have recalled such an incident.

It remains unclear why some people for a long time do not remember sexual abuse and then they do. Certainly, some children who are being abused 'dissociate'. They imagine that they are somewhere else. Consequently, the memory can be split off from the rest of their recollections and resurfaces only in response to some cue. In the most extreme cases, dissociation may lead to multiple personalities as the child creates separate identities in his or her mind as a way of dealing with the trauma.

It is understandable also that some children should entirely repress the memory of the traumatic event. Our capacity to cope with severe suffering depends in part on our ability to make some sense of it, or to place it within some framework of understanding of pain and evil in the world. For younger children in particular, the pain of severe abuse can be overwhelming. It destroys any sense of the world as a place in which adults will care for them and protect them from harm. When the abuse is by a close relative such as a father or stepparent, the child may experience the most profound feelings of betrayal. It should not be surprising that some children respond to very traumatic events by blocking them out from conscious memory. The pain of remembering may be so great that it would overwhelm the child's capacity to develop normally, with trust in parents and other adults, and an optimistic view of the world and their future within it.

If repression is a necessary coping mechanism for some children, this does not mean that it is best for the memory to remain buried forever. Often, the pain of the abuse has all sorts of effects at a subconscious level. Like an internal injury to the body which is very serious even though it is not visible, the childhood wounds continue to have deleterious subconscious effects. The trauma remains unresolved because it has never been dealt with. For most people, remembering child abuse after a long period is not a process that they undergo willingly. The memories may begin to force themselves to the surface in the form of flashbacks, or the adult may be in emotional turmoil without being able to understand why. When, finally, the adult allows the memories to surface, these often come together with powerful emotions, as if the feelings associated with the original abuse had merely been frozen in time. It may take months or even years to be able to deal with the depth of the pain.

Michael's Story: In the Valley of the Shadow of Death

Michael was in his mid-thirties when he first began to remember his childhood abuse. It began one winter when he began to feel a strong sense of emotional pain. Disappointed lovers sometimes describe themselves as having a 'broken heart', and it was this kind of feeling that Michael began to experience. He was also aware of a deep sadness, but he had no idea where it came from. About this time, he sensed during his prayer times that God was telling him he was about to go through a very dark valley. He was reminded of Psalm 23: 'Even though I walk through the valley of the shadow of death, I will fear no evil, for you are with me; your rod and your staff, they comfort me.'[14]

One morning, as he awoke from sleep, he realised he had had a nightmare in which he had been screaming at the top of his voice in utter terror. He had no idea what had so terrified him. All he could remember from his dream was the piercing sound of his own screams.

It was at this point that Michael went to see a professional Christian counsellor, Jonathan. Jonathan listened to the symptoms, and explained that he thought a repressed memory might be coming to the surface. He explained that the sense of emotional pain might be occurring because Michael was beginning to remember some traumatic event, but a part of him was desperately trying to suppress that memory because it was so painful. Jonathan was very careful not to suggest what that trauma could be. The one thing Michael 'knew' was that he had not been abused as a child. Jonathan did not suggest otherwise. He indicated that the painful memory could be one of any number of different experiences.

A couple of weeks later, Michael saw Jonathan again, and this time they went into a darkened room with a mattress in it, where Michael was invited to lie down. In the quiet of the room, they took some steps to help Michael relax, and then Jonathan asked Michael to give voice to whatever thoughts came to mind. Immediately, Michael felt like crying, and saw himself as a boy, about seven years old, in the playground of his primary school. He was very lonely because he was sad, and he couldn't join in the fun of the other children. There was one girl in the playground who was his friend, because she was sad as well. They felt close to one another.

A few minutes later, Michael was overwhelmed by intense and irrational fear. He said, 'Jonathan, I am afraid that you will put your hand on my throat.' Michael was terrified that someone would strangle him. He wanted to scream but he couldn't. He felt a need *not* to give vent to the memories that were beginning to return because he was so scared of them.

In this session, there were also numerous other memories – childhood events, some happy, some sad, other images which didn't have an obvious meaning. Michael gave them voice without needing to make sense of them. He ended that first session emotionally drained.

In the next few days, the sadness continued to intensify. Michael found it hard to concentrate at work with the pervasive sense of heartache he was experiencing. It was agony to suppress the memories, but a greater agony to allow himself to remember. He started to have sensations of being seized by the throat, flashes of memory which he could perceive not merely as a mental image, but as a physical sensation. The fear made him want to vomit, and he would begin to cough violently.

In the next session with Jonathan, Michael began to remember a little more. At first, the images were very confusing. Among all the other childhood memories that came to mind during that session, he became troubled by images of a churchyard at night. As a boy he had grown up beside an Anglican church with a large churchyard, so the scene was familiar to him. The images now were disturbing. Something had happened in the churchyard which made him very afraid. As he began to focus on this image, he became frightened again of being grabbed by the throat. After warning Michael about what he intended to do, Jonathan gently put his hand around Michael's throat. Michael screamed. In that instant, he had an image of a devil grabbing at his throat. It was a child's image of a devil, with black cape and sharp-lined eyebrows, a pointed chin and a hat. The session ended there.

The following session, Michael began to picture himself again as the sad and lonely child at primary school, about seven years old. He was lonely because he had a secret which he could not tell anyone. He could only cry alone. Then he began to see images of the churchyard again. He saw himself beside a gravestone that was about his height. Again, as the fear of being strangled returned to Michael, Jonathan placed his hand gently around his throat. This time, Michael saw, not a childish image of a devil, but a man who was probably in his fifties. He could see the face clearly. He had grey hair, whiskers and a pointed face. He dimly remembered that he had seen this man before hanging around the churchyard.

Slowly but surely, in this session and the next, Michael began to remember the whole sequence of events. He had been at a piano lesson in the vestry of the church. It was only a very short walk from the vestry to his home, down a footpath. The man was standing a few metres from the footpath among the gravestones and tombs. He beckoned Michael over, saying he wanted to show him something that appeared to be hidden in the inside pocket of his raincoat. As Michael came close to him, the man placed his right arm firmly on Michael's shoulder, strongly enough to prevent him from running away. He said that he wanted to play a game. Michael was very scared, and began to cry. The man grabbed him by the throat very firmly in order to stop him crying and told him to keep quiet. He then took down Michael's shorts and began to suck Michael's penis like a starving man having a meal. Something else seemed to have happened after this, for there appeared to be a gap in the narrative which as yet Michael was unable to fill. All Michael could remember was that at the end of the abuse, the man threw him violently to the ground, warning Michael that if he ever told anyone, he would kill him. Michael could not remember the exact words so much as the menace in his voice.

These memories were not merely vague mental images. As the memories came back, Michael would scream at the top of his voice in utter terror. There would be coughing and dry-retching. At times Jonathan and he would have to take a break for Michael to recover before resuming the ordeal of remembering. The feelings of terror were almost as real as if the event were occurring there and then.

Perhaps Michael's most graphic and detailed memories were of what happened immediately after the man had let him go. He remembered crying for a while at the edge of the churchyard before he was able to regain his composure sufficiently to go into the house. He went into the kitchen where his mother was. She noticed he had been crying, but he told her he had fallen down on the footpath and hurt himself a little. He went upstairs to his room and lay down, crying his eyes out. He felt ashamed, worthless and dirty. After a while, he was able to stop crying sufficiently to turn on the electric fire in his room and to sit in front of it, reading a book. It was a colourful book about farms and animals. Eventually, his mother came up to see if he was all right. He assured her he was, and then he came down to eat his dinner, remaining withdrawn and quiet, but otherwise acting as if nothing had happened.

Recovering this memory at last made sense for Michael of certain other experiences in his life which had not adequately been explained before. Michael was seen by a child psychiatrist at about the same age as he had been abused. He appeared to be very unhappy, and all the stories he wrote at school ended in people dying. The psychiatrist thought there must be family problems. As an adult, Michael had also had occasions when he felt vulnerable around the throat, but without knowing why.

Remembering this incident of abuse was just the beginning, not the end. He had to go on to deal with the sadness and the emotional pain caused by the abuse. It was at least a year later in the counselling that Michael began to remember anal abuse as well. This was the missing part of the sequence. He had suspected it because he had physical sensations around the back passage when he allowed himself to imagine being back in the churchyard. Remembering this abuse was the most terrifying aspect of all, and difficult because he did not have a visual image but rather a sensation that something had happened behind. Michael may also have blacked out or tried to imagine himself being somewhere else because he still has little visual recall of the event. The memories were mainly of the physical sensations and the terror.

His first proper recollection of the anal abuse was when he was alone one day and feeling overwhelmed again by sadness. He began to focus on his feelings and saw himself back in the churchyard. The man had told him to turn around. At this point in remembering, Michael began shaking violently from side to side, so terrifying was the memory. On the other occasions when he has tried to deal with the pain and terror of this episode, it has always been in the safety of a room with a counsellor. Only after two more years did he reach the point where he could allow himself to feel the pain associated with this episode without shaking almost uncontrollably. Eventually, he was able to remember more of what happened. The man had attempted anal penetration but had given up in frustration.

It took four years in all before Michael was able finally to overcome the negative effects from the churchyard incident. Just as the sensation of feeling vulnerable around the throat was the first aspect to be remembered, so it was the last of the traumatic effects to abate.

The Reliability of Recovered Memories

If there are situations in which people repress traumatic memories for periods of time and later recover them, the difficult question remains: how can one be sure that what a person recovers as a 'memory' actually happened? Many psychologists and psychiatrists who have raised concerns about recovered memories do not deny the fact that such repression can occur, but they are worried that recovered memories have on occasions been the sole basis on which a person has been convicted of criminal offences, and that recovered memories in general are treated with insufficient caution. There is a particular problem with memories recovered through hypnosis. People who are in a hypnotic trance are highly suggestible, and experts have pointed out the ease with which a person can be hypnotised into believing that something occurred when it did not.[15] Indeed people sometimes cling very strongly to a false memory induced by hypnosis, so sure are they that it really happened. Hypnosis increases people's confidence about a memory, but not the reliability of those memories.

The problems about reliability of memories do not arise purely from the dangers of hypnosis as a technique for their recovery. The concern is that therapists may assume that a person has been sexually abused even though he or she has no recollection of it and then 'help' the person to recover the memories. All of us are suggestible. Under the right conditions, we can be persuaded to believe something which didn't happen. Suggestibility is particularly a problem when the person who is consciously or unconsciously making the suggestion is in a position of influence or authority. Research has demonstrated again and again that even eyewitness testimony is subject to the 'misinformation effect'.[16] If one person in authority introduces a plausible detail that is suggested to other witnesses as true, the witnesses will tend to reconstruct their memories to accord with the authoritative account that has been suggested to them.

The Fallibility of Memory

Memory is also fallible. Many readers will remember well the Challenger disaster in 1986, when a space shuttle exploded into flames within a few minutes of take-off. On the morning after the event, a group of forty-four students was asked to write down where they were when they first heard about the disaster, whom they were with, how they learnt about it, what time it was, and other such details.[17] Two and a half years later they were interviewed again using the same questionnaire and asked to recall the same details. They were also asked how certain they were of their recollections. When the original account was compared with the later account, the researchers found that 25 per cent of the subjects were wrong about every detail concerning how they had heard the news. Another 50 per cent were correct on only one of the major details. However, there was no correlation between people's accuracy and their confidence in their ability to recall the events. Some people were very confident indeed about their recollections, while being wrong in most if not all the details.

Our conviction that something happened at some point in the past, and even the level of detail we are able to provide about it, is not a certain indicator that it occurred. This is so for all memories, and not just those which have been recovered after a long period. The mind does not record events in the way that a computer records data. Everything that we remember goes through a process of interpretation when it is first committed to memory. It also goes through a process of reconstruction when it is recalled from memory.

These examples of the fallibility and selectivity of memory generally should put us on guard about all memories of long ago. Our memories of childhood events may be a combination of what we stored in memory at the time, the stories that our parents told us and pictures we have seen. These different sources of information can blur into a single account of the event or situation, only some of which is the product of a child's direct memory of it.

In a climate in which there is considerable discussion of child sexual abuse, and in which it is understood to be a contributing cause of many problems in adult life, it is certainly possible for memories of abuse to be the product of suggestion, even auto-suggestion.[18] People experiencing depression or other such problems might be induced, with sufficient prompting or incentive, to recall memories of abuse. Such pseudomemories are not, however, very easy to induce, and there is little reason to believe that a few suggestive questions will lead people to invent compelling false memories.[19] In most cases, a therapist interviewing a client with vague presenting symptoms will gently ask a range of questions about childhood experiences and relationships without leading in any particular direction. There is no reason to suppose that there are many therapists who are urging clients to remember sexual abuse on the basis that they suspect it may have occurred.

Indeed, one of the effects of the controversy about repressed and recovered memories has been to make therapists far more cautious about suggesting sexual abuse, or any other form of abuse, as a contributory cause of adult problems. In a large number of cases, the person goes to the therapist because troubling memories of abuse or an unidentified trauma have already begun to surface. In others, the recovered memories build upon a foundation of conscious memories. The person may have had some memory of the abuse but it becomes much clearer as it is dealt with in therapy.[20]

Traumatic Memories

Do the problems about the fallibility of memory generally mean that no one can be sure their recovered memories are real? While there is a need for caution in interpreting recovered memories, most of the research on suggestibility and fallibility of memory has been on memories which are of a very different kind from the sorts of traumatic memories that surface after many years. It is one thing to be mistaken about where you were when you first heard about the Challenger disaster, or what you saw as an eyewitness of an event. It is another thing to have the kind of gut-wrenching memories of traumatic experiences that are quite typical of recovered memories of abuse.

The way in which recovered memories of abuse come to the surface usually differs from the way in which other memories are recalled. They may surface in a fragmented way, which begins with frightening flashbacks, or physical sensations, smells or emotions, rather than clear visual recollections. The power of the memories comes not from their vividness or detail but from the terrible pain that accompanies them. The memories seem to surface from deep within. While most memories from long ago seem distant and do not have much emotional impact in the present, traumatic memories often have an emotional intensity that is overwhelming, at least while the person is focused on them. Very commonly, people who are beginning to recover memories are full of doubt about what they are remembering; they find that the detail is quite unclear and feel that they would rather not remember because it is so traumatic to do so. Nonetheless, the memories break through the person's resistance. Depending on the nature of the trauma, terror, deep sadness, grief and feelings of shame and worthlessness may all accompany the memories. These are not adult feelings of grief and anger arising from the realisation that one has been abused as a child. Rather, they feel like a child's buried emotions, raw and immature although carried by an adult.

There have been occasional reports of people having apparent recollections of traumatic events that they have not experienced. In one case, a man had flashbacks of Vietnam and believed himself to be a war veteran although he had never been there.[21] However, generally there is little research evidence to suggest that such intense feelings can be solely the product of suggestion and without any factual basis at all.

Through a Glass Darkly

Even when real events are remembered, the details of a recovered memory may not be recalled accurately. Frequently, repressed memories return rather as the blind man recovered his sight when Jesus healed him. Initially, the images were blurred. He saw people who looked 'like trees walking around'. A little later he was able to see clearly (Mark 8:22–26). Surfacing memories may be chaotic and fragmented; they may begin to make sense and form a complete picture only slowly. A process of interpretation is involved. Inevitably, the story may develop or change over time as new details are remembered or new interpretations are made of the fragments of memory.

Indeed, we may not remember what happened so much as the way we perceived what happened. In Michael's case, for example, he perceived his attacker as a devil, and the first memories he recalled of the event were of a 'devil' grabbing his throat. Only a little later was he able to go beyond that interpretation of the event to recall the event itself. The 'devil' had a somewhat wizened human face. Where painful memories return, imagined elements may be mixed with real elements. This stems from the child's need to put the abuse into some framework which makes sense.

The nature of recovered memory is such that one may not be able to say in an objective sense that the recovered event is true. We see the past as through a glass darkly, in which much of the detail is obscured. The person who is beginning to recover memories needs to be open to the possibility of different interpretations of what he or she is remembering. Sometimes there is some corroboration. There are abuse survivors who repressed their memories for years and yet had siblings who had always remembered their abuse at the hands of the same perpetrator. In some situations, the perpetrator has confessed that abuse occurred. The memory of the abuse may also make sense of other life events which exist in conscious memory.

For many people though, the memory of abuse can only ever be a subjective conviction, and the account is impossible to verify. Some experts in the field are thus urging caution about how therapists respond to the recovered memories of clients. A Working Party of the British Psychological Society recommended in 1995 that therapists should not form premature conclusions about the status of a recovered memory but should help the client to consider a range of possibilities – that the material might be literally true, that the memory is a metaphor for other non-sexual experiences or that it derives from fantasy or dream imagery. This involves tolerating a certain degree of ambiguity or uncertainty regarding the clients' experiences.[22]

Those who have recovered memories, especially when they were the product of such therapeutic techniques as hypnosis and eye movement desensitisation and reprocessing (EMDR), necessarily have to treat what they recall with caution. In many cases, the feelings associated with the memory are such that it is clear that something very traumatic must have happened. Because the recovery of memories is a process over time, the person should be careful not to try to piece all the fragments of memory together too quickly or to fill in the gaps in the narrative with supposition.

A particularly difficult issue is whether the person should take the recovered memories of abuse beyond the therapist's office. Often the motive is to try to find some external verification or validation of the memories. This may be very helpful to the person, but there are also dangers. In some cases, families have been deeply divided over such memories. Daughters have confronted fathers in the hope that they will acknowledge the abuse and thereby confirm the reality of the daughter's memories. Confession may occur in some cases, but this is likely to be very uncommon, as there are powerful incentives for the perpetrator not to acknowledge the truth. If the father denies the daughter's account, it does not mean that the memory itself was false, and so the family is thrown into a long-term crisis, which is very difficult to resolve and which ultimately may be destructive for all concerned.

Unless there is corroborative evidence, it probably will not be possible to prove the case to others, and certainly the police will have great difficulty in prosecuting such a matter. As time goes on, however, the person who recovers traumatic memories may be able to reach his or her own inner conviction about the truth of what has emerged. In some cases, after a period of reflection, people have concluded that their memories were not real. More often the memories are only too real.

Ritual Abuse

In recent years, there has been growing awareness of, and controversy about, the phenomenon of ritual abuse, or satanic ritual abuse as it is sometimes called. Ritual abuse has been defined as 'abuse that occurs in a context linked to some symbols or group activity that have a religious, magical or supernatural connotation, and where the invocation of these symbols or activities, repeated over time, is used to frighten and intimidate the children.'[23]

Awareness of this problem first began in North America in the early 1980s with accounts from adult survivors of the most horrifying abuse occurring in the context of satanic rituals or other forms of witchcraft. A common element to these accounts was sexual abuse in a ritualised context and, moreover, various other forms of torture involving multiple offenders in the course of rituals. In all such cases a number of people had complicity in the abuse. In recent times significant numbers of people in England, Australia, Canada, the United States and many other countries have reported ritual abuse.

These adult survivors have described people wearing hoods and other costumes, standing around in circles and chanting.

Common elements are altars, robes and pentagrams. There have been reports of orgies, animal sacrifice, the drinking of blood or urine and the eating of faeces. Victims may be drugged in order to secure their acquiescence to the abuse. Most disturbing of all have been the accounts of human sacrifice: babies and children figure in the reports, as do adults in some cases. Many accounts reported that adolescents have been used as breeders and have given birth in secret to infants, a process that provides untraceable children for infant sacrifices. A variation of this is the impregnation, by a member of the group, of adolescent girls who are then forced to have secret abortions before the time when the pregnancy would begin to be visible. The foetus is then used in the rituals.

Typically, the adult survivors, having extricated themselves from these groups and joined churches or survivor groups, have reported that they were powerless as children because all the members of the family were in the satanic cult and were accomplices in the abuse. For children in this situation life is thus an unending torture offering no escape because they are too scared to speak out to anyone outside the group, and their immediate circle of family and friends are part of the group. Silence is reinforced by the threat of death for defection. Many adult survivors have attested to the use of such threats. Not all accounts of ritual abuse involve intergenerational abuse in which parents and grandparents participate. It is believed that in some cases children of pre-school age are being made to take part in satanic rituals.

Most of the accounts have come from adult survivors and relate to events many years before. Such memories have typically been deeply repressed and surfaced only through therapy. A diagnosis of ritual abuse is particularly associated with people suffering from multiple personality disorder or other dissociative disorders.[24] The recovery of memories of satanic ritual abuse is not only terrifying for the person concerned. It also has a profound impact on the therapists who deal with this. They find themselves having to acknowledge a level of evil which they may not have thought was possible.

The awareness of ritual abuse is not entirely dependent on recovered memories. In recent years police or social workers have in some cases concluded that they have uncovered current cases of ritual abuse, including one in Nottingham, England, and another in Oude Pekela, Holland.[25] These cases have aroused some controversy, however. When a prosecution has taken place, the trial has sometimes proceeded solely on the basis of the sexual abuse offences, and the ritualistic context has been downplayed because it might have reduced the children's credibility. Other cases in Britain in which ritual abuse was alleged, including one in Rochdale and another in the Orkneys, have led to court cases or inquiries in which the allegations of ritual abuse have been dismissed and judges have strongly criticised the social workers involved for their methodology in investigating the cases.[26]

The claims concerning widespread organised ritual abuse of children have been greeted with disbelief in some professional circles.[27] When a leading journal on child abuse and neglect published two articles reporting ritual abuse in 1991, it departed from its normal practice by surrounding them with editorials and critical commentaries that questioned whether these accounts could be taken at face value.[28]

Ritual Abuse and Occult Practices

Reports of unspeakable atrocities have of course, through the ages, been greeted with disbelief. The first rumours about the Holocaust were not given credence, and similar disbelief has for centuries surrounded sexual abuse in the family. Our first reaction to anything that suggests that human beings are capable of utter depravity is denial. Denial has been a first stage through which society has passed in coming to terms with many dark secrets. Yet there is a long history of occult activity in Western societies, and while there is some controversy about the origins of the Black Mass and other such rituals popularly associated with satanism, there is nothing new in small groups meeting to practise rituals involving Satan. These rituals include many of the elements described in accounts by ritual abuse survivors.

In recent years, there has been a strong growth in interest in new age practices and the occult. Among the smorgasbord of different occult practices and beliefs are some crafts of the very darkest kind. Books by writers such as Alisteir Crowley have been sources of occult knowledge and practice. Covens and small satanic groups are to be found in many places. Not only is it far from incredible that ritual abuse should occur, it is quite probable that there are occult groups which sexually abuse children in rituals involving animal sacrifice and the drinking of blood or urine. In the writings of some occultists conventional moral values are completely inverted: fair is foul and foul is fair; evil is good and lust is a virtue. This mode of thinking and, indeed, the sadistic physical and sexual abuse of children has a long history. Much of what is to be found in the literature on satanic ritual abuse can also be found in the writings of the Marquis de Sade, particularly a work he wrote in the Bastille in 1789 entitled *The 120 Days of Sodom.*[29]

Reasons for Disbelief

Why then the scepticism? Part of the difficulty of belief comes from the way in which some people have sensationalised the issue. There have been numerous claims of a widespread conspiracy – to engage in ritual abuse and to maintain the silence about it – reaching to the highest levels of society, and that satanic ritual abuse is a very common phenomenon. One American psychiatrist who is an expert on satanic ritual abuse claims that satanic cults form part of an international organisation with a similar structure to that of the Communist party, having local groups, a regional leadership and an international leadership.[30]

A Christian psychologist working with ritual abuse patients quotes a video on satanic ritual abuse as a source of reliable information: 'From the number of pre-school cases alone, it would appear that a massive indoctrination of American children into satanism is going on.' He then cites an estimate from a leading investigator that there have been more than a hundred pre-schools in California implicated in ritual abuse,[31] and quotes suggestions from others that there has been a major cover-up, with evidence disappearing and cases being deliberately mishandled.[32] Such claims generate considerable scepticism and concern among professionals working in child protection who have less invested in the belief that ritual abuse is widespread.

The view that satanic cults have national and international networks, and that they are protected by people in high places, has had a particular reception in evangelical Christian circles. None of these conspiracy theories has been supported by evidence. Law enforcement officers have pointed out that the larger the conspiracy, the more difficult it is for such groups to prevent defections, even under extreme threat. These groups tend to implode.[33]

The sensationalism involved in claiming widespread ritual abuse and cover-up can lead people to dismiss all cases in which ritual abuse is alleged as the product of imagination or highly suggestive interviewing. Christians are sometimes insufficiently cautious and critical in accepting the manifold conspiracy theories about the onward march of evil. Such ideas abound in the popular evangelical literature on the End Times. Rumours about a new and sinister threat from the forces of darkness can spread like wildfire through evangelical and charismatic churches. Commonly, the source of the information is unknown and its veracity not questioned.

Indeed, a serious problem in validating claims of satanic ritual abuse has been the lack of most kinds of evidence. Law enforcement agencies, especially in the United States, have taken these cases very seriously and searched for corroborative evidence but largely in vain. Although there is plenty of evidence that satanic rituals take place in secluded environments, and indications have sometimes been found of animal sacrifices, the police, in America at least, have generally not found evidence to corroborate the most serious charges of human sacrifice, baby-breeding and organised satanic conspiracies.[34]

A major study was conducted in England of all cases

reported to have involved either ritual abuse or other forms of organised sexual abuse of children between the beginning of 1988 and the end of 1991. In total, the investigators found eighty-four cases of alleged ritual abuse. Fourteen cases involved reports of animal sacrifice and thirty-five of human sacrifice, but in none of them was any evidence found to support these allegations. In only a small handful of cases did the police find any corroborative evidence at all of ritualistic elements. In two cases they found robes and altars, in three cases there were candles, and in four cases there were occult books.[35] Of the eighty-four cases studied, only three were confirmed on the basis of corroborative evidence. In each case, there was just one perpetrator of the abuse, although other adults took part in the rituals.[36]

The lack of evidence does not of course prove anything. The groups involved may be particularly adept at covering their tracks. However, some elements of accounts of ritual abuse raise doubts about their veracity. It is common to find reports of baby-breeding and infant sacrifice. Typically, the claim is that the girl in her young teens was impregnated by a leader of the group, perhaps after a satanic marriage. She later gave birth to a child in secret and without the baby's birth being registered. The birth was facilitated by a midwife or doctor who belonged to the group, and the baby was ritually sacrificed soon after birth. In some accounts, the person reports numerous such pregnancies while still under sixteen years old.

While such practices are certainly possible, it is unclear how they could go undiscovered in modern society. It is relatively unlikely that a young girl could carry a baby to term, give birth, and then see the baby killed without anyone knowing, and indeed for this to happen more than once. If such girls were attending school, or had neighbours or friends outside the group, the pregnancy would probably be observed in the latter stages. Modern Western society makes it difficult for individuals or groups to live in total seclusion from other people without any contact with public authorities or the rest of the community. If a baby was born conventionally in a hospital and was registered at birth, it would be very difficult for it subsequently to disappear without trace. It is much more plausible that young teenagers have been impregnated and that they have been forced to have backstreet abortions by members of the occult group.

The problem, then, with accepting the validity of recovered memories of satanic ritual abuse is a paucity of corroborative evidence and the implausibility of some of the claims made. Scepticism has increased as certain well-known specialists in dealing with ritual abuse in the United States have been accused of the most serious professional malpractice. Former patients have claimed publicly that the doctors made a diagnosis of ritual abuse which was not derived at all from the patient's own account, and then 'treated' the patient according to that diagnosis, with enormously damaging consequences.

Beyond Polarisation

The controversy about ritual abuse tends to polarise people into camps of true believers and non-believers, making rational discussion of the issue very difficult. It is not necessary, however, to be locked into positions of either total acceptance or total denial. It is a mistake to focus on the most implausible aspects of the accounts as a way of discounting the phenomenon entirely. Although, in books and seminars, those who have sought to expose the extent of satanic ritual abuse have often focused on the similarities between different accounts in order to suggest that there are recurrent patterns, in reality accounts of ritual abuse vary considerably. Some give indications of satanic worship. In others, the form and purpose of the ritual is not clear, or the occult activity is of a different kind. In some cases the abuse is said to have occurred only within the nuclear or extended family, in others entirely outside the context of the family. In some cases, human sacrifice is apparently involved, in others it is not. Where similarities are observed between entirely unrelated cases and across different countries, this is sometimes the product of interpreting what a child has said or an adult has remembered in such a way that it conforms to the 'typical pattern' of such cases.

In trying to determine whether ritual abuse has occurred in any given case, it is important to keep an open mind and to consider a variety of different interpretations. At the heart of the problem of interpretation is the fact that we do not necessarily remember what is objectively true. We remember what we believe to be true. There is every reason to suppose from the accounts of some adult survivors that, in certain cases, the child has been deliberately confused about what is real and what is not. The child may have been told the blood is human blood as a way of terrifying her, when in fact it is animal blood. A young child may have been led to believe that he has been made to participate in the murder of another child as a way of making him feel guilty by association. Similarly, the fact that a child is told that speaking out is useless because the cult has friends in high places does not mean necessarily that the group does have official protection. The younger the children, the easier it is to create utter confusion in their minds.

There are other potential explanations for some of the accounts. One that needs to be considered is that the child has been the victim of organised sadism rather than being caught up in a satanic cult. It is possible that the extreme cruelty that the child has suffered has been misinterpreted as a new phenomenon of ritual abuse when such abuse has a long history among the most extreme elements of the sado-masochistic subculture. Another possible interpretation is that the child was a victim of a paedophile ring or other organised sexual abuse, in which the ritualistic elements and the references to supernatural power are used to deter the child from disclosure. In such cases, the motivation for the abuse is paedophilic sexual gratification. The method may involve masks, the killing of animals and references to ghosts and demons to ensure that the child is silenced, either by fear or by confusion.[37] A child molester may also say that the devil will get the child if he or she ever tells anyone. This does not in itself mean that the perpetrator is engaging in satanic rituals.

Moreover, recovered memories of abuse may contain a mixture of the real and the metaphoric,[38] or may be 'screen memories' hiding a more difficult truth, that the person did indeed suffer traumatic abuse as a child but perhaps not in the remembered way or context.

Therapists who deal with ritual abuse cases may be overwhelmed by the horror of what has emerged in the counselling room, and for this reason have become convinced about the reality of ritual abuse. They are likely to be opposed to those who question the literal veracity of such accounts, since as therapists they regard it as very important to believe and support their clients. It is not, however, necessary to see any questioning of ritual abuse as an attack on the individuals who have recovered traumatic memories. Whether there was animal blood or human blood, whether there was a satanic ritual group or a sadistic paedophile ring does nothing to change the subjective reality for the person who has been severely traumatised by the experience.

The weight of all the evidence suggests that there are some children who are being severely abused, physically, sexually and emotionally, in small groups which are engaged in occult or satanic practices. It is likely that these are fringe groups in society, which are quite small and may well be intergenerational. It is possible that some groups may have access to children other than through family membership and operate in much the same way as paedophile rings. In contrast to the evidence for sexual abuse generally, there is no evidence that ritual abuse is a widespread phenomenon. Even if the problem is not as great as some people are inclined to believe, that should make no difference in caring for those who have been victims either of ritual abuse or other forms of severe sadistic abuse. They have experienced suffering greater than words can express.

PART II

PASTORAL ISSUES

Chapter 6

The Effects of Child Sexual Abuse

Caring for Abuse Survivors

There are few experiences of childhood more capable of causing serious harm than child sexual abuse. During the course of childhood and adolescence, children who have been sexually abused are likely to show numerous symptoms of distress or disorder including nightmares, sadness, anxiety, poor self-esteem, sexualised behaviour, aggression, suicide attempts, eating disorders and juvenile delinquency. In the long term, child sexual abuse is also associated with depression, mental illness including dissociative identity disorders, compulsive behaviours such as cleaning fetishes, anxiety disorders, sexual difficulties and many other problems. A very large number of people who go to therapists seeking help for emotional problems as adults reveal a history of sexual abuse.

A history of sexual abuse may not be the only cause of mental health problems in adult life. Children who grow up in families in which there is domestic violence, physical abuse or other poor parenting practices are more vulnerable to sexual abuse than those from stable and secure family backgrounds. It is thus difficult to separate the effects on the adult psyche of sexual abuse from those of other contributing factors. Nonetheless, a clear causal link between childhood sexual abuse and mental health problems in adult life has been demonstrated,

111

whatever other factors may have co-existed with this abuse. Furthermore, children from the most loving and secure family backgrounds can be seriously affected by sexual abuse.[1]

It is sometimes difficult for those who care for abuse survivors to understand the profound effects which the abuse has had. Survivors who are struggling with the effects of the abuse years after it has ended are sometimes counselled by well-meaning friends or family members to 'let bygones be bygones' and live for the present. This is particularly a problem in churches, where a belief that Jesus has all the answers can lead to trite counsel from people who simply don't understand the questions.

Good pastoral care can make an enormous difference to abuse survivors. The church family may provide the abuse victim with the first unconditional love he or she has ever known. A church minister or other pastoral worker may also be able to exert a significant influence for good in demonstrating that love and caring need not be sexual. For the Christian who has been sexually abused, a struggle of faith often overlays and compounds the psychological issues that have to be worked through. Loving counsel and non-judgmental support can make all the difference in helping people to find God's comfort in their suffering, and to deal with the painful questions about why he allowed it to happen.

At the same time as Christians can do a lot of good in coming alongside the victim of sexual abuse they can also do a lot of harm. In order to be a positive support for abuse survivors, it is helpful to understand the various effects of sexual abuse, and the way it has impacted upon the survivors' beliefs about themselves and the world.

Do All Victims of Sexual Abuse Suffer Adverse Consequences?

Not all victims of child sexual abuse are badly affected by their experiences. Studies done with children who have been abused have found that on average about 30 per cent show no symptoms of distress.[2] This is not particularly surprising. The one label of 'child sexual abuse' encompasses a wide variety of incidents, occurring in a range of different contexts. A teenage girl's experience of being groped by a stranger on a train or in a cinema may be very distressing, but it is unlikely to affect her as seriously as long-term abuse by her stepfather.

The apparent lack of long-term effects does not mean that the sexual abuse was insignificant. As Browne and Finkelhor put it:

> Effects seem to be considered less serious if the impact is transient and disappears in the course of development. However, this tendency to assess everything in terms of its long-term effects betrays an 'adultocentric' bias. Adult traumas such as rape are not assessed ultimately in terms of whether or not they will have an impact on old age: they are acknowledged to be painful and alarming events whether their impact lasts for one year or ten. Similarly, childhood traumas should not be dismissed because no 'long-term effects' can be demonstrated.[3]

Factors that Influence Outcomes

Generally, there are a number of factors that tend to make the effects of the abuse more or less serious. One of the most significant is the closeness of the relationship between the victim and the perpetrator. Children who are abused by a father or stepfather tend to be particularly affected, and abuse by grandfathers also has very negative effects. The duration of the abuse is another key factor. While single incidents of abuse can be highly traumatic, generally the longer the duration of the abuse the more harmful it is to the child's well-being. Another factor is the severity of the abuse. If intercourse occurred, generally the effects are more severe than those of less invasive forms of sex abuse. The final important factor is the degree of force. If violence was involved, then the level of trauma tends to be greater.

The degree of harm sustained is significantly affected by the level of support that the child receives. Some children tell absolutely no one, and so they are left to deal with their emotions entirely alone. In other cases, the abuse becomes known and the children have strong emotional support from family and friends. Children who gain good parental support tend to do much better than those who don't. Parents who believe their children, act to protect them from further abuse and allow the children to share their feelings about what has happened can do much to assist the child in healing.

An apparent lack of symptoms of adverse effects can be deceiving. Some effects are not seen immediately and appear only later on, as the child begins to deal emotionally with what has happened. Some children develop impressive coping strategies for dealing with abuse, sometimes dissociating and imagining that they are somewhere else while it is happening, at other times putting on a brave face and not allowing themselves to feel the pain and sadness. These coping mechanisms are necessary at the time, but have harmful effects in the long term unless the root problems are dealt with.

Child sexual abuse needs to be understood not merely in terms of the sexual acts that took place but in terms of their emotional effects. Being abused tends to influence children's feelings about who they are, and it is this effect on their core identity that is so significant. Sexual abuse can affect a child's self-esteem, capacity to trust and sexual development, among other things. Whether any or all of these effects are experienced depends in part upon the context within which sexual abuse occurs.

The Effects on Self-esteem

Children who have been sexually abused often show a number of signs of low self-esteem, including self-hatred, suicidal depression and a sense of hopelessness. These effects can be seen particularly in the context of sexual abuse within the family, where the perpetrator is a father or other care-giver. For young children to develop a healthy sense of self-esteem, they need to know that they are loved and respected as individuals. Children learn self-worth from the fact that others close to them love them very much and feel they are worthwhile.

What messages does a father give to a child by abusing her sexually? One of the messages a daughter may hear is that she is not loved for who she is but for her capacity to provide sexual gratification for her father. To be told she is loved by her father means only that he wants to use her sexually, and it is very easy to hear all protestations of love from males as having the same underlying message. Thus the experiences of abuse can affect her capacity to accept at face value the words 'I love you'. The diminution of 'love' to mean little more than that the child's body is sexually arousing can have a profoundly damaging effect on the child's sense of self-worth, sometimes to the extent that their self-worth becomes heavily dependent on feeling that they are sexually pleasing to men.

Just as sexual abuse distorts the child's sense of what it means to love and be loved, so it distorts the child's sense of separate identity. Parents allow their children, even from an early age, to be able to say 'no', to assert an identity independent of the parents. As children grow older, that sense of separate identity includes a knowledge that they have rights concerning their own body. A girl of five may delightedly splash around in the bathtub with mother or father by her side; but as she grows older, she prefers to bath alone and particularly to have a realm of bodily privacy which should not be invaded by others. The parents' acceptance of this growing personal modesty teaches the child that her body is her own and her personal autonomy deserves to be respected. Therapists and social workers often term this an awareness of 'boundaries'.

The incest victim, in contrast, is not allowed to have boundaries. There is no part of her self that is private, no zone which she can say for sure is 'hers' and not 'his', not even the most private parts of her body. Her nakedness cannot be hidden from him, nor can she stop him from touching any part

115

of her. To say 'no' has neither any validity nor any effect, and eventually she gives up trying to say 'no'. It is that constant violation of self, the lack of respect for her as a separate individual that can affect her sense of self-worth at a most fundamental level.

It is no wonder that so many children who have been sexually abused by parents feel that their lives are of no value, that they are worthless and unlovable, for this is the message they have received from at least one parent, sometimes from their very earliest years. While incest usually involves only the father or stepfather and not the mother, it nonetheless affects the child's relationship with the mother as well. She may have tried to tell her mother, and got nowhere. She may have been led to believe that her mother knows and doesn't care, or that her mother is too fragile to learn this news and it is the child's responsibility to protect her by keeping the secret. Sexual abuse often creates estrangement from both parents. The trauma of incest, therefore, is not merely about sexual abuse but about growing up with quite different foundations for life from other children, foundations that become the source of long-term problems. Cathy Anne Matthews refers to the abuse victim as having 'a different basic reference point of defective nurture'.[4] Abuse victims have learnt to see themselves through distorted lenses, and these become the inner beliefs about their identity, which, without therapeutic intervention, may affect their whole lives.

Incest may be particularly damaging, but all sexual abuse can have serious effects on self-esteem. Feelings of worthlessness sometimes derive from what the perpetrator has said. For example, the perpetrator may tell the child that he is doing this to her because she is evil or 'deserves it' or because she is a 'whore'. Sexually abused children sometimes receive the message that they are bad – not just naughty in the way that all children are sometimes naughty, but bad in the sense that they are rotten to the very core of their being. It is a very difficult thing for the victim of abuse to get the perpetrator's voice out of her head. What he says about her can reverberate in the mind for years as a voice of condemnation, and it cuts her down whenever she manages to assert a new confidence in herself as a lovable and decent person.

The message of worthlessness may also be an implicit one. The very fact that the offender is prepared to use the child for his own gratification in disregard of her feelings tells her that her needs, wishes and desires do not matter. She is not important, and it is her place in life to be used by others to meet their needs. Victims who develop such a low level of self-worth during childhood will sometimes go on to make poor choices in adult relationships. Victims of childhood abuse may eventually marry or live with men who also show disrespect for their feelings and bodily integrity. Indeed, research has shown consistently that the victims of child sexual abuse are much more likely than other people to be victims of rape or domestic violence as adults.[5]

Guilt

Guilt is a very common sequel of sexual abuse in childhood. So many victims feel guilty because they believe that they are in some way responsible for the abuse. A sense of guilt keeps many children from telling, and also holds them in cruel bondage in later life. The guilt may be because she accepted inducements from the perpetrator to keep the abuse a secret, or because she didn't say no to his touching, or because she allowed things to go so far before beginning to resist, by which time she felt compromised.

The sense of responsibility for the abuse may also derive from the child's physiological responses to sexual stimulation. Perpetrators often try to persuade children that they were willing participants because it is part of the perpetrator's own rationalisation of the abuse to believe that the sexual pleasure was mutual. Perpetrators thus will often try to arouse the child by stimulation of the penis or clitoris, and many children's bodies will indeed naturally respond. As Anna Salter writes, this can be very confusing and difficult for the child:

If [the boy's] body responds to the abuse, he will find it difficult to resist the offender's interpretation of that response: that he wants the abuse to occur, that he is enjoying it, and that his 'wanting it' was the reason it occurred in the first place. He is unlikely to report the abuse for fear the offender will tell about his physical responsiveness, possibly even his orgasms, and therefore his 'role' in the abuse.[6]

Children's feelings of guilt about their 'role' in allowing the abuse to occur can be profound. They may lead the child to feel utterly bad, and such feelings can become deeply entrenched aspects of his or her self-identity.

Guilt is also a pervasive feature of the experience of sexual abuse victims for other reasons too. Children may feel responsible for the abuse because it is the only alternative to other feelings which are even more difficult to cope with. Guilt is the only alternative to facing up to the unreasonableness of evil. Young children in particular need to have an idealised view of their parents and other care-givers and to be able to trust people. They also need to believe that the world is a safe place in order to grow up feeling secure in their environment.

The sexually abused child discovers, sometimes brutally, that the world is not a safe place, that not all adults will nurture and protect them, sometimes not even their parents. Faced with such a terrifying reality, it is easier to find reasons why he or she is being victimised than to accept that evil needs no reasons. The abuse victim is likely to find those reasons within rather than to locate them externally in a trusted care-giver. If she is being abused therefore, it must be because she is bad or because she is a seductress. Younger children in particular tend to see good and bad situations in terms of themselves. If something bad is happening to them, it is much easier for them to assume that it must be their fault than to come to terms with the fact of evil in a parent or other trusted adult. To the adult, such guilt is irrational, but for the child, it is the only way of making sense of the world while maintaining some shred of faith in it.

Guilt is also an easier burden to bear than a sense of

helplessness. Rape victims and child sexual abuse victims alike have been known to feel guilty because they believe they should have done something more to stop it. Couldn't I have fought back? Wouldn't a swift kick in the right place have given me enough time to run? Why did I remain passive and just let him do it to me? Why did I pretend I was sleeping? These are irrational questions to an outside observer. Of course she could have done nothing when he was overpowering her, of course at her age she could not have stood up to him. And yet, for the victim, such feelings of guilt stubbornly withstand the voices of reason within or without. It is easier to accept responsibility for not using your resources to stave off the abuse than to accept that you were utterly powerless to stop it. For if you acknowledge that you were completely helpless to defend against attack once, at another time in your life you might be utterly powerless again. Feeling guilty for not stopping the abuse is a way of believing that it is possible to have some power and some measure of control even in the face of overwhelming adversity.

Shame

Shame is another very common aspect of the experience of sexual abuse victims. Shame can be healthy or unhealthy. Healthy shame reminds us of our human limitations. We feel healthy shame when we fall short of being the kind of the person we know we ought to be and can be. Healthy shame reminds us of the call to be more Christlike in how we behave and interact with others. Unhealthy shame, or 'toxic shame', as one writer describes it,[7] does not call us on to be the kind of person we ought to be. It condemns us for who we are. It places us in an adversarial position with ourselves.[8]

Toxic shame is a very common effect of sexual abuse. Indeed, it is perhaps the ultimate consequence of many of the other effects. Feelings of valuelessness and guilt translate into a deep sense of shame about one's whole identity. Some abuse victims feel that they are 'damaged goods', that no one could love them after what they have done or have allowed to happen to them. Tamar felt toxic shame when she was raped by Amnon. It is recorded that after the rape, 'Tamar lived in her brother Absalom's house, a desolate woman' (2 Sam. 13:20). She felt that the only way she could cope with life after the rape was to hide away from public view even though she was a princess. Never again could she hold her head up high and walk through the streets with the dignity that should have been her birthright.

The feeling of shame is particularly associated with sexuality. For a girl, the experience of sex may have been of something secretive, dirty, unpleasant, dreadfully wrong. Although it is her abuser's sin rather than hers, she identifies with the shame he ought to feel, and internalises it as her own. She may become ashamed of her body, ashamed of sexual arousal, ashamed of herself for being a participant, even a very unwilling participant, in this secret sexual activity. In its extreme forms, such shame can be manifested in compulsive cleaning disorders, constantly needing to wash hands or genitals, or to rid the house of germs. The abuse survivor feels chronically dirty and yet no amount of washing can make her clean. The sense of being damaged, impure, dirty and bad all work together to make the abuse victim hate herself. The child ought to be angry with her abuser, but so often that anger is directed towards herself. She punishes herself for his sins, crucifying herself for what he has done.

Shame is one of the most destructive feelings associated with sexual abuse. It affects the victims' relationships as they grow up by making it hard for them to believe that anyone could love them. Shame can sap the will to live. It can cripple the heart, robbing the victim of his or her enjoyment of life.

Grief

Another consequence of child sexual abuse for the victim can be a deep sense of grief. Victims grieve over what is lost and can never be replaced. It may be the loss of innocence, the loss of virginity or the absence of the kind of safe and secure upbringing that friends have enjoyed. At its worst, sexual abuse may have blighted the person's entire childhood, and so the sense of loss can be profound.

This was the case for Jane, who was sexually abused for a number of years by her father. At the age of thirteen, when she was in a therapy session, she wrote a letter to her father, in which she spoke about her sense of grief. She felt that she had lost her father at the time when the abuse began. She had very little memory of her father behaving as 'Daddies should behave with their daughters', and wished she could have had 'proper fun' with her father.[9]

Another cause of grief and sadness is the sense of isolation in the abuse. The child who is abused and keeps it a secret for a long time (as so many do) has two realities. There is her private reality, the reality, for example, of what she experiences at night when her father comes into the bedroom, or perhaps the reality of what happens every Wednesday when the uncle comes to babysit. This is a reality that is shared only with the perpetrator, and he will make no mention of it in the company of others. Then there is the reality as perceived by those around her – her mother, brothers, sisters. This world knows nothing of the abuse, and therefore implicitly denies it.[10] The child thus lives some of the time in another world from her close family. It is easy for her to feel isolated, alone, alienated, different. In adult years, the pain of loneliness may well be one of the aspects of the abuse that the survivor most needs to grieve over.

Anger

Anger is another powerful emotion associated with sexual abuse. Healthy anger is the type that locates the responsibility solely with the perpetrator; but it often takes time for an abuse survivor to reach that point. Commonly, when the survivor who has not yet come to terms with the abuse has bottled up the anger, rather than directing it appropriately at the one who was responsible for the pain, it comes out in all sorts of other ways. It may be self-directed, or the abuse survivor may be angry with the world without realising why. When anger is misdirected, innocents can be caught in the line of fire.

For Christians such anger can be difficult to deal with. The abuse survivor may be ashamed of the anger, realising it is misdirected. There may also be guilt about being angry at all. Although Jesus modelled righteous anger at many times in his life, Christians are often very uncomfortable with anger, regarding it as sinful in itself. The abuse survivor who is not given permission to be angry at all may simply bottle up that anger, with internally destructive effects. Identifying the feelings of anger and finding appropriate ways of expressing it are very important steps in the healing process.

Post-traumatic Stress

Post-traumatic stress disorder is most likely to occur when a child has been the victim of a forcible sexual assault or sadistic abuse. The violence may be as damaging as the other aspects of the sexual abuse, and adds another dimension to the harm caused.

For such victims of violent or sadistic abuse, the effects are likely to be similar to those experienced by adult rape victims.[11] Sexual attack carries with it its own trauma. There is none of the subtlety of grooming, none of the befriending and apparent caring; just brute force, violence, violation and, for the victim, feelings of shock, powerlessness, and utter bewilderment.

The trauma of violent sexual assault comes from realising that ordinary human defence mechanisms are useless to protect one from harm. Normally, when human beings are threatened with danger, they experience an adrenalin rush, become alert and are mobilised to meet the threat either by fighting or by flight. Psychiatrist Judith Herman describes what happens when these ordinary adaptations to threat are rendered useless:

122

> Traumatic reactions occur when action is of no avail. When neither resistance nor escape is possible, the human system of self-defense becomes overwhelmed and disorganized. Each component of the ordinary response to danger, having lost its utility, tends to persist in an altered and exaggerated state long after the actual danger is over . . . Traumatic symptoms have a tendency to become disconnected from their source and to take on a life of their own.[12]

Post-traumatic stress disorder is the commonly used term for this. It is a reaction to the threat of annihilation or to the violation of a person's bodily integrity. The responses of body and mind are exaggerations of the normal physiological responses to danger. One of the symptoms is a heightened state of alertness, as if danger will return at any moment, and the person must not relax his or her guard. It is manifested in sleeplessness, irritability and a trigger-fast reaction to anything that is startling.

Another symptom of post-traumatic stress disorder is the persistent intrusion of the traumatic memory. This is typically in the form of repetitive nightmares, but it may also take the form of daytime flashbacks. These recollections of the situation carry a sense of immediacy and vividness, and in extreme cases the person may relive the trauma unaware of present circumstances and surroundings. The traumatic memory lacks the distance of a past event that has been put into perspective. Its pain is not dulled by the soothing voice of reason nor by the rationalisation that comes from reflection. It is not covered over by the passage of time, although some people manage to block it out.

Another symptom of post-traumatic stress disorder is numbness. The victim, unable to flee, surrenders to the attacker but only in her body, not in her mind. She copes with the terror and sense of helplessness by switching off from the pain and entering an altered state of consciousness in which she is somehow anaesthetised from the pain and violation. This numbing of the emotions is a protective reaction at the time, but in post-traumatic stress disorder it survives the period of danger and becomes an intermittent state of detachment from one's feelings, which in the long-term prevents integration and healing.

Post-traumatic stress disorder may be most obvious in the first few months and years of a traumatic event, but its symptoms can be very long-term. Where the memory has been repressed, the trauma remains unresolved and shows itself in symptoms which the person cannot relate to any known causes. The occurrence of flashbacks and nightmares is the beginning of these traumatic memories breaking through into consciousness, needing to be dealt with if healing is to occur.

The victim of traumatic sexual abuse who has not reached the point of being able to deal with the trauma may well be trapped in a state of fear in which the world is seen as a dangerous and unpredictable place and in which she is unable to feel even a reasonable degree of safety.

The Capacity to Trust

Another serious consequence of sexual abuse is the effect that it has on the child's capacity to trust others. Where the abuser is in a position of responsibility in relation to the child, or even where the abuser exploits the child's trust by befriending her and leading her into a place of vulnerability, the child may experience a profound sense of betrayal. The harm of sexual abuse does not lie only in physical violation but in the rape of the child's spirit, that trusting nature which assumes goodness in people and believes that the world is a safe enough place to live in.

The destruction of that trust can have far-reaching effects. At its most extreme, sexual abuse can leave the child with a sense of alienation from the world. It is a terrifying thing for a child to realise that someone who expresses love and affection for the child can be a source of great danger. It is easier to cope with hate than with dangerous love. With hate, you are on your guard, alert to the signs of attack or just wary enough to keep your distance. Children learn from the playground onwards how to cope with that kind of danger. But the dangerous love that hides its true intent makes all relationships unsafe, makes 'I love you' a reason to run and hide, makes the penis something to be feared. Child sexual abuse turns the world upside down for its victims. It makes enemies safer than friends, and those who love them potentially the most dangerous of all.

Because trust is so essential to our humanness, the children who are often the worst affected are those who were abused by people to whom they should have been able to look for nurture. The sense of betrayal, and of being let down, can be very damaging, and can make it much harder to trust again. Sexual abuse can shatter a child's belief in the basic goodness of people. It can have long-term effects on a person's capacity for intimacy. Some victims of abuse put walls up around them, afraid of truly knowing or being known, afraid of loving and trusting again because their sense of betrayal is unresolved.

The harm done by sexual abuse when the perpetrator is in a position of trust may be little related to the degree of invasiveness of the abuse. The damage done is as much a consequence of the perpetrator's identity as of his actions. For this reason, sexual abuse by clergy can be very damaging indeed.

Catherine's Story: The Minister Who Loved Flowers

Catherine has now been a practising Christian for more than fifty years. She remembers attending a Presbyterian Sunday school when she was a small child, and still looks back with affection on the 'angel-ladies' who first taught her songs about Jesus and made her feel peaceful and happy. In her early teens, she became a member of an Anglican church. The minister who taught her about the faith at that stage of her life was a good man who was obedient to the Scriptures and gave her considerable encouragement. She remembers with gratitude those who taught her about the love of God.

Yet for much of her time as a child and a young adult, Catherine had to deal with the predations of men who had a different understanding of love. From the time she was seven until she was twelve, Catherine was abused on various occasions by her uncle, the husband of one of her aunts. Along with her sisters and brother, she was a regular visitor to their home. One day, he followed her to the toilet and undressed himself. He showed Catherine his penis, which he called his 'grasshopper'. Later on, he showed her drawings that were sexually explicit. He put great pressure on her to fondle his penis, saying such things as 'this is a lovely grasshopper, and it needs somewhere warm to rest in'. On numerous occasions in the ensuing years, he would get her to fondle him. He established a routine in which it was his role to take her to the toilet at night, and he would molest her there. She disliked it very much but she had to do what he asked because he was so powerful. He told her it was their secret, and that the only reason he did it was 'because he loved her'.

When she was seventeen, while she was on an interstate holiday, she went with a middle-aged relative to visit some other family members on a farm. On the way back, they were driving along a lonely coast road. The man stopped the car and told her that he wanted 'love' because his wife was ill in hospital. Only by threatening to jump over a cliff was she able to avoid being raped.

It was when she already had this history of sexual abuse that a new minister came into her life. Samuel became the rector of her church when she was about seventeen or eighteen, and he continued in the same Bible-teaching tradition as his predecessor. He was a man in the middle years of life but still of tremendous energy. She had a lot to do with him because she was the parish organist and was involved in teaching the Sunday school. Samuel loved photography and would organise slide evenings when he would show his pictures of beautiful landscapes, interspersed with close-up pictures of flowers. In particular, he would describe in detail the inside of the flowers. His photography exposed their inmost secrets.

Alone with Catherine, he would tell her much more about the flowers. A white lily was one of his favourites. It had a strong and fleshy stamen, and Samuel likened this to the private parts of a man. The flower was not only beautiful in itself. It was also a metaphor for the beauty of sexual love between a man and a woman. The hibiscus was another of his favourite flowers. The inside of this flower too suggested to him a sexual theme. Along with this discussion of flowers, Samuel would quote from the Bible. The love between a man and a woman was natural, it was God-ordained. Even the Church was described in the Bible as the bride of Christ.

Catherine loved flowers, so on one level she warmed to the conversation about them; but she was puzzled by the connections he was making between flowers and erotic themes, and she wasn't quite sure where these conversations were leading.

As time went on, Samuel graduated to writing poetry for her. His poems were about flowers and sexual love. Somewhere among these themes, God could be found too – the God of Adam and Eve, the God who created the natural beauty of the world and human nakedness. When Catherine first went out with a new boyfriend, Samuel wrote a poem about their relationship, and this too had a sexual theme woven in. Since Catherine was a very strait-laced Christian girl, she found this quite disturbing. She began to feel afraid of him, although she was not sure what she was afraid of.

In the vestry one day, he read to her from the Song of Solomon. She had no idea that such poetry could be in the Bible. It was the kind of book that was never studied in the Bible Reading Fellowship Notes which she used to read day by day. Samuel was very interested in nudist colonies, and was keen for Catherine to come with him to one. Catherine kept saying no, and asked him whether his wife minded going to a nudist colony. He replied that she thought it was wonderful.

When he was alone with Catherine in the vestry, perhaps before a wedding or a funeral for which she was the organist, Samuel would show her photographs of his wife in the nude. In the photographs, his wife looked miserable and lifeless. Conversations about these photographs were interspersed with biblical references. Adam and Eve was a favourite theme. Samuel liked them best before they wore fig-leaves.

It was when they were alone in his study one day that

Samuel made his boldest move. His wife and the children were out somewhere, and the house, which was usually bustling with activity, was very quiet. Catherine had been asked to visit him to plan a service, and so they went into his study. She was reluctant to follow him into the study but refusal was not an option under the circumstances. He closed the door behind him. There he showed her pictures of himself naked, close-up photographs of his genitals, and also photographs of his wife and other women naked. He said that he and his wife and the children would run around freely in the nude on the top floor of the house. He intimated that he wanted her to do the same thing with him that afternoon. Catherine was very frightened, but the best way she could cope was to be practical. Wouldn't it be very cold? When he asked her to go to a little summer house in the garden with him in order to be photographed in the nude, she was able to point to the danger that people might see them. Somehow she managed to extricate herself from the situation, and she made sure that she was never alone with him again.

Catherine was deeply shocked. This man was a minister, and she looked to him for biblical teaching and Christian example. His sexual predations brought back to her the memories of another man a long time ago who had insisted that she play with his 'grasshopper'.

The one way Catherine knew to cope with the situation was to go round to every girl in the youth group and to warn them never to be alone with Samuel. A number of girls heeded her warnings and when Samuel spoke to them about the beauty of flowers, they just giggled. Looking back, Catherine now believes that the decision to try to warn the other girls helped her to cope with the overwhelming feelings of powerlessness in relation to Samuel. By warning the others, she gained some sense of power over an otherwise dreadful situation. But Catherine was not the only victim of his predations. A friend of Catherine's with whom Samuel had sexual contact may have been as young as fifteen at the time.

Eventually, Samuel moved on from that parish. Some years later, he left another parish in the same diocese under a cloud.

The rumours that circulated at the time were that secret deals were done with the police. He ceased to practise as a minister in the diocese, although he continued to be a familiar figure in diocesan circles. Nor did he show much sign of change. Thirty-five years later, when he met Catherine again at a funeral of another minister, he told her that he had had a picture of her on his desk for all those years.

Catherine felt utterly betrayed by Samuel. He was a popular evangelist, at one stage of his ministry preaching the gospel in churches all round the diocese. He had set himself up as an example of godliness and had occupied a position of great trust as her pastor. She felt even more betrayed by the church leaders who had covered up for him. The knowledge about the secret deals with the police provoked a crisis of faith for Catherine, and the ongoing failure of the diocese to address the issue of sexual misconduct by clergy properly has made her feel unable to attend church any more.

It is tempting to categorise the seriousness of sexual abuse in terms of the degree of its invasiveness and to treat the sexual abuse of children as inherently much more serious than the abuse of a nineteen- or twenty-year-old girl. What Catherine's uncle did to her as a child could have led to his being imprisoned for many years. What Samuel did when she was a young adult would not have constituted a criminal offence. And yet, more than forty years on, Catherine is as deeply affected by her experiences with Samuel as she is by her uncle's sexual abuse.

Sexuality

Child sexual abuse frequently has profound effects on people's sexuality. Indeed, sexual difficulties are likely to be among the most common of adverse effects of sexual abuse. A large national survey in the United States found that sexual abuse made it more likely that both men and women would report dissatisfaction with their sexual life as adults. This was particularly the case with female victims of abuse.[13]

129

That sexual abuse should be associated with sexual difficulties in adulthood is scarcely surprising. Sexual intercourse is likely to be linked with many unpleasant memories such as finding it difficult to breathe when a man much heavier than yourself presses down upon you during intercourse; the aversive feelings associated with oral sex; the sense of shock and violation for the child when a man first fondles a breast or touches the vagina. Such memories may be triggered in adulthood during sexual foreplay and intercourse.

Sexual arousal may also be a source of problems in adult life. Sexual abuse is very confusing for its victims. On the one hand, they will often be stimulated in such a way that they experience a degree of sexual pleasure. At the same time, the experience of abuse is a very unpleasant one, bringing with it feelings of guilt, shame, fear and betrayal. And so for the abuse victim, sexual pleasure in adulthood may well be associated with negative feelings and emotions as well as positive ones. Anna Salter writes of the effect that sexual arousal in the context of the abuse has: 'Sexual arousal during sexual abuse is one way that survivors become alienated from their own bodies; many see it as a form of self-betrayal. They become angry and distrustful of their own sexual response, and thereafter, sexual arousal in itself becomes aversive.'[14]

Another cause of adult sexual difficulties comes from dissociation during the abuse. Some children cope with the abuse by becoming numb. They do not respond physically; they can only cope by imagining themselves to be elsewhere while the abuse is happening. This numbness can continue as a response to sexual activity in adult life, making it difficult for the victim of abuse to enjoy intercourse.

For some, the consequences of sexual abuse in adult life may be difficulties in arousal or an aversion to all forms of sexual contact. There are some female victims of sexual abuse who have entered into lesbian relationships because the idea of sex with a man is too difficult and painful for them emotionally. There may be links too between male homosexuality and childhood sexual abuse.

Another reaction to sexual abuse is to see sex as something

merely sensual and perfunctory which can readily be separated from the context of loving relationships. It is very common to find that prostitutes have a history of sexual abuse. In one study of 200 street prostitutes in the United States, 61 per cent of them had been sexually abused as children, most of them in the religious family in which they grew up.[15]

Traumatic Sexualisation

Traumatic sexualisation is a process in which a child's sexuality is shaped in a developmentally inappropriate fashion as a result of the sexual abuse.[16] When a perpetrator deliberately stimulates the child sexually, the pleasurable feelings of sexual arousal may be self-reinforcing for the child.[17] So even though the sexual feelings may be mixed with negative feelings such as shame and guilt, a part of her wants the sexual relationship to continue.

This sexualisation may take a number of forms. The child may act out sexual acts of a kind that have been initiated by the perpetrator of abuse and that go far beyond the normal sexual exploration in which children often engage. This might include simulating acts of intercourse or playing games which involve penetration of the vagina with a finger or object. Another indication of sexualisation is compulsive sexual behaviour such as grabbing breasts or genitals. These symptoms can be seen even in pre-school children.[18] Studies of sexually abused children show that inappropriate sexual behaviour is the symptom that most distinguishes sexually abused children from non-abused children.[19]

Another manifestation of sexualisation is that the child has a preoccupation with sexual arousal. Two girls, aged eight and nine, were both sexually abused by their father. In some ways they reacted quite differently. The younger girl enjoyed being around men; her older sister kept her distance from all men and was very perturbed to find that she had a male teacher at primary school. Yet both of them were preoccupied with sexual arousal. This involved masturbating quite openly and finding a variety of ways to achieve sexual stimulation.

Sexually abused children may well go on to form other sexual relationships at a very young age and to become promiscuous as young adults. Some people have learnt as children to associate closeness with sexual intimacy to such an extent that they offer their bodies as a way of trying to find that emotional closeness in their adult relationships. Low self-esteem thus goes hand in hand with traumatic sexualisation. The young person with a history of sexual abuse may not know any other way to feel loved and worth something than to share her body. She can easily be taken advantage of, and some such relationships may be abusive. Since few of these relationships are lasting, she may feel even more worthless as a result of these transient relationships and successive rejections.

For Christians, it can be very difficult to cope with the sexual abuse survivor who is behaving in a promiscuous manner. The survivor who has difficulty in sexual matters is likely to receive only sympathy and support; but the survivor who is showing the effects of the abuse in a pattern of promiscuity is herself violating the Christian moral code. The church minister or counsellor who doesn't understand the reasons for the sexual behaviour may end up judging and rejecting the abuse survivor rather than acting to help her.

Jaimie's Story: The Magic Hands

It is difficult for Jaimie to remember a time during her childhood when she was not being sexually abused. Her abuse did not cease finally until she was twenty-two years old. She can pinpoint very clearly the time when it all began. It was a holiday weekend when she was only four. Her mother did not know about the abuse until many years later, but she remembers that holiday weekend very well. It was the time when her happy and contented little daughter changed markedly. It was a point of no return.

That first incident occurred at her grandmother's house. Jaimie lived with Grandma until she was ten years old, and saw her mother only for about one hour per day. She did not live with her mother because her stepfather didn't want her.

132

Grandma was happy to look after her. It was only one more mouth to feed and there were already several. Grandma had had five children of her own, and all of them apart from Jaimie's mother still lived at home. They had their own children so there were a number of other youngsters in the house. Thus Jaimie grew up in a hive of activity.

Another familiar figure round the house was Harry. As far as Jaimie's grandfather was concerned, Harry was just a close family friend. To Grandma, he was much more than that.

It was during that holiday weekend that Jaimie was first sexually abused by Harry. Jaimie remembers going outside to the outdoor toilet in the evening. Harry lay in wait for her and sexually assaulted her that night. She bled from the attack, and buried her bloody clothes in the sand on the beach. She didn't tell her mother. When the mother noticed some injuries the following day, she made up a story about having damaged herself on the rocks.

Thereafter, the abuse continued for many years. When Harry had the opportunity to be alone with her, he fondled her, sticking his hands up her shorts, or guiding her hand to fondle him. He was constantly in the house.

The family was very isolated. The children's friends were not allowed home to visit them, and they had no telephone. Although the girls at least went to Sunday school (for respectability's sake), they were otherwise not allowed out much. They had a few other outside activities, but for the most part those activities were under the watchful eye of a family member. For example, Jaimie's aunt was the Guide leader.

Jaimie was not Harry's only victim. She saw her male cousin being raped by him while she was in the room. There are reasons to suspect that other family members may have been abused by him as well. It is not certain whether there were victims outside the family, but Harry was expelled from his position as a Scout leader, and it is possible that this was as a result of complaints.

At the age of ten Jaimie moved home to live with her mother and stepfather. The abuse did not stop. On one occasion, when she was eleven, she was raped by her stepfather, a man who was capable of the greatest violence and cruelty. She still remembers the date and time. She 'played dead', and he assumed she was asleep throughout the rape. He tried it again on a number of occasions, but Jaimie managed to avoid it by stirring and indicating she was not fast asleep. He backed off.

The abuse by Harry, however, was constant. Even though he did not have such ready access to her after she moved out of the grandmother's home, he still engineered opportunities to be alone with her. He used to pick her up from school in order to take her to Grandma's, where she normally waited to be collected by her mother. Jaimie used to try to get on the school bus before Harry could get to her, but usually it didn't work. Indeed on one occasion, Harry drove in front of the bus, forcing it to stop, and dragged her off the bus. No one did anything because they thought he was her grandfather.

Harry would take her back to his place before driving her to Grandma's, and there was always some means of explaining the delay. He received mailings from the United States of hard-core pornography, which included scenes of bestiality and sexual acts involving the use of guns. He used to show these pictures to Jaimie and then invite her to do the things in the picture. She knew she had no choice. Sometimes he would threaten her by holding her over the stove and would use force in other ways; but mostly he had no need to threaten her. She was powerless to resist him. He was the boyfriend of the woman who dominated the entire family. Grandma ruled the roost. Harry had power and authority because she did. Jaimie could not tell her grandmother what her boyfriend was doing. She was equally powerless to tell her mother. Experience from an early age had taught her that Mum would not protect her when she needed it. She had often been physically abused by her stepfather, and indeed her mother had been beaten senseless by him on some three occasions. Mum was not going to protect Jaimie from Grandma's boyfriend any more than she had protected her from her stepfather's violence. Jaimie had no place of safety, and no one to run to.

Powerlessness and fear were not the only feelings Jaimie

experienced. As she got older she experienced sexual pleasure as well. Harry had 'magic hands'. He knew how to give her sexual pleasure, and she experienced orgasms readily. She was powerless to call a halt to the sexual abuse. It had been part of her life for far too long to stand up to Harry, and it was also sexually pleasurable. Thus it was doubly difficult to bring it to an end.

The abuse continued even after she left school. She was offered a place in a course at a university in another city, but her parents would not let her go. Instead, she found a job in a bank. Just as he had picked her up from school, he collected her now from work, took her to his place where they engaged in sexual acts, and then drove her home.

Harry eventually died, quite suddenly, when she was twenty-two. The last time they had a sexual encounter was the day before he died. Only after his death did she experience liberation, and the sense of relief was immense. It was as if she could start a new life.

Jaimie was also sexually assaulted by others. As a teenager, she was involved in a ménage à trois which involved intercourse with her aunt's boyfriend. At the age of seventeen, after being in hospital following a nervous breakdown, she was raped by the lodger of a friend she had made in the psychiatric ward. She didn't go to the police because her family had a criminal history. Co-operation with the police was not an acceptable option for the family, nor would she have expected much sympathy from the police if she had reported it.

Through all of this, Jaimie believed in God. She had been sent to Sunday school as a child and had come to believe that God had made the world. When she was sixteen, she became a committed Christian. She responded to the gospel message in part because she believed that Jesus could do something about her situation.

Jaimie did not pray that the sexual abuse would stop, because it seemed impossible to her that Harry would just cease to abuse her. Instead, she prayed that he would die. When he was coming to collect her from school or work, she would pray that he would have a flat tyre or would otherwise be delayed. It was deeply troubling that her prayers for Harry's death were not answered, but she stuck with her faith, hoping that things would come right in the end. Perhaps more Bible study would help. Perhaps God was too busy with the world to attend to her requests.

At the age of nineteen, she plucked up the courage to seek help from the church. She was very involved with her evangelical church and directed the music. She had made friends with the wife of one of the elders. Over lunch with them, she tried to tell them about the sexual abuse. The conversation was not pursued at great length that day, but the following day she was summoned to the minister's office. Present there were the minister, his wife and the two elders of the church. She was questioned at length about her sexual involvement with Harry. They could not understand how she continued to participate in it at the age of nineteen when Harry was not actually coercing her. Still less could they understand why she had told no one. They asked her whether she enjoyed it and whether she was paid for her sexual favours. That night she was expelled from the church for sexual perversion. The church was not told why she had been expelled, but the members were forbidden to have any contact with her.

The experience was devastating. She understood her expulsion from the church in terms of being rejected by God, for the minister had God's authority. In the ensuing months, she tried to commit suicide five times and on four occasions she was nearly successful. It seemed only chance that people had showed up at the right time.

After about six months, she felt able to join another evangelical church and became actively involved in its life and mission. There was, however, a hidden side to her life. One of the effects of her early sexualisation was a lesbian orientation. For many years, while at school, she had an active sexual relationship with another girl who had also been sexually abused. They used to meet at lunchtimes and engage in secret sexual activity. An adult lesbian relationship with another young woman at her church began when she was twenty-two. She was invited into this sexual relationship by the other woman, who had had lesbian relationships before. The relationship met her sexual needs, which had been stirred up so many years before by Harry. It ended only when she disclosed the relationship to the minister's wife. She was told to write to her lesbian partner ending the relationship. Eventually, Jaimie felt so uncomfortable that she left the church. Her lesbian partner was apparently not disciplined.

When Jaimie married it proved to be a disaster. On her wedding night, her husband joined her in the shower. She became terrified. He was a lot taller than she was and thus reminded her of Harry. Furthermore, as her new husband, she saw him as having power and authority over her. No longer could she legitimately refuse him sexually as she had done before their wedding night. She ran out of the shower, dressed herself and made excuses for not having sex that night. She managed to avoid it throughout the honeymoon as well. After a while, her husband understood that there were serious impediments to having intercourse and he did not ask again. Psychological factors were not the only impediments. She also had physical problems. She needed vaginal reconstruction surgery as a result of the effects of her childhood sexual abuse. The marriage broke up after three years.

Jaimie is now living with a kind Christian woman who took her in and treated her as a daughter. She cannot go to church, because she is too ashamed. She does not want people to know about her history, and yet she could not participate in the church family without identifying herself as a survivor. It is so much a part of who she is and what she has been through. She is afraid of being expelled from the church again.

For the present Jaimie is content to be celibate. She regards herself now as a homosexual, although she thinks a lesbian relationship is wrong in God's eyes. Nonetheless, her preference is for sexual relations with women, because she has been so badly hurt by men. The path towards healing has been a slow and painful one. She has been diagnosed as suffering from multiple personality disorder, and although she is able to function well much of the time, she has been in and out of psychiatric hospitals for the last few years.

Jaimie was more sinned against than sinning. From the time she was in pre-school she was introduced to sexual activity. She hardly knew a time of innocence in which she could just be a child without being the object of sexual desire. Like many victims of sexual abuse, she both hated the abuse and found pleasure in it. Harry was very experienced sexually. He knew how to stimulate women and girls. She was sexualised at a very young age, and acted out that sexualisation with her friend at school. The churches to which she turned for help could understand none of this, and in rejecting her, they reinforced the idea that she was to blame for the abuse.

The Bruised Reed

> 'Here is my servant, whom I uphold,
> my chosen one in whom I delight;
> I will put my Spirit on him . . .
> A bruised reed he will not break,
> and a smouldering wick he will not snuff out.'
>
> (Isa. 42:1–3)

The prophet Isaiah foresaw the coming of a Messiah who would be a suffering servant, 'a man of sorrows, and familiar with suffering'.[20] Jesus indicated that he had come to fulfil this messianic role.[21]

The abuse survivor needs to be cared for with the gentleness of Jesus. At times, he or she may be as fragile as a bruised reed. It can take a very long time to be able to put on the garment of praise rather than to be weighed down by a spirit of despair. To learn to feel worthwhile and lovable can be an extraordinarily difficult thing if for much of your childhood you have been abused.

Yet there can be a great strength in abuse survivors, a strength which comes from that determination and resourcefulness that allowed them to survive the abuse – in some cases over many years. The term 'survivor' rather than 'victim' recognises the active role played by the person in moving beyond being a passive victim of another's aggression and exploitation. The abuse survivor does not merely exist like a doormat, to be trodden on by others, but has actively survived the abuse and gained strengths through suffering.

The abuse survivor who has worked through pain can use those resources for the good of others, and become someone who in turn will comfort those who mourn and help them to find their own crown of beauty instead of ashes. It has been said that you cannot really appreciate the highest mountain until you know what it is to be in the deepest valley. The abuse survivor will have known many deep valleys, and once he or she is able to move out of them, the only direction is up, even if it is not always an easy climb.

Chapter 7

The Struggle of Faith

Sexual abuse does not only inflict profound and lasting psychological effects. It is also likely to have a damaging effect on the faith of victims. Sexual abuse can make it difficult to believe any of the major doctrines about God. God is omnipotent, yet he did not rescue. God is love, but he allowed an innocent child to suffer such torment. God hates evil, but he did nothing to prevent it. Sexual abuse has been described as the murder of the soul.

A number of studies have shown that victims of serious sexual abuse are less likely than people in the general population to have a religious commitment in adulthood, even though they were brought up in a religious home.[1] The struggle of faith is a struggle to rediscover belief in a God who orders the world and watches over his children, a God who cares, and who loves even those who see themselves as most unlovable.

When Clergy Abuse Children

The destructive effects of sexual abuse on a person's faith are likely to be considerable where the perpetrator is a priest or minister, for here the sense of betrayal is so great.

Robert's Story: The Priest and the Orphanage

Robert is now in his late fifties. He is a tough man who in his younger days spent two periods in jail. After release from prison he worked on the shop floor in an engineering company, and had a reputation for his explosive temper and his disrespect for authority. Yet when he talks about his experiences as a child in an orphanage, his eyes well up with tears. The grief he still feels about his lost childhood is intense.

Robert's mother gave birth to him when she was only twelve years old, and because she could not possibly care for him, he was placed in an orphanage run by an order of nuns. There was also a resident priest at the orphanage. Robert is sure that the nuns in that orphanage must have shown him some kindness, but he honestly cannot remember it. All he can remember are the ceaseless beatings and the merciless mental cruelty of these nuns. They must have known his birthday, because he was sent away from the orphanage on his fourteenth birthday. But he never knew his birthdate until that time, and never was his birthday celebrated. The only Christmas present he ever received was an empty box which had once contained caps for a toy pistol. He was told that empty boxes are for empty heads.

Worst of all was his experience of sexual abuse at the hands of the Catholic priest. This priest first molested him when he was an altar boy and aged about eleven or twelve. He was travelling with the priest to conduct a mass in a country village. While they were driving along, the priest unzipped his trousers, took Robert's hand and got him to fondle his penis. The penis became erect. Robert was shocked, and said to the priest that this was wrong, since he had been taught to be ashamed of anything to do with genitals and nudity. The priest replied that since he was a priest, it was not wrong.

Later, Robert was called to the presbytery. The priest said that he wanted to improve Robert's Latin. The priest took him into the bedroom, took off his clothes, bent him over, and then sodomised him. Robert left, bleeding, sore and crying. This happened frequently thereafter. Sometimes, the priest would push Robert's head down towards his penis and make him perform oral sex. If he tried to refuse, the priest would beat him about the head.

When Robert went to confession with this priest, he began by saying, 'Father, I have committed a sin of impurity.' The priest replied, 'What a priest does to a child is not a sin; but if you tell anyone, that would be a mortal sin and if you die you will go to hell.' Robert did tell people, even though he believed what the priest said about going to hell. He told an older boy, who assured him that the priest was committing the sin. He also told the nuns. In response to this, however, they beat him severely for 'telling such lies' about the priest. It seems clear that some at least must have accepted that he was telling the truth, but did nothing to protect him. On one occasion, he showed two nuns his bleeding and bruised anus after he had been sodomised by the priest at the presbytery. They did not confront the priest. When Robert resisted going for his 'Latin lessons', the nuns would beat him, and he was often crying when he reached the presbytery. On occasions, after the sodomy, Robert would soil his trousers. He still remembers, with great bitterness, that his regular punishment was to stand naked in front of the other boys with his dirty sheets surrounding his head. On one occasion, a nun rubbed his faeces in his face and into his mouth.

As well as apparently being complicit in the abuse, the nuns played their part in ensuring that the secrecy was maintained. When this priest went overseas for a few months, and another priest came to the orphanage, Robert was not allowed to go to confession at all. In all, the sexual abuse lasted about two years. Robert was not the only boy who was sexually abused by this priest. One of his friends was also sodomised regularly, and there may well have been other victims. Certainly, the priest's sexual interest in little boys was the subject of a rhyme, which went the rounds of children at the orphanage.

Robert left the orphanage when he was fourteen, and subsequently worked on farms. Throughout his childhood, his mother had been looking for him and had asked the state children's department where he was. They never told him. It was only after he was thirty-five that he was finally reunited with his mother through a chance conversation with a friend, and he discovered that he had a number of siblings, as well as nieces and nephews. This discovery changed his life. From then on he lived for his family, treasuring his new-found relationships. The mother who was lost had been found, and that meant more to Robert than anything in the world.

Robert says that the orphanage robbed him of his manhood. All sex became abhorrent to him. He had no interest whatsoever in homosexual intercourse, but nor could he ever make love to a woman, since he would be afraid that he was hurting her as the priest had hurt him. The memories of the orphanage still haunt him, particularly the anal abuse. He likens his experience to that of a prisoner of war or an inmate in a concentration camp. He has had counselling, but nothing can take away the pain of the memories.

Robert's experiences of abuse by the Church have left him extremely hostile to organised religion. He cannot see a nun or priest on television without becoming incredibly angry. He believes that if he hadn't found his mother, he might have ended up arbitrarily killing a priest or nun. On the very few occasions on which he has attended the Catholic church since he was a boy, perhaps on the occasion of a wedding or a funeral, he has had to remind himself that the priest celebrating the mass is not the same priest who abused him.

His experiences have also made it very difficult for him to believe in God. If there was a God, he would have told the priest or the nuns that what they were doing was wrong. Nor is it a help to know that Jesus suffered as well: 'When Jesus carried his cross to Calvary, at least the women were along the side of the road to comfort him. But when I was sodomised by that priest, no one came to my aid. No one wiped the tears from my eyes or the sweat from my brow.'

The God Who Was Not There

There are few victims of sexual abuse who find it easy to maintain faith as a result of their suffering. Some, like Robert, find it difficult to believe in God at all. Others continue to hold on to their faith, but not without difficulties. For many abused children, God is the God who was not there, the God who remained silent through all their tears and cries for help and protection.

This struggle of faith is an experience shared by a number of those whose stories have been told so far in this book. Jaimie (chapter 6) has experienced such struggles. Throughout the long years when Jaimie was used to fulfil the sexual needs of her grandmother's boyfriend, she believed in God's love and prayed for his intervention. Yet her prayers went unanswered. Even after all her experiences of abuse, and her difficulties with churches, Jaimie still believes in God. Her beliefs have not changed. God created the world, and she accepts God as he is revealed in the Bible. God is who he is, but she cannot pray to him, or call him Lord at this time. It is too hard to pray to a God who took years to answer her prayer that Harry would die. She cannot relate to the God who allows little children to suffer. She finds it a little easier to relate to Jesus, who was betrayed by a kiss, and who hung naked and in shame upon the cross. Someone once said to her that God is weeping for her. But for her, it is like a mother weeping when her son is injured. The child needs healing, not his mother's tears. Jaimie has yet to find that healing in her life.

Michael (chapter 5), who had repressed the memory of being attacked in a churchyard until he was an adult, found that one of the hardest aspects for him to deal with was his sense of abandonment by God. One day, about a year after he had first begun to remember the sexual attack, he was alone in his house, experiencing a time of quiet reflection. Without warning, he found himself in floods of tears, saying, 'Lord, you abandoned me!' He wept uncontrollably for more than an hour. The next day he found himself crying in this way again, unable to stop. For Michael, it seemed as if he was experiencing the inconsolable grief which he must have felt as a child, and which had been trapped within for so long, unable to find expression. As an adult Christian, he could understand the reasons why God doesn't intervene to stop evil, but how could that be explained to a seven-year-old boy? Michael had been brought up to believe that Jesus looks after little children as a shepherd looks after his flock. How could the good shepherd allow such a thing to happen to him?

No suffering is easy to deal with. Many Christians go through great struggles as they try to relate their faith to their experience of pain and of unanswered prayer. For the child who has been abused, the confrontation between faith and experience is particularly difficult, and occurs at a much earlier age than for most other people. In our Sunday schools and Scripture classes we teach children so many things about God which are seemingly contradicted by their experiences. We teach them, in the words of the old children's song, that if they 'trust and obey' they will be 'happy in Jesus', and his smile will wipe all their sadness away. At an age which for most children should be an age of innocence, they are assaulted with the reality that adults are capable of the greatest cruelty towards them and will exploit them for their own gratification. When they pray, it seems that God is silent.

Loss of Meaning

Facing up to the fact that God wasn't there brings with it a loss of meaning. Judith Herman sums up this aspect of traumatic experiences: 'Traumatic events destroy the victim's fundamental assumptions about the safety of the world, the positive value of the self, and the meaningful order of creation.'[2] Sexual abuse challenges our most fundamental assumptions about the world, about what we can expect from caregivers, about what we can expect from God. Such loss of meaning is particularly difficult to deal with for people who have repressed the memory of the abuse entirely, and who are then troubled in adult life by terrible memories about sexual abuse. Remembering sexual abuse in this way can shatter so many illusions. The person may have had illusions about an idyllic childhood, in which he or she was safe and protected from harm. The memories may shatter the idea that the world is a safe enough place, that the Lord is the good shepherd who watches over us.

What do people do when all their ideas about the world and their place in it, all their ideas about God and his place in relationship to them, are destroyed by the recognition of a traumatic event that casts everything into doubt? Is anything familiar any more? Is anything certain? What doctrines and assumptions of faith is it possible still to believe? What hasn't changed? Loss of meaning is a profound experience for survivors of abuse, and it can leave them drowning in a sea of uncertainty until they find life rafts to which they can cling, new certainties that they can believe. This process can take a long time to come about. It involves integrating the fact of the abuse into one's interpretation of life, giving that abuse some meaning within one's understanding of the world. During this time of coming to terms with the loss of meaning, church can seem at best irrelevant and at worst painful. The messages which used to comfort or inspire, the worship which used to uplift, seem no longer to be in tune with their needs and present reality. To attend worship may be to experience a sense of great alienation.

In this process, first of coping with the loss of meaning, and second finding new meanings through the pain, the abuse survivor is likely to be more hindered than helped by comforters who can only remind the person of the old meanings, the old explanations and beliefs. Those are the very things that have caused the grief of loss. Scripture may remain for the person the inspired word of God, but his or her interpretation of it may change, and so perhaps may ours as we listen to the person's struggles and reflect on their meaning. Walking with the abuse survivor may indeed be a privilege from God, as we learn to wrestle with things which hitherto we have only thought about in theory. Theory is useless to the abuse survivor in the midst of pain; but God is not useless, and, in working through the loss of meaning, the survivor may be able to come to a deeper faith.

Anger with God

Anger with God is not a universal experience for survivors. Some have been able to find God's comfort in their suffering, and blame men rather than God for their pain. Sarah (chapter 2) who was molested for years by her father wrote: 'As a teenager I felt that the abuse I suffered was "my trouble" and that everyone had troubles – that Jesus was separate from them and helped me with them, but never was the cause of them. I saw God in his character as totally wonderful – absolutely no relationship to my abusive father.'

Yet even Sarah had to struggle with issues of faith in later years. On the one hand she recognises the hand of God in carrying her through. She is particularly thankful for the church members who gave her emotional support when she was a teenager, not realising how very much she needed it. On the other hand, she has posed the question that so many other victims ask: if Jesus was in some way 'there' and he was not powerless to prevent the abuse, why didn't he do so? She continues today to hold the reality and truth about God in tension with her pain and suffering.

Being Honest with God

In dealing with a history of child sexual abuse, and in finding healing, the survivor needs time to grieve, to acknowledge her emotions and to allow herself to feel them without trying to block them out. Just as it is very important to allow other emotions to surface, such as shame, fear and anger, so it is important for people to be able to express their feelings about God, as a way of beginning to work them through.

This is not an easy thing for pastors and Christian friends to cope with. It is hard to hear someone you know and love, who is a committed Christian, express rage against God, or even to doubt that he exists. It is tempting to rush in with Bible verses, or to admonish the person gently for the sin of doubting God, even perhaps to call for repentance. But this is likely to be of little use. The survivor's problems with God are not merely at the cognitive level. It is not a problem about doctrine. It is at the dimension of the heart that the Holy Spirit must do a gentle work of healing, helping the abuse survivor to work through the feelings of sadness, loss and abandonment by God. The danger to the survivor is that these emotions will remain repressed. If they remain hidden because the survivor does not have a supportive environment in which they can surface, then they will continue to affect the believer's life and faith in subconscious ways, and the process of healing will be hindered.

Particularly damaging to the abuse survivor can be the triumphalism that characterises so many evangelical and charismatic churches in particular. The encouragement to believe, to forgive, to triumph and to claim the victory of the Lord can sound hollow in the ears of the sexual abuse victim, who longs to be free from the hurt and the pain but who has lost any faith in easy answers. Jeremiah expressed this sort of pain when he cried out to God in anguish and disappointment: 'Why is my pain unending and my wound grievous and incurable? Will you be to me like a deceptive brook, like a spring that fails?' (Jer. 15:18). Jeremiah was honest with God. And the Psalms are full of that same honesty and questioning, which is often a necessary stage on the way towards acceptance and healing. Yet few such voices of pain and rage are heard in our churches today. We emphasise the victory of faith and not its trials, we give testimonies of the answered prayers while saying nothing about the unanswered ones. And in so doing we are in danger of painting a false picture of the Christian life. It silences those whose experience does not equate with the joyful life of faith as it is portrayed.

I sometimes wonder how, as modern believers, we would have reacted to Jesus's passion in Gethsemane. No doubt the music of our choruses would have prevented us from falling asleep. But how many of us, dismayed and uncomfortable at Jesus's tears, would have encouraged him to trust and obey, to believe that God had a good plan for his life, that everything works out for good for those who love God and have been called according to his purposes?

The Bible does not hide from us Jesus's anguish as well as his humble submission to the will of the Father. His despairing cry of God-forsakenness on the cross was a cry from the heart and not a clever allusion to Psalm 22 for the benefit of modern preachers. There are many victims of sexual abuse who feel that they also were forsaken by God at a time of great need. The pain is very real, and there is perhaps nothing we can say that will truly explain where God was when they prayed and he did not answer. This side of heaven, God has been gracious to give us only glimpses of an explanation, clues to reconciling what we know of his love with the reality of our pain.

Expressing rage at God is actually an expression of great trust and faith. The young child who is secure in his parents' love can say that he hates them. He can rage against them because he knows that they will not strike him down, that they will love him anyway.[3] Rage is the response of the loved child to profound disappointment, and the disappointment arises because the child's experience seems to contradict what he knows of his parents' goodness and love. So for the Christian, rage is an expression of disappointed faith. It affirms in its own way the goodness of God.

Caring for the abuse victim means standing with her in her pain, lovingly conveying the presence of God without trying to produce answers.[4] Through the rage, through the pain, through the confusion of faith, God is able to bring his peace, and to comfort those who mourn. We can only watch and pray, and be awake for those who need us in their night of doubt and sorrow.

Distorted Images of God

Some abuse survivors struggle to deal with the lessons they learnt about God from the perpetrator. Those who have been abused in Christian homes may well have been brought up with distorted ideas about Christianity. One Catholic man claimed that it was all right to sleep with his daughter because God had told Lot to sleep with his daughter. Of course, this is nowhere in Scripture (see Genesis 19), but such ideas are no less destructive to the child for being false.

One of the more common attitudes to be found in offenders is the notion that women have a subordinate role in society. In Christian families, this can translate into very rigid ideas about the father's role as head of the household, and of the need for women and children to submit to his authority. Men who sexually abuse children are characterised by a lack of empathy, and thus the idea that men should be in a position of headship becomes distorted into the notion that women and children are possessions to be used for the man's gratification. Another common distortion is to emphasise to a daughter some of the negative images of women in Scripture – Eve as temptress, woman as seductress, and so on. These images may be used to reinforce the idea that the child is to blame for tempting the adult.

There are endless ways in which Scripture can be distorted and Christian teaching perverted by men who are rationalising their abusive behaviour.[5] From the pastoral point of view, the importance of this is in realising that some victims of sexual abuse who were abused in a religious context may well have distorted images of God and the Christian life. If they are rejecting Christianity, it may be because they are rejecting what they have learnt, rather than what Christ taught.

The 'Maleness' of God

For some victims of sexual abuse, one of the most difficult aspects of faith is coming to terms with the revelation of God in the Bible in terms of male images. God is revealed as Father, and Jesus as his Son. Jesus came to us as a man. Yet for many of those who have been sexually abused, maleness carries with it feelings which are the opposite of the feelings we ought to have about God. We are told that God is love, but what abuse survivors have known is a perversion of love. We are told that the perfect love of God casts out fear, but maleness is associated with fear.

For those who were abused by their own fathers, the Fatherhood of God may be particularly difficult to come to terms with. What they have known is a father who has betrayed them, and abused his position of trust. The negative images of God as Father are not only associated with the abuse of a paternal role. God the Father, as creator of the universe, is associated with absolute power, and this power can be terrifying for those who do not know its benevolence. Victims of sexual abuse have experienced the most serious kinds of abuse of power. They may well be threatened by the power and authority of a heavenly Father.

The problem that some sexual abuse survivors have in dealing with the maleness of God has been one of the reasons why churches have suggested referring to God in ways other than as a male figure.[6] Some alternative translations of the Bible and of liturgical prayers now refer to God as a heavenly parent, and to Jesus as God's child. It is important to recognise that God is, in essence, beyond gender. The Bible says that 'God created man in his own image . . . male and female he created them' (Gen. 1:27). God's attributes are reflected, however dimly, in human form, and both men and women share these attributes. As a pastoral response to the sexual abuse victim, it may also be important to emphasise the maternal aspects of God's character. Through Isaiah, God tells his people: 'As a mother comforts her child, so will I comfort you' (Isa. 66:13).

And yet there are dangers in going beyond this to delete references to God as Father and to remove all other male images of God. It was Jesus himself who so emphasised the Fatherhood of God. The Old Testament writers had largely contented themselves with more majestic and regal terms for God as Lord and King. Jesus showed us God's intimate love, and he revealed God as *Abba*, Father, even though he must have known how many fathers would abuse their trust, and how many more would show to their children almost all the opposite characteristics of those which God himself wanted us to understand.

Children who were sexually abused by their natural father are not the only ones who may find difficulty relating to God as Father. Those whose fathers left home when they were very young, or who were emotionally distant, or who worked so hard outside the home that they were rarely there for their children, all may experience a sense of grief and loss. So often, this grieving is for the father that they wish they had had, for the father who never fails. And it is significant that God should have revealed himself to us in terms of the characteristics of perfect fatherhood.

God's Fatherhood need be an obstacle to his grace only if we are unable to separate him from the fathers in our lives who have let us down. Instead of being a source of pain, God can be the Father who never fails, the one who will never abuse the trust we place in him, who will always act for our good. For a time, it may be very difficult for the abuse survivor to cope with God's revelation of himself in terms of male images. Yet ultimately, it may become a source of healing, as God the Father demonstrates that absolute power may be absolutely benevolent, and as the healing balm of his love seeps into the sorest wounds and deepest hurts.

Making Worship Sensitive to Survivors of Abuse

Facing up to the extent of sexual abuse in the community brings us back to a Biblical world-view. The Bible recognises that the world is utterly sinful, that Christians can be victims of the most terrible crimes (and may even commit them), that the God who watches over us without sleeping does not always protect us from harm. In the letters to the seven churches in Revelation there are only two churches which were commended by Jesus. To the church in Smyrna he wrote that they were not to be afraid of what they were about to suffer. 'Be faithful, even to the point of death, and I will give you the crown of life' (Rev. 2:10). To Philadelphia, he wrote that, since they had kept his command to endure patiently, he would keep them from the hour of trial that was coming upon the world (Rev. 3:10). Two faithful churches. One is to be prepared to suffer and to die. The other is spared from suffering. Both are seemingly in God's will.

Suffering is a part of the Christian life from which few are entirely spared. Some suffer very deeply. How well does our worship minister to the reality of people's life experiences? To what extent are the sermons we preach relevant? Do we acknowledge the searing emotional pain of those in our congregations who are suffering, or do we hide from it?

These are important questions for churches. In music, the treble clef and the bass clef together create harmony. The treble clef may provide the melody, while the bass clef brings depth to the music. Without the bass clef, the melody line can sometimes seem shrill or trite. The bass without the melody is sonorous and tuneless.

Too often, abuse survivors feel left out by our worship because they hear only the treble clef. The worship does not allow them to feel the depth of sadness or pain. It does not recognise their trials and tribulations. It is worship which does not mention the dark side of life unless it is blaming the Evil One. It is worship which relates in an unreal way to an unreal world.

For worship to be sensitive to survivors of sexual abuse and those who have experienced another form of suffering, there needs to be a greater recognition of the bass clef – that if God brings victory it is neither easy nor cheap for the believer. We need to talk more about emotional pain and about being angry with God. This is an issue for evangelical and charismatic churches in particular. Child abuse, sexual assault and domestic violence are too rarely named as serious human problems. Sermons on suffering tend to focus on such issues as disasters and serious illness or disability. Perhaps because as Christians we are so supportive of the traditional family, and perceive it to be under threat, we are silent about the darker aspects of family life such as the abuse of wives and children.

One approach which has been very meaningful to survivors

of abuse is to hold an occasional special service for the victims of abuse. This can be a time for those who grieve to be able to acknowledge that pain before God, and to find comfort and healing in his grace. In recent years, a number of liturgies have been written and prayers composed for the survivors of abuse.[7]

As we minister to the abused, we will reflect the love of God who is 'close to the broken-hearted and saves those who are crushed in spirit' (Ps. 34:18).

Chapter 8

Forgiveness

One of the most difficult problems that Christians have to deal with in coming to terms with childhood sexual abuse is forgiveness. Again and again, Christian abuse victims are urged to forgive the offender. For many victims, at an early stage in their journey towards healing, that causes real conflicts, since they feel they are not yet in a position to forgive.

Forgiveness is something that Jesus emphasised strongly in his teachings. In his teaching in the Sermon on the Mount, Jesus linked the forgiveness of others to God's forgiveness: 'For if you forgive men when they sin against you, your heavenly Father will also forgive you. But if you do not forgive men their sins, your Father will not forgive your sins' (Matt. 6:14–15). The command to forgive is sometimes interpreted as a command to forgive promptly. Didn't Paul write, 'Do not let the sun go down while you are still angry' (Eph. 4:26)? Furthermore, forgiveness is sometimes understood to mean that the person should be reconciled to the offender without conditions.

Christians who have been abused are often made to feel that they are the wrongdoers if they are unable to comply with the demand to forgive. So what does forgiveness mean in the context of child sexual abuse? There is much confusion about the nature of forgiveness. A starting point in considering this important issue, therefore, is to examine what it is and what it is not.

The Nature of Forgiveness

Forgiving and Forgetting

When people urge victims of sexual abuse to forgive, frequently this is tied up with other issues which confuse the picture. One area of confusion is between forgiving and forgetting. The command to 'forgive and forget' is not found in Scripture. It originates in Shakespeare's play *King Lear*.[1] God may be able to forget, but he does not ask humans to do so. Forgetting is a divine quality. Victims of child sexual abuse cannot easily forget. It is too significant an aspect of their formative experiences as children.

As Dan Allender says, 'forgiveness built on "forgetfulness" is a Christian version of a frontal lobotomy'.[2] People cannot wipe out a part of their history and just pretend it didn't happen. The most that can be done is to leave the abuse in the past, to find some relief from the pain, and to gain some perspective that helps the person to move on. Indeed, forgetting is the worst thing a person can do. Children may block out the memory of the abuse by repressing it because that is the only way they can cope, but the abuse is not forgotten. Its effects continue at a subconscious level. The process of healing involves facing up to the abuse and the emotions associated with it, rather than trying to block them out, integrating the experience of abuse into one's personal history.

Forgiveness and Trust

Sometimes, forgiveness is confused with trust. In seminars for Christians on the subject of child sexual abuse, I have sometimes heard people say that if the Church has forgiven someone (to the extent that it is the Church's place to forgive), that should be the end of the matter. There should be no obstacle to that person's continuing to work with children. This confuses two distinct issues. Forgiveness is about the past, trust is about the future. Forgiveness by the victim (or in the pronouncement of absolution by the Church)

156

cannot in itself bring about any change in the perpetrator. The only thing that can bring about change is heartfelt repentance together with expert therapeutic intervention. The perpetrator must take responsibility for controlling his abusive tendencies and needs considerable assistance in doing so.

It is possible to forgive someone for the sexual abuse of a child and yet never to trust him again in ministry with children and young people. Indeed, such is the compulsive nature of paedophilia that, even after surrendering to the police, accepting punishment and successfully completing an offender treatment programme, the only responsible course will be for the person to avoid situations of temptation in the future. Repentance and forgiveness may help the offender in finding peace with God. They may open the way for restoration to the fellowship of God's people. That is a quite different issue from trusting him with the care of children. To confuse forgiveness with trust is to place children at great risk of abuse.

Forgiveness and Punishment

Forgiveness does not mean exemption from punishment. A parent may forgive a child for his or her wrongdoing and yet still impose a punishment. As one writer has put it:

> The opposite of punishment is not forgiveness, for the opposite of forgiveness is resentment and ill-will. To forgive is to refuse to nurse resentment, or to try to refuse to nurse resentment: it means that one no longer says to the person 'you have done me an injury which I shall always remember and hold it against you.' . . . Forgiveness is a moral sentiment where ill-will is no longer retained. It may occur before or after punishment, but does not affect it.[3]

Because punishment is not revenge, forgiveness is not its opposite. Punishment is a means by which a society enforces its moral standards. It affirms the offender's personal responsibility; it acknowledges the seriousness of the harm done to the victim; it acts as a deterrent to others. Paul affirmed the role of the State in punishing wrongdoing, and identified this as something that is done on God's behalf (Rom. 13: 1–5). The one in authority 'does not bear the sword for nothing. He is God's servant, an agent of wrath to bring punishment on the wrongdoer.'

Punishment plays an important role in protecting the community. In the case of child sexual abuse, this occurs in a number of ways. There is a temporary protection for the community if the person is jailed. This is reinforced by the procedure adopted by many organisations that work with children and young people of checking to see if any applicant has been convicted of offences of sexual assault or violence. The criminal process also provides a framework within which treatment can occur. Experts maintain that treatment programmes, to have a chance of success, must be mandatory for offenders. In New South Wales, for example, some perpetrators of child sexual abuse are eligible to enrol in a pre-trial 'diversion of offenders' programme. If judged suitable, they must be accepted into the programme and must plead guilty to the offences. The 'carrot' is that they avoid jail. The 'stick' is that if they do not comply with the conditions of the two-year programme, they can be returned to court for sentencing.[4]

Forgiveness and Repentance

Forgiveness is closely tied in with repentance. Paul instructed Christians to 'forgive as the Lord forgave you' (Col. 3:13). God forgives us freely because Christ took the punishment that we deserved. God's forgiveness, however is not unconditional. It is just undeserved.[5] It is conditional upon the repentance of the offender. Jesus said, 'If your brother sins, rebuke him, and if he repents, forgive him' (Luke 17:3). Repentance involves fully acknowledging one's wrongdoing and making a commitment to turn from it.

When people pressure victims of abuse to forgive without insisting on the repentance of the offender, they fail to see the important connection between forgiveness and the offender's responsibility to make amends. As Peter Horsfield writes:

> Many survivors of assault find that they cannot forgive, not because they don't want to, but because the injustice and trauma they have experienced which has terrorised, degraded, and diminished them has never been acknowledged and never been put right. We have tended to explain this resistance to forgiveness by branding the woman as a vindictive or unforgiving person. But there are other ways of seeing this . . . When a survivor of sexual assault refuses to forgive . . . it is frequently the only way they have to resist the evil that has been done.[6]

Forgiveness which is pronounced without repentance is not an act of love to the offender. Rather it glosses over his sin.

The responsibility to seek forgiveness lies with the offender. Jesus instructed the wrongdoer: 'Therefore, if you are offering your gift at the altar and there remember that your brother has something against you, leave your gift there in front of the altar. First go and be reconciled to your brother; then come and offer your gift' (Matt. 5:23–24). The only responsibility of the wronged is to make the wrongdoer aware of his fault (Matt. 18:15).

The Ethical Conditions for Forgiveness

The forgiveness pronounced between one person and another is relational forgiveness. Relational forgiveness may not even be an issue when the abuser was a stranger or there is no continuing point of contact between them. Many victims neither wish to see the offender again nor need to, since they are not brought together in the same matrix of familial or church relationships. Relational forgiveness becomes an issue only when there is a relationship such as that between father and daughter, or where the offender asks to be forgiven for his wrongdoing.

Some victims of child sexual abuse are pressured very strongly into relational forgiveness. This pressure may come from ministers, family members or even from the offender himself. It is most likely to be exerted in the context of intrafamilial abuse where there is or, in. some people's minds, ought to be a continuing relationship between the victim and the offender. Forgiveness, in this situation, frequently gets mixed up with other agendas. The mother may want the daughter to forgive the abusive father or stepfather so that they can be one big happy family again, as if nothing has happened. The minister may believe that it can never be right for a father to have to leave the home even if there has been ongoing sexual abuse of a daughter or son. Forgiveness by the child is therefore a better alternative for dealing with the situation than breaking up a marital relationship.

Not surprisingly, offenders may also want to be forgiven for similar reasons. The problem with this pressure to forgive is that it can be used by the offender as a means of avoiding responsibility for his wrongdoing. Forgiveness is a continually recurring theme with Christian offenders.[7] Some assert their right to be forgiven personally by the victim, often in a face-to-face meeting, so that their relationship can carry on. Forgiveness, in the eyes of the offender, may mean that the victim who has forgiven should not press charges, or that the church which has forgiven should not take disciplinary action. Forgiveness becomes a spiritual argument for avoiding the consequences of his crimes, and for negating the need to deal with his offending behaviour. If everyone will just forgive him, he can put the past behind him, and achieve a quick resolution of the 'problem' without facing up to all its implications.

One minister who had sexually abused his daughter over a considerable period of time demanded that she forgive him. As far as he was concerned, he needed to remain with the family because he was still in a position of headship over his daughter. When his daughter first disclosed the abuse, he had contacted the church hierarchy and sought forgiveness from them. Now, if his daughter forgave him, the case should be closed, and family life should be able to return to normal.

He seemed to have no insight into the enormous changes he would need to make in order for it to be safe for him to live with his daughter. First and foremost, he needed to stop sexually abusing her. Yet even after he demanded forgiveness from her, the abuse continued. Forgiveness that is seen as a means of avoiding repentance is dangerous. And repentance for sexual abuse means much more than saying sorry. It requires a determined decision to turn away from the sin.

If there is to be relational forgiveness, there are certain ethical conditions that have to be met by the offender. These are recognition, repentance and reparation. All three conditions are explicit or implicit in the teachings of Scripture.

Recognition

Recognition is otherwise described in Scripture as 'confession'. It involves the full acknowledgment of the wrongdoing. This is not an easy thing for offenders. Typically, when first confronted, they will minimise the seriousness of the offending, by, for example, acknowledging only the offences which they think the questioner already knows about, or admitting to less serious criminal offences as a way of trying to avoid responsibility for the more serious ones. Honesty about the extent of the offending behaviour when it first comes to light is about as rare as snow during summer. It is only as the offender begins to face up to the magnitude of his problem in a counselling programme that he will confess or acknowledge the scale of his offending. Another means of minimising is to shift the blame on to the victim by claiming that she wanted it. Still another way is to deny that the abuse has had harmful effects. Most offenders are not sadists, but they lack empathy for the victim and rationalise their behaviour by regarding it as harmless.

Apologies

Recognition involves an apology for the hurt caused. An apology can be very helpful for the abuse victim if it is properly expressed and makes no demands of its own. In most situations where child sexual abuse is ongoing, the child and the perpetrator are the only ones who know about what has been happening. The child may experience feelings of shame and humiliation, but the only other person who can interpret what is happening for the child pretends there is nothing wrong with what he does. Parents, priests, teachers and others with similar responsibilities have the power to define for children what right and wrong are. Thus the confession and apology of the perpetrator are a confirmation for the victim of the truth of what happened from the only other person in the world who has first-hand knowledge. A true apology redefines the child's experience as abuse rather than love, evil rather than good, exploitation rather than caring. It gives validity to the child's feelings. As a recognition by the offender of his responsibility and the victim's pain, it can be a step on the road towards healing.

However, an apology which still minimises the offence and tries to share blame with the victim does not provide a basis for forgiveness. Furthermore, some apologies which may be sincerely meant can also do harm if the offender shows little insight into what he did wrong. This can be seen in Adam's story of abuse by a Brother in a religious order.

Adam's Story: Betrayed by Brothers

Adam was sexually abused by members of a religious order at two different stages of his life. The first period began when he was just ten years old. The second occurred when he was seventeen. Adam was a very religious child. He remembers at the age of seven devoting his life to the service of Jesus. He prayed to Mary, pledging himself to serve her Son and not to do anything naughty. He was a very happy child then, and he believed in a Jesus who was gentle and kind. At first he was educated by nuns. Later he was transferred to a boys' school run by an order of brothers.

The man who sexually abused him was the principal of that school. At first, the abuse occurred in the classroom, in front of other children. The principal would come over to his desk, put his hands down Adam's pants and play with his genitals. Adam was intensely embarrassed. As time went on, the principal would regularly call Adam into his office and abuse him there. A number of different forms of sexual abuse occurred. The principal would usually bring himself to orgasm, ejaculating over Adam. Oral sex occurred regularly. On two occasions, anal penetration occurred. On one of those occasions, Adam was left bleeding. He bathed in a stream to wash it off and was then punished at home for getting his clothes dirty.

Adam hated what was happening to him. When the abuse occurred, he was like a motionless puppet in this man's hands. It was as if his body was there but his spirit was elsewhere. At the same time, he had no frame of reference to understand the sexual nature of the abuse. He was too young to know much about sex, particularly homosexual sex. He did not know what semen was. The first time he realised that what the principal was doing was wrong was when the abuse occurred, not in the principal's office as normal, but in another room where there was a statue of Mary. The principal covered it over with a black raincoat. He was too ashamed to let even a statue see what he was doing to this child.

The principal may have justified the abuse to himself by a selective reading of Scripture. At one time, Adam asked the principal whether homosexuality was a sin. He replied, 'Christ never spoke about it'. That was the end of the discussion.

The only place of sanctuary for Adam was the chapel where he would go to pray and contemplate. Although his faith was a source of great comfort and support to him, Adam found it difficult to relate his faith to the sexual abuse. On the one hand, he didn't blame God for it. On the other hand, he couldn't pray about it either. The man was a brother in a religious order. Adam couldn't complain to God about one of God's consecrated servants.

The sexual abuse was not a secret. Other boys at the school knew what was happening and thought Adam went along for these private meetings with the principal willingly. Consequently, they excluded him from their social group, and he remained very isolated. In all, the abuse lasted for three years. It stopped only when the principal was transferred to another school.

This terrible experience of sexual abuse did not deter Adam from later wanting to join a religious order himself. He felt a strong sense of calling on his life, and at seventeen he joined a small religious order. The experiences of his childhood began to repeat themselves – first an unwelcome sexual advance from his novice-master, then a couple of more serious incidents of a sexual nature which he was later to report to the police. Adam left in disgust, and his dream of serving God through a religious vocation lay in tatters. Many years later, he went to the police about his experiences as a novice in the religious order. The subsequent investigation led to numerous charges being made against members of the order.

The sexual abuse has had a profound effect on Adam's life. Although he married, the emotional pain associated with sex was unbearable. Eventually his marriage broke up. The sexual abuse has continued to take its toll. Adam is often very depressed, and has a compulsive cleaning disorder. He washes his hands constantly. He cannot go to church because it is too painful for him, although he still believes very much in Jesus.

For Adam, it was important that the Church should recognise his pain and that there should be an apology, although it took some effort to achieve this. The head of the religious order that had run the school where Adam was abused as a boy wrote to Adam's mother acknowledging that the principal's behaviour was 'sinful and shameful' and that the parents, as well as Adam, had been 'betrayed by a person who was believed worthy to be trusted'. The offender also wrote, asking for forgiveness for each and every act of abuse, and expressing deep regret for the hurt which he had caused. It appeared to be a genuine expression of sorrow. However, he didn't seem to understand how abusive his behaviour had been. To Adam he wrote: 'It seems strange what started off a very close friendship turn into hurt and very wrong doing on my part has cause you such great pain [sic].' To Adam's mother, the offender wrote: 'It is strange how a friendship can turn into something that can hurt an other person.'

For Adam, there was absolutely no friendship. He likens his experience of abuse to being in a Nazi concentration camp, trapped in an abusive situation and powerless to escape. In any event, to speak of a 'friendship' between the principal of a school and a young boy seems not to show insight into the power differential between them. In a letter to the head of the order, Adam wrote: 'I am still very angry over the way Brother . . . can so easily dispense with the emotions of the situation . . . Why can he not further explain . . . why it was so easy to betray me? I can not accept it as a misdirected consequence of a close friendship.'

Preparing the Offender to Apologise

Because apologies have the power to wound as well as to heal, therapists working with offenders and victims take great care in preparing for apology sessions in which the offender says sorry to the victim. In one treatment programme in Australia, counselling is provided to the whole family, but the offender is kept apart from the non-offending parent and the child. Considerable preparation goes into the first resumption of contact between the offender and the child. The overall aim of this meeting is that the child should have control in the proceedings. The offender is expected to set an agenda detailing exactly what he intends covering or saying, and this is provided to the victim before the meeting. He is expected to address not only the detail of what he has done, but also its impact. If he cannot validate the account of the child, it is unlikely that a meeting will be permitted.[8]

Repentance

The second ethical condition for relational forgiveness is repentance. Forgiveness can have little meaning if the offender has no intention of stopping the abuse. Forgiveness means saying that there is an end to the matter. That cannot be if the offender is not prepared to change.

In the area of child sexual abuse, repentance is often confused with remorse. Remorse is what happens in the back of a police car. Repentance means taking full responsibility for the offending and walking the painful road of lasting change. Offenders may well express deep remorse when the abuse comes to light. Mixed in with shame may well be a considerable amount of self-pity. Discovery potentially involves enormous losses: the loss of family, liberty, reputation and perhaps profession. The offender may well feel devastated by the prospect of losing these things. Such deep remorse may well be taken for repentance, but the signs of true repentance are in the deeds, not in the tears. Relational forgiveness expressed to an offender would at this stage be quite premature, because the offender is still trying to avoid responsibility rather than accepting it.

The repentant offender ought to be willing to acknowledge to the police and the courts that he has done wrong, that he has committed grave criminal offences and deserves to be punished. What then the courts do with that repentant confession is up to them. They may well have mercy, coupled with a requirement that the offender go into a recognised treatment programme in which his progress is supervised through the parole system. They may determine that a prison sentence is warranted. The offender who voluntarily submits to the judgment of the court by turning himself in and pleading guilty demonstrates clearly by his actions that he is repentant.

Reparation

The third step that must be taken is reparation. An apology is meaningless if it is not accompanied by an offer of reparation. Even as children, we learn when we break a neighbour's window that an apology needs to be accompanied by an offer to pay for the cost of repair. Many sex offenders have hoped that an apology, unaccompanied by an offer of reparation to the victim, will be accepted – either because the offender is trying to smooth things over with as little pain to himself as possible, or because he has very little idea how much damage he has done to the victim.

Reparation, which compensates the victim in some way for what he or she has lost, is a sign of true repentance. It is repentance that hurts, repentance that acknowledges the extent of the harm caused, repentance that declares that the offender is entirely responsible for the harm. Zacchaeus, amazed to have been accepted by Jesus despite all that he had done wrong, promised to pay back to anyone he had cheated four times the amount that he had taken from them (Luke 19:8).

At the very least, reparation ought to involve paying for the counselling costs of the victim, which can be substantial. While some counselling is provided in England and Australia free of charge through the health system or charitable agencies, many survivors of abuse have to pay for their own counselling over a long period. Such therapy with an expert counsellor is necessary to help the victim deal with the effects of the abuse. In the case of a victim who is still a child, reparation may mean not only some compensation for the present, but also contributing money towards treatment for the time when the victim is an adult. The offender may have to sell his house or his car to raise the money. It is costly, but it is also just. No amount of compensation can ever truly make up to the victim for the harm caused by the most serious kinds of sexual abuse.

The survivor of abuse may not want to be compensated. That is for her to choose. She may decide that there is a basis for relational forgiveness without the need for the offender to do anything tangible to right his wrongs. She may be satisfied with the fact that he has repented and sought treatment. Nonetheless, reparation ought normally to be expected from the offender as a condition of forgiveness. Many survivors of abuse have been so trampled upon that it is difficult for them to make claims on their own behalf. To stand up and say, 'I deserve to be compensated', even just for therapy costs, may be to demonstrate a level of assertiveness which is quite out of character. The church, while encouraging relational forgiveness, ought to insist on reparation on behalf of the victim as a normal course, unless the victim makes an informed decision to the contrary.

Forgiveness and Reconciliation

When the victim of sexual abuse says to the offender, 'I forgive you', it is a way of saying that it is all over, that there is no continuing bitterness. This kind of forgiveness involves making peace, ceasing hostility. Such forgiveness is always a remarkable act of grace. It does not, however, necessarily mean that there can be reconciliation, in the sense that there is restored warmth in the relationship. If the offender shows the signs of recognition, repentance and reparation, that may go a very long way to restoring the relationship, but the offender needs to have realistic expectations.

Forgiveness does not mean that relationships can be restored as if the abuse had never happened. The father who has sexually abused his child for a long time cannot expect that his daughter will be able to relate to him with the same love and respect as exists in a 'normal' father-daughter relationship. The grown-up daughter cannot relive her childhood in a restored state of innocence. Forgiveness may mean letting go of the past, but it cannot alter it.

Furthermore, even if she is grown up and is not personally threatened by him any more, she may be unable to trust her father with her own children. Whether relationships can be restored, or ought to be, is a question of making a realistic judgment, not about forgiveness but about trust. Sexual abuse creates lasting changes in the dynamics of family relationships. The worst of sins may be forgiven, but their consequences may be permanent.

The Church and Forgiveness

The ethical conditions for forgiveness in a case of child sexual abuse may appear to place the hurdle so high that a great many offenders will be unable to jump it. Yet these conditions are only an expansion, within this given context, of what confession and repentance ought to mean. Even if these conditions are met, forgiveness cannot be demanded of the victim. It can merely be made possible. Relational forgiveness can hardly be possible where the offender is still denying the victim's reality, or reiterating the cognitive distortions that he used to rationalise the abuse. Still less can it be possible where all that the offender is demonstrating is regret at having been discovered rather than repentance, which involves a real commitment to change.

Christians who have been sexually abused are very commonly urged by ministers to forgive the offender and to make peace in the relationship without any of the ethical conditions being met. The minister who puts pressure on the victim in this way may find that he is indirectly helping the offender to avoid responsibility for his actions. Such forgiveness proclaims peace when there can be no peace.

The focus of so many churches on the victim's forgiveness rather than the offender's repentance stands in stark contrast to the teaching of Jesus that the Church needs to serve as an advocate on behalf of the victim, stand with her in confronting the offender and demand that he make amends. Jesus was clear in his teaching that if a wrongdoer refuses to listen to the complaint of someone who feels wronged, and also refuses to listen when friends come along to support her, then the Church itself needs to confront the wrongdoer. If he refuses to listen to the Church's call to repentance, he is to be treated 'as you would a pagan or a tax collector' (Matt. 18:17).

The same need to have ethical conditions for forgiveness ought perhaps to apply to the Church's own pronunciation of absolution. The Church that tells the offender that his sins are forgiven and forgotten by God before there is real recognition and repentance may actually be doing more harm than good. Rev. Marie Fortune, of the Centre for the Prevention of Domestic and Sexual Violence in Seattle, reports interviewing twenty-seven incest offenders in a secular treatment programme. Of the twenty-five active Christians among them, every one told her that, once the abuse was discovered, their minister had immediately pronounced forgiveness and prayed for them before sending them on their way. They said that their church had failed them by immediately declaring their sins 'forgiven'. It was only the secular treatment programme that was confronting their wrongdoing and holding them accountable for what they had done. Their message was that the churches should not forgive them so quickly.[9] Cheap grace is not grace at all if it leaves no incentive for the offender to take responsibility for his offending and to turn away from sin. Forgiveness which demands repentance is forgiveness grounded in concern for the offender.

Unilateral Forgiveness

Even if there is no repentance by the offender, there is still a place for unilateral forgiveness, but this is a question of victims' relationship with God and with themselves, not with the offender. It is significant that much of Jesus's teaching on forgiveness is in the context of his teaching on prayer. When Jesus said, 'if you do not forgive men their sins, your Father will not forgive your sins' (Matt. 6:15), it was an explanation of the words in the Lord's Prayer, 'forgive us our trespasses as we forgive those who trespass against us'. A similar message is given in Mark 11:25: 'And when you stand praying, if you hold anything against anyone, forgive him, so that your Father in heaven may forgive you your sins.'

Forgiving others for their sins is a way of recognising that however much we may have been wronged, we also are sinners. We also need to be forgiven for things. God's forgiving grace is available to all who seek it, whatever they

170

have done. Forgiving others in prayer is a way in which we can ensure that our attitude of heart is more like the self-humbling tax collector than the self-righteous Pharisee (Luke 18: 9–14). It also helps us to ensure that 'no bitter root grows up to cause trouble' (Heb. 12:15).

This kind of forgiveness can be unilateral. Indeed, very often it must be. It does not assume any ongoing relationship with the offender, for he or she may be dead or living far away. This kind of forgiveness is independent of the offender's repentance, and is not a response to his apology. Because this unilateral forgiveness is solely for the victim's benefit, it needs to be in her time. One writer calls this 'psychological forgiveness'.[10]

Unilateral forgiveness is enormously important in the process of recovering from childhood sexual abuse. It is something a person may perhaps do only in the grace of God. Starting on the road towards healing, it may be possible to do nothing more than to set one's sails towards forgiveness. In the course of time, and in God's grace, there comes a point when it is possible to say, 'it is finished', and to leave the abuse in the past. For this reason, it is usually the end of the process of healing, not the beginning. Only the abuse survivor knows when the time has come that she is able to forgive. Forgiving involves letting go of bitterness and anger, leaving justice to God (Rom. 12:19–21), and being able at last to wish good for the offender.

Letting go is a process. Often, abuse survivors have first to forgive themselves; not because they have anything objectively to be forgiven for, but because it is so common for abuse victims to feel guilty and ashamed. The abuse survivor also needs to be clear what it is that is being forgiven. It is very common for abuse victims to begin therapy many years after the abuse ended. In some cases, they have convinced themselves that it wasn't very important, that it was long ago, that it can't have been that bad because there was no intercourse, or because it happened only once. Far from exaggerating the significance of the sexual abuse, the typical pattern for the child sexual abuse victim who has not yet come to terms with the abuse is to understate its importance. It is often only in therapy that the victim begins to realise the serious effects of the abuse. A female survivor may come to understand better her own reactions, why she is so wary of men or has problems with intimacy. Anger follows from this awareness. Such anger is righteous. It is being angry about something that also makes God angry. It names sin for what it is. It does not minimise it or excuse it. Only when you have been able to be really clear about the sinfulness of the abuse can forgiveness be truly meaningful.

Anger is important for the victim because it allows long-repressed emotions to be given expression. Sometimes children internalise their anger because it is not acceptable to be angry with an adult. Another important reason for anger is that, through it, the victim places the blame for the abuse squarely where it belongs – on the offender. Child victims sometimes take all the blame themselves because they have been socialised to believe that a trusted adult such as a priest or a teacher can do no wrong. Being angry is a way of transferring responsibility. Where the offender has explicitly laid the blame on the victim, calling her a 'whore', or claiming that she wanted his sexual attentions, anger is a way of breaking free of the offender's damnation and turning it back on his head.

Unilateral forgiveness for sexual abuse takes time and grace. The longer the emotions have been buried, the more that the victim has internalised the offender's rationalisations and excuses, the longer it takes to come through the process to be able to place the blame where it lies and yet to forgive.

Even so, forgiveness does not mean forgetting, it does not mean trusting the offender and, most important of all, it cannot in itself be the basis for a restored relationship with the offender. If the latter is to occur, the offender has much that only he can do.

PART III

THE CHURCHES' RESPONSE TO CHILD SEXUAL ABUSE

Chapter 9

Issues in Child Protection
for Christians

It is an unfortunate reality that churches need to be prepared for cases in which child sexual abuse is disclosed in church families or in the life of the congregation. We would all wish this never to occur in our church. But it is quite clear now from all the evidence that sexual abuse does occur even in devout Christian families, and that it is also quite common in situations such as church youth groups and other church activities. Sex offenders are found in all denominations and among people of many different theological persuasions. There are sex offenders in fundamentalist churches and in pentecostal churches. There are sex offenders who claim to be born again and to have been baptised in the Holy Spirit. No denomination is exempt. No congregation can say, 'it won't happen here'.

In coming to terms with the problem of child sexual abuse in church communities, a starting point is to recognise the mistakes and sins of the past. For it is a sad reality that until recently churches have been more a part of the problem of child sexual abuse than a part of the answer.

The Sins of the Past

In the course of researching and writing this book, I have come across numerous situations in which church members and leaders such as bishops and ministers have responded to cases of child sexual abuse in ways that leave much to be desired. In the past, a typical response of church leaders to complaints against ministers of sexual abuse was to move them to another parish or to send them off for a period of prayer and contemplation. Everything was done behind closed doors, false explanations often being given as a cover for the real reasons behind the minister's abrupt departure. The major motivation was to avoid scandal.

Inappropriate responses to the problem are not confined to one denomination or to churches of one theological persuasion. While the Catholic Church has been identified most publicly as falling short in the way it has dealt with child sexual abuse in the past, some of the worst problems now are in the evangelical and charismatic churches. While things are changing, especially in Britain, in my experience of child protection in Australia, children are less likely to be protected in churches than in almost any other group in society.

My assessment is not alone. Rev. Marie Fortune, who for twenty years has led the way in the United States in combatting sexual abuse by clergy, has said this:

> When I first began to help address the issues of professional misconduct and sexual abuse, I believed that the real problem before us among the administrators, the leaders, the bishops etc., was one of ignorance . . . I no longer believe the problem is ignorance. I now see institutions more interested in secrecy and damage control than justice, more interested in protecting themselves from survivors than healing for survivors, more interested in avoiding liability than doing the right thing, more interested in protecting perpetrators than in holding them accountable.[1]

Why? Why is it that churches find it so difficult to deal with the problem of child sexual abuse? Until we face up to the reasons why we do not act protectively towards children, when everything in our faith and doctrine suggests we should, we will make little progress in developing suitable child protection policies and procedures.

Some of those reasons have already been suggested in this book. One is the naivety of church leaders, who are unaware of the compulsive nature of much sex offending. Another is that counselling has its limitations. Another important issue is forgiveness. The confusion between forgiveness and trust is one reason why offenders have been allowed to continue in positions of pastoral responsibility even after they have been known to have abused children.

Moreover, churches' concern to avoid or to limit legal liability has sometimes led them to take an adversarial approach to abuse survivors, rather than to respond out of pastoral concern. The problem has been evident in the Catholic Church in particular. Not infrequently, bishops have sought to respond sensitively to abuse survivors, but the lawyers, acting ostensibly in the best financial interests of the Church, have done everything possible to prevent the Church from being held legally responsible. In this way, the lawyers have negated any positive good being done by the pastoral response of the church leaders. Sometimes, this strategy is counter-productive even in a legal sense. I have known a number of survivors of clergy abuse who are not so much interested in compensation as in being heard by the Church and ensuring that action is taken to prevent such abuse from happening again. An adversarial approach to them just drives them into a litigious response because the Church is unwilling to resolve the issues in the manner which is expected of people motivated by Christian love.

In any event, the concern with legal liability is sometimes misplaced. In England and Australia, churches are not likely to be held vicariously liable for sexual assaults committed by employees[2] since, generally speaking, employers have been held liable for assaults by employees only if the assault occurred in the furtherance of the employer's business (for example, a barman ejecting a drunken customer from a pub).[3] They are unlikely to be held responsible if they neither knew about nor suspected the offending behaviour. The most likely situation in which the Church as an institution will be liable is if it knew about the propensity of one of its members for abusive behaviour, or ought to have known, and did not act to protect children by removing the person from a position where he had ready access to children. The Church might well be liable then for negligence. It might also be negligent if it appointed someone to a position knowing of the person's history of abusive behaviour.

There are other reasons also for the Church's failure to protect children properly. These include: denial, discomfort, Christian isolationism, confidentiality, spiritualising and concern for the preservation of marriages.

Denial

Church members may recognise child sexual abuse as a problem in the community at large, but there is an enormous reluctance to accept that it could happen in a good Christian family or in congregational activities. When the churchwarden who has faithfully served the church for years is charged by the police with the sexual abuse of his nephew, everything within us is likely to want to deny it. The allegation of abuse confronts us and challenges us. It confronts our theology. We know this man is a dedicated Christian and therefore he could not do such a thing. It confronts our picture of evil. Men who molest children are dirty old men hanging around public parks. They are not the people who lead the worship on a Sunday morning, or pray earnestly for the salvation of souls in our Wednesday night prayer meeting. It confronts our judgment. This man has been a friend of ours for years. Only last week he came to lunch and our daughter sat on his knee. It confronts our ideas about sexuality. He is a happily married man. Why would he want to molest children? It confronts our ideas about Christian sinfulness. Christians, of course, commit all kinds of sins, but only 'little' ones, and certainly not serious criminal offences. It confronts our faith. How could God allow him to do this?

Given these powerful reasons for denial, it is no wonder that sometimes children are not believed. This is particularly the case if we have heard only the offender's side of the story. There are very good reasons why children who disclose sexual abuse should not be subjected to repeated questioning by adults. Such interviews should be kept to the minimum necessary to protect the child. A consequence of this is that church leaders who may need to make judgments about how to respond to allegations of sexual abuse by church members may not have had the benefit of speaking to the child personally. The account of the disclosure is second- or third-hand. In contrast, church leaders may have listened personally to the vehement denial of the alleged perpetrator, his distress and indignation at the allegations, his explicit or implicit demand to be believed by the church leader, his utter confusion that anyone could say such a thing about him, his longing for comfort and support. It should hardly surprise us that Christians so often seem to side with the alleged offender.

There are a number of other reasons why people may find it difficult to believe that abuse has occurred. One is a belief that children lie about such things or that they are prone to making unfounded accusations. These are certainly possibilities, and it is the task of the professional investigator to consider them. But unfounded allegations are very uncommon. People also have a natural reluctance to accept an allegation without corroborative evidence.

Lying and Truthfulness

Children have a reputation for telling lies to a much greater extent than adults. Some of us are more willing to believe that a child has done something seriously wrong than an adult. Faced with a stark choice between believing a child who discloses abuse and a friend of ours who emphatically denies it, we may prefer to believe that the child is lying or mistaken. After all, children lie frequently, don't they?

Yes, children do lie. Usually it is to avoid getting into trouble. Whether they lie more frequently than adults is open to question. The ability to lie successfully is a developmentally acquired trait.[4] The older we are, the more successful we are at concealing deception. Young children find it difficult to lie successfully because they are not good at inventing plausible alternative explanations for the known facts, and they give the truth away by verbal or non-verbal signals. As children get older, their ability to lie plausibly increases. Thus we may not detect a lie in an older adolescent or an adult. We may assume that children lie more than adults because their lies are more detectable. All things being equal, adults are more likely to lie successfully than children. Furthermore, because the behaviour of adults is less often subject to correction than the behaviour of children, adults have fewer occasions when they may feel a need to lie than children.

Do children lie about sexual abuse? Fundamentally, we need to ask why they would wish to lie about such a thing. It is not to get them out of trouble. Usually, it brings them a heap of trouble. They have to cope with police interviews, questions from social workers, distressed parents, and a whole range of other consequences of revealing the secret. Of course, they may not anticipate such consequences. Claiming to have been sexually abused may theoretically be a way of getting attention. But children who have not been sexually abused are unlikely to be able to provide the detail necessary to sustain such a story.

Interviewers who investigate possible sexual abuse are listening for a range of things, not just what the child says. One is knowledge and awareness about aspects of sexual behaviour which would not be expected of a child of that age. Another is detail about feelings, smells, sights and other aspects of sexual activity which indicate that this is a real experience, not something seen on television or on a video, or which has been suggested to the child by inappropriate questioning. Children who have been sexually abused display a range of emotions such as sadness, shame and guilt. They may be very confused about the abuser's behaviour, and very reticent to tell. The full story does not necessarily come out straight away. The experienced interviewer will be able to deduce from these kinds of details whether the child really has been sexually abused.

Unfounded allegations of sexual abuse generally originate from adults connected with the children rather than from the children themselves. Concerns about sexual abuse are far more often unsubstantiated than unfounded. There are many times when adults have cause to suspect that a child has been sexually abused on the basis of the child's behaviour and when it is proper for them to involve professionals in the assessment of the child's problems. When the child has not made any clear disclosures of abuse, the concern about the child may have to be left at that, and the suspicion of abuse cannot be substantiated.

Truly unfounded allegations of sexual abuse made by children are very unusual. In a major study in Denver of 576 cases of suspected child sexual abuse reported to the social services department, about 40 per cent could not be substantiated because there was insufficient information to show that abuse had occurred. There was a legitimate suspicion of abuse but nothing more. In only 6 per cent of the cases did actual reports of sexual abuse turn out to be unfounded. Five per cent of the cases were judged to be fictitious allegations by adults, and 1 per cent were fictitious allegations by children. Describing them as 'fictitious' does not necessarily mean that they were deliberately invented or that the accusers were motivated by malice. Deliberate falsifications, misconceptions and confused interpretations of non-sexual events were all included in this category. Eight fictitious allegations were made in total by five children. Four were quite disturbed teenage girls who had been sexually abused in the past by someone else. The fifth was a four-year-old boy who with his mother produced an account which appeared fictitious.[5] A child is most likely to make a false allegation of abuse when he or she has been sexually abused previously and is showing signs of serious effects from that abuse.

A higher percentage of false allegations occurs in disputes between parents following divorce or the breakdown of a cohabiting relationship. Such allegations are sometimes made in litigation about where the child will live and how much contact the other parent will have.[6] While the popular mythology about these false allegations is that they are motivated by malice or are an attempt to find a trump card in the legal dispute, the reality is probably more complex. The breakdown of a marriage often generates enormous hostility between the parents, particularly when one feels abandoned, abused or betrayed by the other. In such a climate of hostility, innocent behaviour by a father may be misinterpreted as abusive, especially if the mother was the victim of domestic violence during the marriage or had very negative sexual experiences. An exaggerated fear for the child's safety while staying with the father may cause a mother to worry about what the child tells her about activities at bathtime and bedtime. False allegations of abuse may sometimes arise when, on access visits following marriage breakdown, the father may for the first time routinely engage in parenting activities such as bathing a daughter, which hitherto were done only by the mother. He may also be insensitive to a child's growing modesty and independence concerning personal hygiene.[7]

It is possible also that false allegations of abuse will be made by teenagers as a means of revenge, or in order to gain greater liberation from parental authority. Again, the demeanour of the young person and the level of detail are significant factors. The teenager who has the confidence and malice to make up such an allegation is likely to present to an interviewer quite differently from a typical abused teenager, who is likely to be diffident, embarrassed, tearful, traumatised or sullen.[8]

If a child gives a clear account of behaviour towards him or her by an adult, such as an adult would recognise as sexual abuse, by far the most likely interpretation is that the child has been abused. Other interpretations and explanations have to be considered and evaluated before reaching a firm conclusion on this, but such assessments need to be left to professionals. It ought not to be for a minister or other church leader to discount the child's story without that professional assessment.

Corroborative Evidence

It is often said that an allegation of sexual abuse is easy to make but hard to disprove. The opposite is closer to the truth. The allegation of sexual abuse is incredibly difficult for the child to make given all the incentives she has not to tell, such as the threats of the perpetrator and the fear of the known consequences. Because sexual abuse happens in secret, it is also very difficult to prove to the satisfaction of people who will not believe the child's word on its own and insist on corroborative evidence. Such evidence is difficult to find. In most cases of sexual abuse of children, the abuse takes the form of fondling, oral sex or masturbation, not penetration. Such activity does not usually leave physical signs. Vaginal or anal intercourse is more likely to occur with the older child who is sufficiently mature physically to make penetration possible without causing serious damage. Even when there has been penetration, it may be difficult to find evidence with the post-pubertal child, unless the abuse is disclosed or discovered soon after the event. The presence of semen will be detected only if the child is examined within a day or two after an act of vaginal intercourse took place. In the case of anal abuse, the time-frame is much shorter.

The absence of medical evidence does not mean that the abuse has not occurred. In most cases of sexual abuse there will not be any medical evidence or it will be equivocal. Again and again, allegations of sexual abuse have been disregarded by church leaders and others because 'there is no evidence'. This assumes that the child's own account of the abuse is not 'evidence'. Yet the uncorroborated testimony of a child is sufficient to convict a person in the criminal courts if the jury is convinced beyond reasonable doubt that the child is telling the truth.[9] Some children are able to provide an account which is so obviously true that juries do not hesitate to believe them.

It used to be the case at common law that if a child was too young to give evidence on oath, then the evidence carried no weight unless it was corroborated by sworn evidence. That is no longer so. Prosecutors prefer to have corroboration of some kind, such as the evidence of another person who saw aspects of the event, medical evidence consistent with sexual abuse or, if it is admissible, evidence of a similar pattern of abuse of another child.[10] They may decide not to prosecute without that corroboration; and judges may warn juries about the dangers of convicting a person on uncorroborated evidence. Nonetheless, while in Scottish law corroboration is essential,[11] in the rest of Britain and Australia, there is no barrier in law to convictions on the basis of the child's evidence alone.

If corroboration is not an essential requirement even in the criminal justice system, we should not dismiss a child's word merely because 'there is no evidence'. We have to look to see if there are any reasons why we should not take the child's account at face value. Generally, our difficulties in accepting what children tell us about sexual abuse usually have much more to do with our own reasons for denial than the lack of credibility of the child's account. We need to examine our desire not to believe in the light of the known facts of any given case and ask why it is that we have doubts. In the light of that careful examination of the facts, we may not be able to sustain our disbelief.

Discomfort

Another reason why churches deal with child protection badly is their great discomfort with the issue. As long as the problem remains only in the women's magazines or the newspapers, we can cope with it. But when it ceases to be 'out there', when it comes into our living rooms and into our vestry, we are not sure how to deal with it. The discomfort in facing the issue squarely is the discomfort of admitting that sexual abuse is not just a problem of the unconverted.

Discomfort may cause someone who learns of sexual abuse to attempt to get rid of the problem. One respectable Christian woman in an evangelical church responded by trying to get it out of the family. She had asked her daughter-in-law why she had had to be admitted to a psychiatric clinic. The daughter-in-law explained that she was suffering from the adverse effects of sexual abuse as a child. The woman was visibly taken aback. She responded by saying that her daughter-in-law should divorce her son. 'How dare you contaminate him like that?' she said, and walked out.

Churches tend to get rid of the problem by expelling the offender. That may appear to be a firm, unequivocal response to sexual abuse. The church demonstrates by its immediate, decisive action that it will not tolerate the abuse.

Maybe. But on closer examination this may turn out to be a way of getting rid of the problem rather than dealing with it. It is a church protection response rather than a child protection response. The quiet resignation or the expulsion of the offender removes the problem from that particular congregation or diocese, but nothing more. It does nothing to help the repentant offender to deal with his problem, nor does it protect other children from the unrepentant offender. The minister who resigns quietly once his abusive behaviour is discovered does so with his halo intact. It is not uncommon to find ministers or lay workers who have left one church or denomination turning up in another city or denomination a few years later where they resume work with vulnerable children and young people. The peripatetic offender is a serious problem in churches.

It may be easier to get an offending minister to resign quietly, but the cost of that approach is that the victim's experience of abuse is classified only in the nether world of 'allegation' or 'rumour'. Years down the track, when the offender is working again in ministry and questions about his conduct arise, all that can be said about the past is that there were 'complaints', but 'nothing was substantiated'.

Christian Isolationism

One of the most damaging aspects of Christian responses to child sexual abuse over the past few years has been the tendency to hush it up, to deal with it 'within the church family', and not to involve the secular authorities in the process of investigation. Sometimes, even today, policies and procedures of churches do not emphasise adequately the role of the civil authorities. This tendency can be seen in a church protocol on how to deal with sexual misconduct by church workers, which states: 'Where the contact person is provided with reasonable evidence of a complaint of sexual misconduct by a church worker involving a minor, the contact person will report the substance of the allegation to the police and government agencies if required to do so by applicable law.'[12] This implies that the person need not report a case of sexual abuse of a child by a church worker unless he or she is required to do so by law.[13] Nowhere else in the document is it stated that, even in the normal course of events, the police will be informed about the suspected commission of serious criminal offences.

There are many reasons why there is such a reluctance to involve the police in investigating child sexual abuse. The good reputation of the church is at stake. If the abuse has occurred in the Sunday school or youth group, then people may be afraid that disclosure could be a source of shame and embarrassment for the church congregation, whether or not the church could have done anything to prevent the abuse. It is easy to mistake the need to protect our own reputations with a desire to protect the work of the Lord.

A second reason is to protect the offender. Christians sometimes have a great reluctance to see matters taken to the criminal courts. It is argued that the Christian message is about forgiveness rather than judgment, and we should aim to restore the offender to a position of grace rather than to see him punished. This assumes that forgiveness is the opposite of punishment, when, as has been seen (chapter 8), forgiveness and punishment may occur together. While everyone would want to see an offender restored to grace, this cannot happen unless he is able to take responsibility for his wrongdoing. Accepting legal responsibility is a means by which the offender can acknowledge the seriousness of the offence, the harm he has done to his victims and the necessity for change. It is very difficult for an offender to accept the seriousness of his wrongdoing if others minimise it.

There are deeper reasons for Christian isolationism however, which go back to aspects of church history and culture. The problem tends to affect all churches, although for different reasons in different denominations.

The Catholic Church

In the Catholic Church, the tradition was established centuries ago that the Church and the State exist as parallel legal systems and structures. This distinction between Church and State can be traced back to the eleventh century. Prior to that, the political rulers saw both Church and State as their domain. Charlemagne, who was crowned Holy Roman Emperor in AD 800, regarded the Pope merely as his chaplain, and told him that it was the Emperor's business to govern and defend the Church and the Pope's duty to pray for it. This situation was brought to an end in the Papal Revolution of 1075 in which Pope Gregory VII asserted his ultimate authority over the church in all its aspects.[14] The Pope was to be the supreme authority in the Church and to be responsible for its governance without interference from political rulers.

Thereafter, canon law emerged as a distinct body of law, which paralleled the state's jurisdiction. Canon law was a vast system of law that governed the Church, and also covered moral and spiritual matters for the population such as laws concerning the validity of marriages. The Church had its own ecclesiastical courts, separate from the common law courts.[15] The ecclesiastical courts were not subject to the other courts of the land, and in this sense, the Church was not subject to the laws of the State at all, even in relation to such matters as church property. Where the matter was within the jurisdiction of the ecclesiastical courts, the Church dealt with the matter in accordance with its own laws and without reference to the civil law of the State.

By the canon law, the Church dealt with its own people. It exercised disciplinary functions over clergy. The legacy of that tradition remains quite strongly today. The Catholic Church has frequently responded to cases of child sexual abuse in the past by treating it as a moral and spiritual matter, not a criminal one. Clergy against whom complaints have been made have been moved from one parish to another or sent off for counselling. Reporting to the police has neither been done nor encouraged by the Church. At most, complainants have not been *discouraged* from taking matters to the police.

This separateness from civil authority has been a major contributing factor in the past in the Church's failure to respond appropriately to cases of child sexual abuse. In Australia, the best-known problems this century have occurred within the institutions run by the Christian Brothers of Western Australia. The Order's own historian has recorded that complaints by boys of sexual abuse in these institutions were taken seriously, but investigations were ineffectual. In one case in 1959, a leader in the Order in Melbourne wrote to a Brother in Western Australia, asking for his response to a boy's report that this Brother had interfered with him. The Brother replied: 'In answer to your letter referring to my behaviour towards a boy at . . ., I am pleased to say that the accusation is completely untrue as far as I am concerned. I am deeply grateful for this opportunity to clear myself of any doubt in your eyes.'[16] That was all. He did not explain why the boy might have been making these allegations. No other attempt appears to have been made by the authorities in this situation to investigate the matter further. That was not unusual. Typically, if the alleged perpetrator denied the allegation, then it was the boy's word against the Brother's, and usually no further action resulted other than to give a warning to the brother concerned.[17] Such internal investigations were unlikely to be very effectual. If the matter had been seen clearly as one of alleged criminal misconduct, and the police had been called in to investigate, a different result might have been reached.

Protestant Churches

Christian isolationism takes a different form in Protestant circles, but it is no less of a problem. Indeed, the more evangelical the church is, the stronger is the sense that churches are separate from the world and need to respond to spiritual laws, not human ones. The Bible is sometimes used to justify Christian isolationism. This is based upon Paul's first letter to the Corinthians in which he urges believers to judge matters for themselves:

> If any of you has a dispute with another, dare he take it before the ungodly for judgment instead of before the saints? Do you not know that the saints will judge the world? And if you are competent to judge the world, are you not competent to judge trivial cases? . . . The very fact that you have lawsuits among you means you have been completely defeated already. Why not rather be wronged? Why not rather be cheated? (1 Cor. 6:1–2, 7).

This commandment has perhaps been underemphasised by churches. In the United States, the Christian Legal Society has taken the initiative of setting up a Christian conciliation service to engage in mediation and arbitration of disputes between Christians.[18] Other Christian groups provide similar services. They deal with a great range of disputes such as commercial disputes between Christian organisations, custody battles and disputes about debts. These are the kinds of disputes that Paul most likely had in mind. The law makes a distinction between civil disputes, which are lawsuits between individuals, and crimes, which it is the role of the State to punish. In a civil matter, the State is acting as an independent and neutral player, which can decide cases on which the parties are unable to reach agreement. In a criminal matter, the case is brought by the State itself against the individual. The State is upholding its laws, and punishment of wrongdoing is a moral act. A criminal prosecution is not a 'dispute' between the defendant and the victim of the alleged abuse. It is a matter between the defendant and the State.

The idea that Christians should tell it to the Church rather than going to the police can lead ministers to make grave mistakes which expose children to continuing risk of abuse and which may expose the church itself to legal liability. I have been told of numerous instances in evangelical and charismatic churches when sexual abuse has been disclosed and when the response of the minister has been to pray with the offender, pronouncing forgiveness, and to do no more. In one case, the leader of a youth group who had abused children within the group was sent by the minister to a counselling programme. He participated on a voluntary basis for a while, but did not complete the programme. He continued to be involved in the youth work. About two years later, he offended again. This was not only a tragedy for the children who should have been protected from abuse. It also exposed the minister personally, and perhaps the church, to an action in negligence. The church owes a duty of care to the children in its youth activities to protect them from harm. By allowing the youth leader to continue in youth ministry knowing that he had a propensity to offend, the minister could be regarded as negligent.

Telling it to the church may also be abusive. In one case where a complaint of sexual abuse was made by a child against a prominent member of an evangelical church, the mother was persuaded to take the child to visit the pastor of another church who was said to have the 'gift of discernment'. The church leaders quoted the verses from 1 Corinthians about taking disputes to the brothers. This pastor would be able to discern whether the little girl had been sexually abused or whether the alleged perpetrator was telling the truth in denying wrongdoing. When they got to the church where this meeting was to take place, the mother was asked to wait outside while the little girl went into the room with four men, including the alleged perpetrator of the abuse. She felt as if it was four against one. She was being asked to meet the perpetrator face to face. She screamed. The meeting ended in disarray.

The notion that Christians should deal with cases of child sexual abuse themselves and should not involve the police cannot be supported by Scripture. It is certainly not fulfilling Paul's instruction to the Romans that Christians should accept the governance of the secular authorities: 'Everyone must submit himself to the governing authorities, for there is no authority except that which God has established. The authorities that exist have been established by God. Consequently, he who rebels against the authority is rebelling against what God has instituted, and those who do so will bring judgment on themselves' (Rom. 13: 1–2).

Paul's teaching does not give any support to the kind of Christian isolationism that sees the secular world as the devil's domain. Nor does the teaching of Jesus, who accepted the validity of civil authority in commanding his followers to 'Give to Caesar what is Caesar's' (Matt. 22:21).

It should hardly be necessary to emphasise that Christians have a duty not to cover up crimes. And yet it is astonishing how reluctant Christians are to involve the police, and how often ministers take it upon themselves to counsel child sex offenders when they have no qualifications for so doing and no idea of the pitfalls.

Confidentiality

What does a minister do if a member of the congregation admits confidentially that he is abusing children? If the perpetrator discloses abuse to a minister in the course of a conversation in which he explicitly demands confidentiality, then the minister may be torn between his or her obligations of confidentiality and the moral obligation to the child to help bring the abuse to an end. It is a central principle that anything divulged to a minister in the course of private counselling or confession should not be disclosed to anyone else. It is for this reason that ministers and priests are not usually subject to mandatory reporting laws concerning child abuse in countries which require other professionals to report.

Confidentiality and the Law

The question of maintaining confidentiality requires closer scrutiny. Do ministers have a greater obligation of confidentiality than other professional groups which also are bound by an ethic of confidentiality? In law, this duty of confidentiality is not an absolute one.

The law recognises that there are valid reasons for breaching confidentiality. In some jurisdictions, the law allows professionals to report child abuse, even if they are not required to do so. Such laws stipulate that a report of child abuse does not constitute a breach of the professional obligations that person has. It cannot be the basis of any disciplinary procedures.[19]

It is also an accepted defence to a legal action seeking damages for breach of confidence that the information disclosed related to a crime.[20] Some judges take a broader view that the disclosure of the confidential information is legitimate if this is necessary to protect the community from destruction, damage or harm.[21] An important case in England concerned a psychiatrist's disclosure of confidential information concerning a patient who had been detained in a secure facility after being found guilty of causing the deaths of a number of people.[22] The psychiatrist was worried about the patient's continuing capacity for violent behaviour and provided information to a review board which had to consider whether to release the patient. This disclosure was without the patient's consent. It was held by the Court of Appeal that the breach of confidence was justified in the public interest. In Australia, a man who was being counselled by a mental health nurse for depression and anxiety revealed that he had sexually abused his step-daughter. The police requested a written statement from the nurse on what had been revealed in the counselling sessions. The man's attempt to stop the nurse from revealing this information was rejected by the NSW Supreme Court on the grounds that it would be contrary to public policy to enforce a right of confidentiality which would impede the investigation of a serious crime.[23]

Thus if a professional who is bound by an ethic of confidentiality found it necessary to reveal something told in confidence in order to protect a child from further sexual abuse, then the law would not treat it as a breach of confidence for which damages could be awarded. If no child were presently at risk of abuse (for example, where the abuse happened many years ago and the person is no longer in a position where he has ready access to children) then the public interest in disclosing this information would not be as great. Whether a professional person could be compelled to give evidence in court in cases where children are presently at risk of serious harm is another matter. In some Australian jurisdictions, ministers or priests are not required to testify about information given to them in their professional capacity. Some of these jurisdictions limit the legal 'privilege' to communications made in the context of a ritual confession.[24] Britain does not have special statutory rules protecting confessions to priests, and so a minister might be required to testify.[25]

The Church and Confidentiality

Does the Church have reasons to insist that it is unethical to reveal confidences in circumstances in which for other professionals it would be lawful? Perhaps; but this varies from one denomination to another. In the Catholic tradition, and in some Anglican churches, the confessional has a sacramental quality, and the priest is sworn to complete secrecy. Indeed, the punishment for priests in the Catholic Church who break the seal of the confessional is excommunication. Other denominations do not have a sacrament of confession and arguably the reasons why communications between a minister and a parishioner are to be kept confidential are the same as apply to doctors, counsellors and other members of the helping professions. Confidentiality encourages honesty of communication. The counsellor is entrusted with information for the benefit of the client, and it is shared so that the counsellor can assist the client.

In this respect confidentiality differs from secrecy.[26] A

193

promise of secrecy is a promise never to reveal the information, at least without the express permission of the person concerned. The promise of confidentiality implies that the information may be disclosed for the benefit of the person making that disclosure. General practitioners routinely consult with specialists, for example, disclosing information which they hold in trust for the benefit of the patient. The purpose of confidentiality is to enhance, rather than to diminish, the professional's capacity to assist the person making that disclosure. In the long term, keeping child abuse secret does not help the offender to deal with his problems.

The notion that confidentiality should be subservient to the best interests of the patient is recognised in the advice given to doctors in Britain by the General Medical Council. Its *Guidance to Doctors: Professional Conduct and Discipline* (1993), para. 83, states that where a doctor believes that the patient is a victim of physical or sexual abuse, 'the patient's medical interests are paramount and may require the doctor to disclose information to an appropriate person or authority'.[27] In another document on child protection produced by the Department of Health and doctors' associations, doctors are advised to make a balanced judgment between the justification for breaching confidence and the distress that this might cause.[28]

If a member of the congregation tells a minister that he is sexually abusing his daughter, that is likely to be a cry for help, and it may be possible to persuade him to end the secrecy surrounding the abuse without the minister's breaching confidentiality. The perpetrator may need help in accepting that he may be unable to stop himself from abusing his daughter if he insists on maintaining the secret. The power of the offender lies in the secrecy of the offences. While that secret is maintained, the conditions in which abuse may occur continue to exist.

Furthermore, sharing the secret with the minister is unlikely to give him the assistance that he needs. This is because counselling offenders is such highly skilled work. It also helps to prevent a recurrence of abuse if work is done with the children and a non-offending parent so that they recognise the patterns of grooming behaviour and the children are better able to say 'no'. If secrecy is maintained, these goals cannot be accomplished. A promise not to do it again is as worthless as a promise by an unreformed alcoholic not to drink. The private confession of sin may actually decrease the chances that he will stop offending. The confession may temporarily assuage the offender's guilt without bringing about lasting change.

The minister who is entrusted by a perpetrator of sexual abuse with confidences concerning his abusive behaviour needs to encourage the offender to end the secrecy. The case that can be made to the perpetrator for breaking the silence is compelling. The truth may well come out anyway, eventually. Children grow up, and it is much more common now than it once was for young adults to go to the police complaining about the abuse even many years after it ceased. Lapse of time is not intrinsically a barrier to successful prosecution and there are many men who are behind bars today because adults have courageously reported their childhood experiences of abuse. Furthermore, for the father or stepfather abusing his daughter, ending the secrecy will be the most loving thing he has ever done for her. It gives him at least a possibility that he could salvage some kind of relationship with his daughter when she is older.

Such arguments may not in the end persuade the perpetrator to bring his crimes into the open. That takes great courage. At the very least, however, he may be willing to co-operate with the minister in ensuring that the abuse comes to an end and that the safety of the child is ensured. Neither is assured unless he moves out of the home while he goes into counselling. If he is unwilling to go to the police he may at least admit the abuse to his wife and family.

Should clergy break confidentiality even if the abuser insists on maintaining secrecy? This is, of course, for each church to consider. Some churches have adopted the position that confidentiality will be maintained unless disclosure is necessary to prevent a crime. Many counsellors resolve the issue of confidentiality by stating at the outset that all matters will be regarded as completely confidential unless disclosure is necessary in order to protect a child from harm. A clear policy, made known in advance, can absolve a minister from the ethical dilemma that might otherwise arise. Even within the sacramental tradition of confession, the priest may take the view that in cases of sexual abuse, absolution should be conditional on a penance, which involves either an admission to the police or other steps that will ensure that the silence is broken and the child is protected from further abuse.

In the ultimate analysis, the confidentiality of pastoral communications is not a biblical principle. It has grown up, for good reasons, within the tradition of both Catholic and Protestant churches. The protection of the vulnerable is a biblical principle. The poor, the fatherless and the widow are regarded in the Old Testament as requiring special consideration. If the law recognises that there are exceptions to the ethic of confidentiality, so perhaps should the churches.

Spiritualising

Churches have in the past usually spiritualised the problems of offenders; that is, they have treated sexual abuse as a moral and spiritual failure, with the consequence that they have responded to the offender with moral and spiritual counselling. As in medicine, if there is a wrong diagnosis of the problem, the proposed course of treatment is doomed to failure. So it has been with much of the spiritual counselling and prayer that has been the pastoral response to offenders.

Counselling is sometimes put forward as a magic solution to sex offending. Indeed, it has been the traditional response of churches, which have tried to deal with sex offending as an internal matter. Counselling can, of course, mean all sorts of things. It may involve just one or two sessions with a person who may or may not have any qualifications or experience of working with sex offenders, or it may be a properly recognised and respected treatment programme. Successful counselling requires qualified, skilled and experienced counsellors and a willingness on the part of the offender to change. It takes time.

Moral and spiritual counselling will not, on its own, achieve what is necessary. This is not to say that there are not spiritual issues for those who sexually abuse children. Rather, the problem needs to be dealt with as a psychosexual and behavioural problem. Christian paedophiles are, in this respect, indistinguishable from non-Christian offenders.

Spiritualising the problem of child sexual abuse takes all kinds of forms. One variation on the theme is for the offender to believe that 'the devil made me do it', and thus to locate the problem externally. One pastor of a charismatic church took this line when his daughter disclosed that he had been abusing her. He saw himself as a victim of spiritual warfare, and insisted that he needed prayer counselling, rather than to participate in a more conventional treatment programme. Such explanations may readily be adopted by the offender because they make him the victim. He seeks sympathy and support as a casualty of a spiritual war rather than identifying himself as the perpetrator of a serious crime. Such victim-stancing raises problems if it means that the offender takes no responsibility for his own behaviour. The cognitive distortions will remain, and so will the tendency to abuse again.

Another form of spiritualising is to see the problem as an illness from which the offender has been 'healed' by prayer. Of course, God may choose to liberate an offender instantaneously from any tendency to abuse children again. God may also move mountains. The difference between them is that we will know when God has moved a mountain. There is no way of knowing when a religious offender pronounces himself 'healed' whether or not this is so. It may be something he deeply desires to be true, or believes is true. The issue for those who are considering whether an abuser should be allowed to work with children again is not whether God has healed him, but how we will know he has been healed.

In any event, the notion of spiritual healing in this area is highly suspect, because transformation is not merely a question of being liberated from sexual desires for children. The cognitive distortions need to be dealt with. There may be

important issues about offender's views of women and children and his ability to recognise the warning signs that mean
he may be about to offend again. These long-term issues
cannot be dealt with in a few minutes of prayer. The patterns
of thinking that led the man to overcome the internal re-
straints of conscience before need to be addressed for the
future.

Spiritualising the problems or the solutions is dangerous
because it can lead people to believe that problems are
resolved when they are not, and thereby children are placed
at continuing risk of harm. The offender can avoid taking
responsibility rather than be encouraged to face up to the
issues within. Counselling may well need to address a range of
spiritual and moral issues in the life of the offender, but this
needs to be in addition to, and not in substitution for, the
expert treatment programmes that exist.

The Sanctity of Marriage

The importance that Christians rightly place on the sanctity of
marriage may make it difficult for them to respond protectively towards children. In a world in which nearly four out of
ten marriages end in divorce, Christians want to do everything
possible to keep marriages together. Christ's teaching on this
seems unequivocal. Adultery is the only ground on which a
person is justified in ending a marriage. Paul adds to this the
desertion of an unbelieving partner. Certainly, if adultery is a
basis for divorce because it breaks the covenant of marriage,
how much more does sexual offending against children constitute reason to regard the marriage covenant as broken? Is
there any greater example of unfaithfulness?

Where a father or stepfather abuses his children sexually, it
makes it very difficult for the relationship with the mother to
continue, at least without a significant period of separation
while counselling occurs. Among child protection workers, it
is regarded as an established principle that where child sexual
abuse is discovered in a family, either the perpetrator has to

leave or the child must be removed. It is too great a risk to leave the two together in the same household. The separation between perpetrator and child needs to last at least until it can be established, after a reputable treatment programme has concluded, that reconciliation is possible. This may take a very long time indeed and, in a great many cases, even in the best treatment programmes, reconciliation is contraindicated. Because the discovery of child sexual abuse leads so often to the departure of the perpetrator, child protection workers are sometimes accused of breaking up families.

There are important reasons why separation is necessary following the disclosure of sexual abuse in a family.[29] First, it deprives the perpetrator of physical proximity to the child and other children in the household. Second, it breaks the psychological hold of perpetrator over the victim. The removal of the perpetrator from the home makes visible for the child the breaking of his power over her.[30] It gives her, perhaps for the first time in years, a sense that she can at last be safe at home.

Separation and the denial of contact for a time are also necessary to ensure that the child is not pressured by the perpetrator to retract his or her account of the abuse. The pressure may take the form of blaming the child for the family break-up, threatening violence unless the child retracts, or using emotional blackmail such as suicide threats.

Another factor in subsequent recantation is that, in the early stages after a disclosure, the child may have a fragile confidence in his or her knowledge that the father's behaviour was wrong and that it was good to tell someone what was happening. As part of the process of grooming, children will often be told by the perpetrator from an early age that intimate sexual contact is part of growing up, or that this is the way fathers always behave towards sons or daughters. In order to recognise that the perpetrator's behaviour is wrong, the child must undergo a massive cognitive readjustment, which involves the recognition that the relationship has been abusive. Sometimes, when children disclose abuse, this cognitive readjustment has begun to occur. In many other situations, the child's initial disclosure of the abuse is accidental, and the child still accepts the father's version of what is and is not normal within the father-child relationship. If the child continues to live with the perpetrator at a time when his or her concepts of right and wrong in regard to the abuse are still fragile, and the perpetrator is maintaining a vehement denial of any wrongdoing, then the child may come to accept that the father's denial represents the reality that he or she should accept. Thus the pressure to recant need not be overt. It may result from being in the presence of a hitherto all-powerful and all-knowing parent who rejects the child's version of events and insists the child must be mistaken in his or her interpretation of what has occurred.[31]

Separation in the aftermath of the disclosure of sexual abuse also allows time for the relationship between the abused child and the non-abusing parent to change. The perpetrator's tactics of isolating the child may be highly destructive for the relationship between the mother and the child.[32] The father may implicate the mother as responsible by saying that if the mother were more responsive sexually, it would not be necessary for him to use the child to satisfy his sexual needs. The child may also be told that the mother knows about the abuse and does not care. The child may thus blame the mother for the abuse. Alternatively, the father may try to prevent the child from confiding in the mother by saying that the mother will have a nervous breakdown if ever she finds out. Thus the child is made responsible for protecting the mother from harm by maintaining the secret.

With such a strong dynamic in place when the sexual abuse is disclosed, it is crucial for the well-being of the child and family that the mother's authority and parental role have the chance to be re-established without being subjected to continuing negative influences from the perpetrator. This is vital if rehabilitation is ever to be a consideration or if the new reconstructed family is to have a chance of survival. For the child, learning to confide in the mother again after being distant from her for so long may be a slow process. While the perpetrator is absent, the family as a whole is given a chance to adjust to what has happened and to re-establish relationships, unaffected by the dominance of the abusing parent.

Such steps are necessary in the long-term interests of the whole family. The necessity of separation may be difficult for Christians to accept. Child sexual abuse, together with domestic violence, make us face up to the question of the validity of preserving marriages at all costs. The need for separation underlines just how serious child sexual abuse is. Sexual abuse destroys so much that cannot be restored. Realising this should make us the more determined to prevent it, and to act responsibly and decisively when it is discovered.

Taking Child Protection Seriously

When a case of child sexual abuse comes to light it often provokes an immediate and very serious crisis among everyone concerned. Events may move quickly, circumstances change constantly. It is very easy in these circumstances for church leaders to be pulled in a range of different directions and to have a number of conflicting instincts. Responding appropriately to cases of child sexual abuse requires us to put the interests of children ahead of concerns about avoiding scandal or other such issues. The decision we make in principle about whether we are willing to take child protection seriously is likely to colour our response to the crisis that arises when abuse is disclosed.

Taking child protection seriously does not mean that we need to abandon our concern for the perpetrator or that we assume a person to be guilty of child abuse when he denies the allegations. It does mean that we need to respond to situations in a way that is protective of children, and not merely protective of the church or the perpetrator. This the churches have in the past too often failed to do.

Chapter 10

Disclosure, Investigation and the Legal Process

If churches are to be prepared to deal with problems of child sexual abuse in the congregation or in Christian families, then it is necessary to be clear about how they will respond if abuse is disclosed. The chances that a minister or priest will have to confront a case of disclosure of sexual abuse at some time in his ministry are so high that training in the relevant legal and pastoral issues ought to be included in all theological courses. Understanding what to do about disclosures is also important for anyone else working with children.

A first stage in being prepared to respond to the abused child is to be aware of the indicators of sexual abuse.

Are There Any Signs of Sexual Abuse?

Some books and pamphlets on child sexual abuse publish a list of indicators of sexual abuse. These include certain physical and behavioural symptoms. While such lists may be helpful, it is important to realise that many of these signs could equally be indicators of a range of different problems. The behavioural indicators in particular are equivocal. We shouldn't jump to conclusions about what they suggest.

There are very few physical signs of sexual abuse which point to that diagnosis and no other. The presence of semen or

202

pubic hairs are obvious indicators of sexual abuse, as are the symptoms of a sexually transmitted disease, and of course, pregnancy. Bruises or bleeding in the genital area or the buttocks indicate that the child needs at least to be taken for a medical examination. The younger the child, the more likely that any attempt at penetration of the vagina or anus will cause tearing. A vaginal infection may also be a cause for concern.

Behavioural symptoms include sexualised behaviour, although this should not be taken as a clear sign of sexual abuse. Pre-pubertal children are much more aware sexually than most people realise, and with the saturation of sexual images in television programmes, cartoons and films which are accessible to children, awareness of and interest in sexual behaviour are only to be expected. The great majority of boys and a majority of girls will engage in some form of sexual exploration before the age of twelve. This may be sexual activity involving just their own bodies, such as masturbation, or activity that involves a friend. Most of this activity takes place when adults aren't looking.[1] Some forms of sexual activity are a cause for concern. The acting out of inter-course, repetitive and open masturbation, preoccupation with sexual matters or genitalia as indicated through the child's language or activities, engaging in sexual activity with another child which goes beyond 'playing doctor' are all reasons to seek professional assessment. A child may also give indications of sexual abuse through drawings, although these can be difficult to interpret. Drawings of men with very large penises may at least suggest that the child has been inappropriately exposed to an erect penis, and other drawings with sexual themes may be indicative of sexual abuse.

Other behavioural signs are that the child is afraid to be alone with a particular adolescent or adult, or is afraid to go home. Sudden regression in the child's behaviour may also indicate some form of abuse.

Many behavioural problems have explanations other than sexual abuse. Some symptoms such as recurrent nightmares, withdrawn behaviour or, alternatively, delinquent or aggressive behaviour could be indicators of a range of problems including physical abuse, emotional abuse and exposure to domestic violence. All behavioural oddities should, however, ring alarm bells for the parent or care-giver, who may be able to give the child space to talk about her feelings or to explain where she learnt a particular kind of sexual behaviour. If there are a number of behavioural symptoms of abuse it will be worth talking it over with someone who has experience in that field, such as a social worker or psychologist.

If there is sufficient cause for concern, or the behaviour persists, then a parent may want to take the child to see a child psychologist or paediatrician with expertise in child abuse. This course is not open to others who observe symptoms of abuse; but if there is reason to believe the problem may be at home, the appropriate course is to notify the relevant child protection authority. Reports may also be made to the police. In Britain, the child protection authority that has the statutory responsibility to intervene in cases of child abuse is the Social Services Department. In Australia, it is the government department in each State or Territory responsible for family and community services. Staff here have the training to interview the child and may have the power to refer the child to a psychologist or paediatrician with suitable expertise. In all parts of Australia except Western Australia, certain professional groups are required by law to report the matter if they have reason to believe a child is being or has been abused. There is no mandatory reporting in Britain, but people are encouraged to contact the social services if they believe that a child is at risk of significant harm.

How Children Disclose

Because perpetrators often take such elaborate precautions to ensure the compliance and silence of the child, it can be very difficult for adults to discover what is happening. In most cases, the only way that we can know that a child has been sexually abused is if he or she tells us. While some children become worried about the perpetrator's behaviour and cry out for help, and others pluck up the courage to speak, many disclosures of abuse are not intentional at all in the sense that the child deliberately tells an adult. A child tells a schoolfriend the secret in the way that children share secrets, the friend tells her mother; a young child's drawings appear to depict oral-penile contact and prompt questions; one girl talks to a friend and discovers that not all Daddies do what her own Daddy does to her, so she asks her mother about it. In all these ways and more, the sexual abuse can come to light without any intention to disclose on the part of the child.

Commonly, a child's disclosure of sexual abuse is a process which occurs over time and has a number of stages. One study examined carefully the process of disclosure in 116 cases in which sexual abuse was confirmed.[2] In 94 per cent of these cases, the offender was convicted of abuse. In the other 6 per cent of the cases there was medical evidence highly consistent with abuse. In 74 per cent of the cases, the children did not make a purposeful disclosure of the abuse. Adolescents were most likely to make a purposeful disclosure. In those whose disclosure was accidental, the first indications that there may have been abuse were that a known offender had spent time with this child, that the child demonstrated sexualised behaviour uncharacteristic of the age group, or that the child said something to a parent that suggested the child had been introduced to activities of a sexual nature.

While some children who disclosed accidentally did give a clear account of what had occurred once they were asked about it, in general it was uncommon for the whole story to come out straight away. More frequently, there were initial stages of denial and tentative disclosure. In 72 per cent of the cases, the children denied the abuse when first questioned. For most of those who initially denied the abuse, the next stage was a very tentative acknowledgment that things had been happening, but frequently the child appeared confused or uncertain, vacillating between acknowledgment and denial. Thus the child might say that it happened only once, or that she had forgotten about it before, or that it had happened to someone else. Eventually, as she began to trust more, she would give more details and acknowledge what had happened. This third stage is the stage of active disclosure.

Following an active disclosure, there was often a further stage. In 22 per cent of all the cases, the child at one stage recanted the allegation. The main reasons were pressure from the perpetrator or from the family, or negative reactions to the process of investigation and prosecution. The final stage among this 22 per cent of cases who recanted was that, in nearly all cases, the child reaffirmed the story again. In these cases, the prosecution went ahead. In many cases where a child recants his or her story, prosecutions will be dropped even if the child confirms the story again, because the child's veracity will be too vulnerable to attack under cross-examination.

THE STAGES OF DISCLOSURE

Stage 1   Denial
Stage 2   Tentative disclosure
Stage 3   Active disclosure
Stage 4   Recantation
Stage 5   Reaffirmation

Source: Sorenson and Snow, 1991.[3] 116 confirmed cases of sexual abuse.

Children thus find it difficult to disclose sexual abuse. Creating an environment in which children feel safe enough to tell someone what is troubling them is part of what it means for churches to care for children, whatever the problem may be. Younger children in particular may need 'permission' to talk. If they are looking sad or seem to be depressed, we need to give them the opportunity to tell us why, and we may need to ask them some open-ended questions to prompt them. It may be something which they don't feel they can tell Mum or Dad about, but they may be willing to tell a Sunday school teacher. There could be a multitude of reasons why they are unhappy, some trivial, some very serious. There may also be many reasons why they haven't been able to tell their parents. Children may keep secrets from the best of parents. Following up on a child who seems distressed or withdrawn is a matter of Christian caring. It does not imply any criticism of the parents, nor that they may be the cause of the child's unhappiness.

When Children Tell

WHEN A CHILD DISCLOSES ABUSE

1. Don't panic.
2. Don't ask many questions. Let the child tell you in his or her own words. Ask questions only if you need to establish a bit more before you have reason to suspect abuse.
3. Try not to show you are upset or anxious. Be there for the child.
4. Reassure the child that it was a good thing to tell, and that he or she was not to blame for the abuse.
5. Don't make any promises you can't keep.
6. Explain what you will do next on the basis of the information, who will be told, and why.
7. Notify the relevant authorities, giving as much information as possible.
8. As soon as possible after the disclosure, write down a record of what you said and what the child said.

How then should an adult respond to a child's initial disclosure of abuse? When a child begins to talk it is important to try to stay calm, or at least to appear calm. Your calmness will help relieve the child of the stress of telling and make him or her feel more comfortable about the situation. There is no need to panic.

It is important when a child makes an initial disclosure to allow the child to tell you as far as possible in his or her own words, and to ask as few questions as possible. This is because in some cases defence lawyers argue that the adult unwittingly led the child by suggestive questioning. Questions such as 'did he touch you on the vagina or the bottom?' may imply to the child that he did one or the other. By contrast, if the child is allowed as far as possible to describe things in his or her own words, then there is much less chance either of improperly influencing the child, or of the child's story being successfully challenged by defence lawyers.

Most children will need some encouragement to tell, even if only by such questions as 'what happened then?' or 'how often did this take place?' Usually with younger children some questions may be necessary just to clarify that the child is indeed describing sexual abuse and not something more innocent.

However, it is not your job to investigate, and therefore you do not need all the details. All you need is to be sufficiently sure that the child is describing sexual abuse for it to be appropriate to report the matter to the police or the child protection authority. Once that is sufficiently established, it is best not to press for a lot of details. Others will need to ask these specific questions.

When children disclose abuse, it is helpful to offer reassurance by saying to them that it was not their fault and that it was good for them to tell someone, because now you can do something to help them. Children who disclose abuse may feel very vulnerable. They may believe that they have done something very bad, and feel dirty or ashamed. They may be very worried about the consequences of telling because of what the perpetrator has said will happen if they tell. Reassurance and comfort are therefore an important way in which children can be helped when disclosing abuse.

Reassurance should not go too far, however. It is important that you do not make any promises that you cannot keep. You cannot promise that the offender will not be punished or that Mum won't ever find out. What you can do is to try to allay the child's very legitimate fears about the future. As a church, we can promise always to be there for her, no matter what.

The child should also be told what will happen next, who will be told and why. This does not need to be in any great detail, but the child needs to be able to feel that things are happening with her and for her, not just all around her.

After you have reassured the child and ensured that she is in a safe place with appropriate support, it is important then to notify the police or the child protection authority as soon as possible. They will take action from there. If the abuse has occurred quite recently, then the child may need to see a paediatrician for a medical examination. If the child is living with the perpetrator in the same household, then it can be expected that the police or social services will act swiftly to ensure that the child is safe from further abuse.

Finally, it is good to note down the main elements of the conversation as soon as possible after it has finished. How the conversation began, what she said, what you said may all be helpful to the police or the social worker who speaks to the child about the abuse.

When the Child Wants to Maintain the Secret

What if the child insists that she doesn't want you to tell anyone else? The child may well be desperate for someone to help while at the same time being very afraid of the consequences if the secret is made known, not least if the perpetrator has made threats. If the abuse was by a parent or step-parent, the child may be afraid that the family will break up. It would be easier if the child could be assured that this will not happen. The reality is, though, that where incestuous sexual abuse has been occurring, the family may indeed break up when the secret comes out. In very serious cases of abuse, the child protection authority will need to remove the children if the non-offending parent is unable or unwilling to protect them. The assurance that can be offered is that the child will be looked after whatever the consequences and that the church family will be there to help. The unknown need not be a deeper abyss than the child is in at present, and the child needs to be assured that those who intervene will be motivated by his or her best interests.

Children's concerns about confidentiality need to be fully acknowledged and respected. If the adult rides roughshod over the child's fears, the child will feel this as a betrayal by the adult to whom he or she has entrusted this darkest of secrets – which may just add to the damage resulting from the abuse. Sexually abused children will probably have experienced already what it is like to be betrayed by the offender, whom they should have been able to trust. They may also have known feelings of great powerlessness in being unable to stop the abuse and to make themselves safe. At the same time, help and support for the child are going to be available only if the secrecy surrounding the abuse is broken and there is a clear acknowledgment of the gravity of what has happened.

A child who begins by insisting that no one else be told needs to be helped sensitively to advance to the point where he or she gives permission to the adult to tell others who can help to bring the abuse to an end. As far as is consistent with ensuring the child's safety, the child needs to be allowed to control or have some say in who knows about the abuse and when they find out.

In the ultimate analysis, should the adult report abuse against the express wishes of the child? This is a real dilemma. Clearly, the younger the child, the more it is necessary for adults to decide what is in his or her best interests even if this does not coincide with what the child wants. Sometimes, a child may be able to accept that the secret is one which the adult cannot maintain and that the only way the abuse will end is if the secret is revealed. If you are mandated by law to report the abuse, you can explain that the law requires you to tell. Even if you are not required to report, the question may be not if the secrecy should be broken but when.

The problems of balancing the child's need for protection against his or her request for secrecy indicate that it is inadvisable to invite children to share problems with a promise that the adult will not tell anyone. Some counsellors get around this by saying to the child that they will not tell anyone without telling the child first, or unless someone is doing something against the law.

When Sexual Abuse Occurs within a Church Activity

What happens if sexual abuse occurs in the context of a church activity such as Sunday school, a youth group or a church camp? Procedures need to be in place for dealing with such situations. These should be known about and understood in advance, at least by the key leaders to whom such an occurrence would be likely to be reported.

In a number of places an Adviser or Co-ordinator has been appointed in the diocese, presbytery or other denominational structure, whose role is to provide expert support to ministers and churches when these situations occur. In England, the House of Bishops' Policy on Child Abuse (1995) recommends that each bishop should appoint a representative to advise and support him in dealing with issues of child abuse. This person would be asked to fulfil a number of functions including providing advice and training to ministers and parish councils, advising on cases as they arise and liaising with the statutory authorities (police and social services). The Anglican Diocese of Southwell, for example, has a Diocesan Co-ordinator for Abuse Procedures who is appointed by the Bishop and reports to him. It is specified that this person should be lay, preferably female, and from outside diocesan management structures.[4] One of the co-ordinator's functions is to ensure that as far as possible the Church's response to a child abuse case places the interests of the child above those of the institution, and that the Church co-operates fully with the police and social services in the investigation. The co-ordinator's specific roles include advising the Bishop with reference to any incident or allegation, providing appropriate support for those affected by allegations of sexual abuse and liaising with the police and social services with regard to the investigation. Such a person can also play a very important role in the pastoral response to situations of abuse. Abuse cases can affect not only the victim and alleged perpetrator and their immediate families, but often also the congregation as a whole.

A number of principles about responding to cases of child abuse in congregational settings may be identified. The first is that the police and child protection authority should always be notified. The second is that, in all but the most exceptional circumstances, the person against whom the allegation has been made should be suspended from a position of work with children while the investigation is continuing. The third is that church leaders should avoid conducting their own investigations while the official investigation is going on. The fourth is that appropriate pastoral support be provided for both the victim and the alleged offender.

Involve the Police

The first principle is that the police and the child protection authority should always be notified. Investigating child abuse is a matter for professional skill and judgment and if any prosecution is to occur, the police will be the body responsible. Additionally, the child protection authority has the legal power to remove children from a home or to seek a supervision order if the child is being abused within the family. Even though it may not have any statutory authority to take any legal action where the abuse occurred in a church setting, the social services department or its equivalent is usually involved in child protection investigations so that it can provide or coordinate supportive services for the victim and the family.

What if the child or the parents do not want to involve the police? Often they don't, for a variety of reasons. Children may be reluctant to have the police involved because they are afraid of having to give evidence in court, or because they do not want the perpetrator to be sent to jail. Parents may have the same concerns. These concerns need to be respected, but it may be helpful to the child and to the parents to look at it in terms of taking one step at a time. When abuse is first disclosed, it is a distressing period for all those who are close to the situation. People won't be ready to take all the decisions at once, or to think clearly about all the issues. Nevertheless, reporting the abuse is very important even if eventually charges are not laid. It makes what has been secret public and thus helps to break the power of the perpetrator over the victim. Whatever may happen subsequently, involving the police is a means of protecting the child from further abuse.

It is also very important from the church's point of view to tell the police of alleged abuse in the course of church activity. The church needs to think about the protection of all the children in its activities. If one child has been abused, then there is a real possibility that other children are at risk of abuse by the same alleged perpetrator. It has its own responsibility to ensure that those who work with children are not likely to offend, and it will be liable in negligence if it fails to take proper action to protect children from sexual abuse. The church cannot keep such a matter private, even if the parents wish to.

Furthermore, the church needs to be aware of the adverse criticism which it may attract (quite rightly) if it is seen to be covering up criminal offences and thereby endangering the safety of other children. If a minister or a church employee has been accused of a criminal offence, the inference will be almost inescapable that the church is protecting its own if it fails to encourage and facilitate a full independent investigation.

If we are going to tackle the problem of child sexual abuse it is important to deal with these cases as criminal offences. Whatever compassion there may be for the offender, it does not help the problem to minimise the offence.

Churches therefore must involve the police as a matter of course in all cases of child sexual abuse in church activities and in every other situation in which a child discloses to a church worker or volunteer abuse that is occurring at home. In other situations in which the parents are not implicated in the abuse and have no interest in protecting the alleged perpetrator, it probably ought to be for them to decide whether to report the abuse. They should be encouraged to do so.

Disclosure of the abuse to the police does not mean that the matter will go to court or that the child will have to testify. The child can be reassured that he will not have to give evidence if he doesn't want to, but it is better to cross that bridge when he comes to it. Children are not forced to testify in court. Generally, prosecutors seek the permission of the parents (or non-offending parent). Furthermore, if the offender pleads guilty, there will be no need to testify.

Children's worries about having to give evidence in court are quite understandable. Giving evidence in court is easier than it was, but is still quite difficult and stressful. In recent years, many reforms have been introduced to help children giving evidence in court. What children generally fear most about testifying is seeing the perpetrator again in the court-room. Consequently, one of the major reforms has been to make this unnecessary. In Britain, and in most parts of Australia, it is possible for the child to give evidence by closed circuit television. This means that the child is placed in another room which is linked by video to the courtroom. The child is able to see the judge and the lawyers (though not the defendant) and the people in the courtroom are able to see the child. The child's evidence is then given by question and answer through the closed circuit TV system. It may be necessary for the child to appear briefly in the courtroom to identify the defendant and to be seen by the jury, but in the main his or her evidence is given elsewhere.

Another reform that has been introduced in Britain and in some other places is to allow videotaped evidence. This is a videotape of the interview which is conducted at an early stage of the investigation. In Britain, it is usually conducted jointly by police and social services. There are special centres for such investigative interviews which are separate from the normal police interview rooms, and these are designed to be more comfortable and appropriate for children. In Australia, videotaping of interviews is not as common, and they may or may not be used in court, but this varies from State to State. In Britain, if a videotape of the interview has been taken, then this may be used instead of the child's giving evidence in response to the prosecutor's questions. However, the child needs to be available for cross-examination by the defence. Closed circuit television and videotaped evidence may be used together. Thus the child's account of what happened will be told by playing the videotape, and then the child will answer any defence questions through the medium of closed circuit television. Whether these facilities are available in any particular case will depend upon the decisions made by the prosecutor or the judge.

It is thus not as frightening an experience for children to give evidence as it was a few years ago. Prosecutors, judges and other court personnel are much better now than they once were about looking after child witnesses properly and making sure that they are not harangued or distressed in other ways by the process. It still isn't easy, and there are some cases both in England and Australia where the child witness has a bad experience that could have been avoided. Nonetheless, giving evidence should not be seen as necessarily distressing. A great many children give evidence these days. It can even be therapeutic for some children if they get to tell their story and the jury convicts. On the other hand, they need to be prepared for the possibility of an acquittal.

If a criminal conviction is secured, then the sentence is up to the judge. Jail sentences are not imposed in all cases of child sexual abuse. It depends on the gravity of the offences and what is known about their frequency and duration. If a jail sentence is imposed, that is the judge's decision and responsibility. It needs to be emphasised that the child is not responsible for the punishment that the perpetrator receives.

Suspend the Alleged Perpetrator from Working with Children

If there has been a complaint made of sexual abuse within a church activity which is under formal investigation, the alleged perpetrator must be suspended from involvement in children's ministry. Suspension is a protective measure not only for the children but also for the alleged offender who would not want to be subject to further allegations of misconduct. It is also an important way of reassuring church members if the situation becomes known in the congregation.

In many cases in which the accusations of child molestation are not public knowledge, a volunteer may be able to withdraw quietly from children's work without reasons being given. The situation with regard to an employee or office-holder is more complex. A temporary suspension from duty on full pay pending an investigation may not need to comply with any principles of natural justice, such as having a hearing,[5] but if the suspension may involve a loss of pay, status or reputation, then the person would need to have some kind of hearing with a senior official before it was implemented.[6] This requirement of natural justice (otherwise known as procedural fairness) is due to the prejudicial nature of such a suspension. Although it is not appropriate, while an investigation is occurring, for the senior official to reach a conclusion on whether abuse occurred, he or she must at least be satisfied that there is a case to answer before suspending a person. Suspension is not the only option: reassignment to other responsibilities that do not involve work with children is another way of ensuring the safety of the children. A minister who is accused may be allowed to continue such of his pastoral work as does not involve children. Where, however, the circumstances of the allegation are known in the congregation, it may be impossible for the minister to continue in any capacity, and an open acknowledgment that he has withdrawn from congregational ministry while the police investigation is under way may be the only way to handle the situation.

The timing of any suspension is critical and requires close liaison with the police. It can be very important in a police investigation for the alleged offender to be caught by surprise without foreknowledge of the arrest or investigation. Normally, the police will gather statements from the victims before confronting the offender and that may take some time. A church leader who learns of the allegations at a very early stage and then suspends the alleged perpetrator without first consulting with the police may give the offender advance notice of the police investigation and thereby jeopardise it. There have even been cases in which, following a complaint of sexual abuse, the police have engaged in covert surveillance within the church of an unsuspecting alleged offender. There should be early collaboration between the church and the police on all aspects of the investigation and the church's response to the situation.

Leave it to the Police to Investigate

When sexual abuse is alleged in a church community, church members are likely to experience a range of emotions including shock, disbelief, anger and sadness. Some people may desire very strongly to get to the truth of the matter. They may find that they cannot move on in their lives without having made their own decision on the matter. There may even be some who feel they will be unable to come to terms with it unless they hear the story personally from the lips of the victim. The desire to investigate is likely to be particularly strong for the leaders of the congregation, since they are charged with the well-being of the church community and may have to make important decisions about the church's response to the crisis.

It is important, however, that, having involved the authorities, the church members leave it to them to conduct the investigation in the first stage. This is for two reasons. First, it is essential that the stress on the child be minimised to the greatest extent possible. One of the most difficult aspects for the child to deal with is the necessity to keep repeating the story to adults. In the past, it was not unusual for children to give a large number of accounts of what occurred. The child disclosed first, perhaps, to a teacher, who then involved the school counsellor. Then the child had to repeat the story to the principal. A parent or parents may then have been informed, and no doubt asked the child all about it many times. The police and social workers then interviewed the child separately, and then the child would repeat the story in therapy.

Then, if the matter went to court, there were further occasions on which the story was raked over in minute detail.

Child protection workers are well aware now of the negative effects all this can have on a child, and professionals practising in this field endeavour to keep to a minimum the number of times the child is required to tell the story. Ministers and other church leaders do not need to add to the difficulties children have by asking them to repeat the story to them. Nor are they likely in any case to be skilled in interviewing children about such sensitive and shame-filled matters.

A second reason to avoid taking on an investigative role is that it may detract from the investigation by the police or other authorities. Suggestive interviewing by adults needs to be avoided. The more that the child is interviewed by people who are not experienced in this field, especially in the early stages of an investigation, the greater the potential for a prosecution to be undermined.

When the abuse has occurred in a church setting, it may be very important for the minister to determine at the earliest possible stage who should learn about the incident or allegations and why. The general principle is that such information is shared on a strict need-to-know basis. If the situation is already known in the congregation, there may be a need to talk to the key leaders in the church and those close to the people concerned, explaining to them the importance of leaving the matter with the police.

Provide Pastoral Care to Both Victim and Alleged Offender

Providing pastoral care in the aftermath of a disclosure of sexual abuse raises some difficult issues. The circumstances of individual cases vary enormously. In some situations, there will be no question about whether the abuse occurred. The pastoral challenge is to cope with the shock of discovery and help the various people affected to come to terms with the situation, for which they probably need professional counselling to help them work through the anger and grief.

It is not only the victim and his or her family who may be affected in this process. If the abuse has occurred in a Sunday school or youth group, many parents will be asking whether their children were abused as well as the known victims. If the alleged perpetrator is a minister, youth leader or respected member of the congregation, then people are confronted by the terrible dichotomy between what they have hitherto believed about the goodness and faithfulness of that person and the alleged wrongdoing. It is often difficult for these two quite different pictures to be reconciled.

The need for pastoral care includes the offender and his immediate family. A Christian who has molested children does not cease to be a child of God. The family of the offender may also become victims of the abuse, although other church members do not recognise this. The family may feel guilt by association or may battle with a sense of vicarious shame. The spouse and children of an offender are likely to need particular support. There will be the shock of what has been revealed about a man they loved, and feelings of grief and loss, particularly if a jail sentence is imposed. They may indeed feel exiled from the church community. All of these feelings are likely to be there irrespective of the way in which other church members actually respond to the offender's family. They can be exacerbated however, by insensitive behaviour by church members. In one small church, the pastor was convicted of sexual abuse of his teenage daughter. The church dismissed the pastor immediately that the abuse came to light. It also expelled the wife from both the manse and the church, accusing her of 'keeping an immoral household'.

How should the minister respond in a situation where the alleged perpetrator strongly denies the allegations and remains within the congregation, and both the complainant and the accused are looking for pastoral support? The pastoral situation then can become particularly difficult. It is not uncommon for two rival camps to form very quickly, as both the complainant and the accused look to friends for affirmation and support, demanding that their friends declare their loyalties. The minister can be caught between a rock and a hard place in a situation in which there is genuine uncertainty about what occurred and where the case is beginning to make its long and arduous journey through the court process.

This situation arose in one church where it was alleged that a prominent church musician had molested a teenage member of the church. Friends of this teenager also subsequently alleged that they had been molested as well. The allegations were strongly denied by the man concerned. The church leaders were very uncertain what the truth of the matter was. On the one hand, the allegations had to be taken very seriously indeed, and the police certainly felt there was sufficient evidence to lay charges. On the other hand, there were certain reasons to doubt the veracity of the teenagers' stories. Eventually, indeed, the accused man was acquitted after significant inconsistencies in the testimony of the teenagers who gave evidence. While the police investigation was continuing, the church leaders came under considerable pressure, particularly from the mother of the boy who first made the allegations, to remove the alleged offender from the music ministry and to deny him any other visible role in the church services. Properly, they declined to do so. While some members of the congregation were convinced that he had done what was alleged, others had the strongest doubts. If the church leaders had removed him from all visible ministry, it might have looked as if they were taking sides and assuming him to be guilty. His music ministry in the church did not involve any work with children or adolescents.

Instead, the church leaders resolved the issue by drawing up a roster. The mother concerned was told in advance when the accused man was playing in the group, and could then choose not to attend that service. At the same time, the minister took steps, with the co-operation of the alleged offender, to ensure that this man was not alone with children.

The other difficulty which the minister faced in this situation was the demand to be believed by both sides. He resolved this by telling them that he believed them both. He also told them that this was what he was saying to them both so that he could not be accused of duplicity. He took the further step of involving other people in the work of pastoral care, so that he did not need to handle matters on his own.

One suggested approach to the dilemma of providing proper pastoral support is to involve different people in the primary pastoral care of the claimed victim and of the alleged offender, the minister playing a supportive role in the background. There are good reasons for this. First, the minister, working alone, is likely to find it very difficult to support both sides pastorally. Both will want the minister to believe them, and all uncertainties and hesitations may be taken as a sign of disloyalty or lack of belief in the person's story. Second, the minister may well feel compelled by the circumstances to come to a conclusion about the truth of the matter one way or another, in a situation where the truth may be murky and hidden. This poses the danger that the minister becomes another investigator rather than a pastoral carer. Third, the minister who has tried to pastor both sides may find great difficulties if the investigations end either without a charge or in an acquittal. Where both families remain in the church or even in the district, the work of caring for everybody in the aftermath of the crisis may be made easier if the minister has not taken sides.

The Church of England House of Bishops' Policy on Child Abuse recommends that the 'person responsible for the pastoral care of the accused person should have no contact with the person who offers pastoral care to the person making the allegation or the victim of the alleged abuse and his or her family.'[7] This is to ensure that information does not travel from the complainant to the alleged offender through the pastoral supporters in a way which undermines the police investigation of the case.

It is an advantage to have an expert adviser in each diocese, presbytery or other denominational structure to advise and to liaise with the civil authorities. Indeed, there may need to be a small team of people with different disciplinary backgrounds and skills who can be called upon to assist the local church in coping with the situation. Fortunately, most denominations can call upon a great number of people with relevant expertise.

Most denominations are well supplied with social workers, psychologists and paediatricians who have expertise in child protection. Some lawyers also have relevant expertise which can be called upon.

The Question of Future Involvement in Ministry

At the end of the investigation by the police criminal charges may be laid, and at the end of the criminal process there may be a conviction. But what if charges are not laid? What if, although the police press charges, the prosecution is dropped? Or what if, although there is a prosecution, the defendant is acquitted? Does the absence of a criminal conviction at the end of the process resolve the matter completely for the church?

It is here that many church child protection policies fall short. For there is an assumption implicit in them that the police investigation will resolve the issues one way or another. If the person was sexually abusing the child then he will be prosecuted and convicted. If, for whatever reason, there is no conviction, then the abuse allegations must be regarded as unfounded and the accused person will have been vindicated.

In the fictional courtroom dramas on television, the truth always emerges clearly from the courtroom process. Television's best known defence lawyers, the Perry Masons and Matlocks of this world, are not merely defence attorneys but private investigators. Seemingly, they always win. They do so by finding the real villain. They are able to present an accurate account of the murder by a mixture of careful investigation and brilliant cross-examination, which leads the real culprit to confess on the witness stand. Justice is done. The innocent client is vindicated. The viewer never gets to see the lawyer's bill.

Perhaps we need to believe that there are only two alternatives in life, guilty and innocent, and that the courts are always able to determine the issue one way or the other. The reality is more complex. Sometimes the legal process does get

222

to the truth of the matter in determining that a person was not guilty of the offences. The truth emerges through the process of forensic examination and careful scrutiny of the evidence. It can be shown that the key witness was lying or that crucial forensic evidence does not in fact prove the prosecution case at all. There are some child sexual abuse prosecutions which may have been brought on the basis of evidence that simply does not stand up to careful scrutiny. With very young children in particular, it can be difficult to say with certainty whether the child has been sexually abused. The child may be too young to say very much about what happened, or the account could be open to a variety of interpretations. The conclusion that the child has been sexually abused in these circumstances is necessarily a process of ruling out other alternative explanations for the symptoms the child displays.

But there are many other cases in which the child has given a clear and explicit account of sexual abuse to investigators, and cannot be shown either to be lying or indeed to have any motive for lying. Many acquittals for child sexual abuse are achieved by creating a reasonable doubt. It may be enough if the defence can demonstrate some inconsistencies in the child's account through the process of cross-examination. After all, the prosecution must prove its case. The defence needs to prove nothing. All it needs to do is to cast doubt on the evidence put forward by the prosecution, sufficient for the jury (or in some cases the magistrate or judge) to conclude that it would be unsafe to convict the defendant. The criminal trial is focused on a specific question. Is there enough evidence to prove beyond a reasonable doubt that this defendant was guilty of the crimes charged?

In most areas of the criminal law, the decision of the police not to press charges, or an acquittal following a prosecution, would be the end of the matter. Punishment in a civilised society should be imposed only when the case is proven to a very high standard of probability. The consequences of conviction are so serious that the rules of evidence and procedure are weighted in favour of the defence, and the defendant is given the benefit of a reasonable doubt.

However, in the area of child sexual abuse, the question whether an alleged offender should be allowed to continue working with children cannot be resolved on the simple basis of a conviction or a lack of it. For one thing, only a minority of cases which investigators regard as substantiated result in convictions in a criminal court. Often, this has little to do with the real strength of the evidence. For another, because those who sexually abuse children tend to be locked into a repetitive pattern of behaviour, and will offend again, we have to make a realistic assessment of the risk to children if a person who is believed to be an offender is allowed to continue working with them, irrespective of the outcome of the criminal process.

Why So Few Sexual Abuse Cases Result in Convictions

If one examines all the cases in which children make an apparently clear disclosure of abuse, there is, at every point in the system, a continuous dropping off in the number of cases that proceed.[8] First, there are some cases in which the child does not repeat the story to strangers such as the police or child protection authority. The child's account therefore cannot be substantiated and it is doubtful that the matter will be taken any further. Then there are cases in which, after interviewing the child, the investigators, be they the police or the child protection authority, are convinced in their own minds that the child has been sexually abused. They may also be certain of the identity of the perpetrator. In this sense, the report of sexual abuse is substantiated. This does not mean, however, that a prosecution will ensue. Before bringing a prosecution, the prosecutors must be sure that there is a realistic chance of conviction. In the area of child sexual abuse, there are a variety of different reasons why this test may not be met.

One reason is that the parents do not want the child to give evidence, or the child is unwilling to do so. Some parents are understandably concerned about the stress on the child of giving evidence and therefore do not press charges. There may be a long interval between the date of the arrest and the time it goes to court, a time in which the prospect of court proceedings continues to hang over the child. Police don't usually pressure parents about this. If the parents don't want the child to testify, it may mean that no charges are laid.

A very young child cannot of course be a strong witness. Some young children do give evidence, and do so very well, but in general it is very difficult to prosecute if it is necessary to rely on the evidence of a child under the age of seven or eight years. Young children may clam up in the witness box, not answering the relevant questions, or they may be easily confused by cross-examination.

A decision not to prosecute may be made if there is no corroboration. As was noted in a previous chapter, it is possible in both England and Australia for a defendant to be convicted on the basis of the testimony of a child who is too young to take an oath, as long as the jury are convinced of the case beyond reasonable doubt. In practice, however, there is a reluctance to prosecute if the case rests solely on the evidence of a child. In a great many cases, that evidence isn't there. Consequently, there may be no prosecution.

Another reason for not prosecuting is that the child cannot provide sufficient detail. Young children in particular often provide very little detail about what has happened, and the criminal courts require not only that the offence be proven beyond reasonable doubt but that the elements of each offence charged be proven specifically.[9] For the criminal justice system, each separate act of molestation or penetration is a separate criminal act, just as each robbery or car theft is a separate criminal act. The witness does not have to give exact dates, but he or she must describe each act of sexual violation with sufficient specificity that each individual incident is proven beyond reasonable doubt. This involves providing the details that constitute the elements of each criminal offence.

For many victims of child sexual assault, however, it may be very difficult to remember each specific instance of violation. They may be able to describe with painful detail the abuse they suffered over a period of time. But what exactly happened when, what he did on one occasion or another may be quite difficult to describe in a way that does not appear suspect under cross-examination. Over a long time, one incident of abuse may blur with another, details may become confused, and descriptions vague. The stumbling block to pressing charges may be the child's inability to give the detail required about any specific incident of abuse.

Even when there is a prosecution, there may not be a conviction, for reasons again unrelated to the real strength of the evidence. Many offenders plead guilty, but if there is a trial, then there are a number of ways in which defence counsel may create a reasonable doubt in sexual abuse cases. One is to point to apparent inconsistencies in the child's account, even if they are inconsequential. Another is to concentrate on the child's vagueness or inconsistency about peripheral details as a way of casting doubt on his or her testimony concerning the central events.

A particular problem is the use of language that is beyond the linguistic capabilities of the child to comprehend and answer properly. Defence counsel are particularly guilty of this, and the confusion and uncertainty created are one means of creating a sufficient doubt.[10] In one Australian study, the researchers took thousands of questions from the transcripts of trials in which children were witnesses. They deleted the ones which it would be inappropriate to ask children who had not been abused, and then put these questions to other children of the same ages. In order to provide a point of comparison, they asked counsellors and teachers to provide sets of questions that would be appropriate to children of a similar age. The children in the experiment were asked simply to repeat the question. If they could repeat it, or repeat the sense of it, then it was assumed that they had at least understood the question. Children were able to understand almost all of the questions asked by counsellors and most of the questions put by teachers. They were much less successful in understanding the questions put by lawyers. Indeed, in the case of about a quarter of the randomly selected questions from lawyers, the children were unable to preserve any of the sense of the question at all.

Despite this, there are still many convictions for child sexual abuse. The numbers are quite small, however, compared to the numbers of cases in which children disclose abuse. Prosecutors have to make judgments about whether they think they can win the case. For this reason, a lot of cases fall by the wayside.

Some indication of the proportion of substantiated cases of sexual abuse that result in a conviction can be gained from figures available in Australia. In New South Wales, the Department of Community Services keeps records of the number of notifications of sexual abuse (and other forms of child abuse) which are treated as substantiated after investigation. To be substantiated, the social worker investigating the case must consider it 'highly probable' that the child has been abused. In 1992–93, 3,886 children were recorded on the database as having been sexually abused. In 1993–94, the number of substantiated cases was 3,302. Thus there was an average of 3,594 substantiated cases during each of those two years. When these figures are compared with the numbers of people convicted for child sexual abuse offences in all New South Wales courts in 1994, it is apparent how few cases result in convictions. There were 297 persons convicted of sex offences against children in that year, and in addition ninety-eight juveniles were convicted of sexual assault offences. The age of the victims is unknown, but it is probable that most of these offences by juveniles were against minors.

Of course, the figures cannot be compared exactly. The criminal cases represent persons convicted. Some of them could have abused more than one child. The departmental figures represent the numbers of children abused. Furthermore, some of the criminal cases could have involved abuse which happened some years earlier, and so are not drawn from the cases investigated in the year or two before 1994. Nonetheless, the figures give a rough indication of the proportion of substantiated cases in which convictions are secured. If all the juvenile cases were cases of child sexual assault, then there were 395 convictions achieved in 1994 out of an average of

3,594 substantiated cases in the previous two years. The New South Wales figures are not unusual. Professional estimates of the numbers of substantiated cases in which convictions are achieved in England are relatively similar.

It follows that it is a mistake to rely on criminal convictions as our sole criterion for determining whether someone should be permitted to continue to work with children. Convictions are recorded in a minority of substantiated cases of abuse only. The absence of a criminal conviction, for whatever reason, at the end of the process of investigation should not mean on its own that there are no obstacles to that person's being involved in ministry with children.

Balancing the Rights of Children and the Alleged Offender

A second reason why reliance should not be placed solely on the criminal process to determine a person's suitability to work with children is that the criminal process does not purport to weigh the interest of the adult against the need of children to be protected from risk. The criminal trial has a quite different focus.

In the criminal process, the case must be proven beyond reasonable doubt because our society regards it as unacceptable to take the risk that an innocent person could be imprisoned for a crime he did not commit. The criminal justice system is weighted strongly in favour of the accused because we place the highest possible value on the protection of fundamental human rights. The potential punishment that could flow from a criminal conviction is a grave enough prospect for us to err on the side of caution and demand that all reasonable doubts be dispelled before convicting.

The law strikes a different balance of interests in different contexts. Whereas the criminal standard of proof is the 'beyond reasonable doubt' standard, and the rules of evidence are very strict, in civil cases (where usually damages are sought), the standard of proof is the balance of probabilities. An acquittal in a criminal case does not prevent a civil case from being brought. In America, for example, when O. J.

Simpson was acquitted of the murder of his wife and another person following the most publicised murder trial in history, the victims' families announced that they were suing Simpson for damages in civil law for the deaths of their loved ones. His acquittal in the criminal trial was irrelevant. The civil case falls to be determined separately, on the balance of probabilities. So it is in child protection work. In England, for example, the acquittal of a father for causing serious injury to his daughter did not inhibit a judge from finding that he was responsible for the abuse when an application was made to the court exercising its civil jurisdiction to ensure the child's safety.[11]

The balancing of interests in deciding whether someone should be permitted to work with children has to be struck quite differently from the way it is struck in the criminal justice process. No one has a right as such to work with children. In law people have certain rights to be protected from unfair dismissal, and these need to be respected. However, these rights are not given the same protection as a defendant receives in a criminal trial. An employee must be treated justly and must be given a chance to respond to the complaints against him. He may need to be warned about unsatisfactory performance. But it is not necessary to go through a quasi-criminal trial before dismissing a person for serious misconduct. The law recognises that while people's interests in employment are important interests to protect, the balancing of rights and interests should not be weighted in favour of the defendant in the same way as it is when imprisonment could be a consequence of an adverse finding.

While no one has a right to work with children, children have a right under international law to be protected from abuse. Article 19 of the United Nations Convention on the Rights of the Child provides that governments who have signed the Convention (as Britain and Australia have done) shall 'take all appropriate legislative, administrative, social and educational measures to protect the child from all forms of physical or mental violence, injury or abuse, neglect or negligent treatment, maltreatment or exploitation, including sexual abuse, while in the care of the parent(s), legal guardian(s) or any other person who has the care of the child.' Article 34 provides in addition that governments 'undertake to protect the child from all forms of sexual exploitation and sexual abuse'.

The balance of interests and rights between children and someone who, it is believed, has a propensity for sexually abuse ought therefore to be weighted strongly in favour of child protection. While in the criminal justice system it is unacceptable to take the risk that an innocent person will be convicted, in making decisions about working with children it is unacceptable to take the risk that children may be sexually abused. In the criminal justice system, we say that it is better that nine guilty men should go free than that one innocent man should be convicted. In thinking about child protection, we would deny that it is better for nine men who are guilty of child sexual abuse to be allowed to work with children than that one innocent man should be barred from this kind of work.

The Unacceptable Risk Test

Having encouraged an independent investigation by professionals working in the field of child protection, having gathered as much reliable information as it is possible to gather, the church needs to make its own assessment of that information and to determine the question of that person's future involvement in ministry with children.

I suggest that the criterion we should use is that a person should not be permitted to work in youth ministry in the church if, on the basis of all the known facts, this would expose children to an unacceptable risk of abuse. The determination of unacceptable risk ought not to be based on mere suspicion, worries or doubts. A sober assessment of all the facts needs to be made. For example, it is a fact that Susan, aged eight, said that Jim, who ran a children's club, took her off to a secluded corner while she was waiting to be picked up by her mother;

that she said that Jim played a game with her in which she had to pull down her pants; that she said that he touched her on her private parts; that she was very distressed by the incident; that Jim's claim that he examined her private parts because she was complaining that she felt sore down there cannot be reconciled with her account; that a social worker or psychologist has spoken to Susan and has determined that she was sexually abused by Jim. These are all facts. One need not necessarily conclude from those facts that Jim sexually abused Susan. In the absence of any reason to disbelieve Susan's account, it would be an unacceptable risk to allow Jim anywhere near children.

The unacceptable risk test is based upon the decision of the High Court of Australia in *M v M* (1988).[12] This case involved sexual abuse allegations in a quite different context, that of making decisions about whether a father should have contact with a child following the breakdown of a marriage. The High Court of Australia stated that 'a court will not grant custody or access to a parent if that custody or access would expose the child to an unacceptable risk of sexual abuse.'

In English law, the key element that should be emphasised here is that any assessment of risk must be made on the basis of known facts, not possibilities, rumours or suspicions. In a case in England under the Children Act 1989 concerning removal of children from the care of parents, the House of Lords had to decide whether it could be said that children were 'likely to suffer harm' if no harm had been proven in the past. They held in that case that the court must act on evidence, and if no relevant facts that would lead to concern about the children's safety had been proven on the balance of probabilities, then there were no facts upon which to conclude that the children were at risk of harm in the future. Nonetheless, it was emphasised that the court could consider a range of facts, which together might lead to an assessment that a child could be harmed in the future, and that such a conclusion might be reached even though no misconduct had been proven in the past.[13]

These family law cases are mentioned only for the light that they shed on the approach that courts take in the context of child protection. It is a very serious thing indeed to deny a man access to his children. It is even more serious for children to be removed from their parents. It is much less serious for a person to be denied involvement in children's ministry within a church congregation. No one has the right to be trusted by the church with the care of its children. If the church is clear in its determination to make the welfare and safety of the children its highest priority in organising children's ministry, then this may make it easier for church leaders to reach an appropriate decision when there is real concern about an adult's behaviour towards the children. It is also a relevant factor, of course, that, irrespective of whether there was sexual abuse, there may be sufficient concern among parents about the behaviour of the person that it would not be in the interests of the gospel to have him in a position of youth leadership.

The unacceptable risk test is straightforward to apply in the case of those who are working with children and youth on a voluntary basis. It hardly needs stating in most churches. They would not want a person to continue in ministry with children after an incident of sexual abuse which they regard as substantiated even if no charges were laid. However, in situations where the church is deeply divided about the truth of the allegations, the unacceptable risk test is a circuit breaker. Stating this principle in policy manuals or as a resolution of the elders or parish council means that there is an agreed basis for dealing with this situation should it ever arise. It can also be applied in situations in which someone abused a child many years ago. The argument about forgiving and forgetting may seem a strong one until one examines the repetitive nature of sex offending against children. It would be an unacceptable risk to allow a person who has sexually abused children in the past to work with children. This is not about forgiveness. It is about trust. There are plenty of other ministries in the church.

The unacceptable risk test also makes sense for legal reasons. The church may be liable in negligence if a child was abused by a church volunteer, and the church had reason to believe that he may have a propensity to abuse children. Another advantage of the test is in terms of the law of defamation. Making a decision that there is an unacceptable risk if the person is allowed to continue in ministry with children does not involve stating categorically that he has been guilty of sexual abuse in the past. The assessment of risk can take into account a range of factors which together lead to a decision that the risk of allowing the person to continue in children's ministry would be too great to be countenanced.

The issues are much more difficult when the alleged offender is a minister or paid employee of the church. Here, the balance of interests and rights needs to be struck differently because depriving a person of his employment or profession is a much more serious matter than not allowing someone to run the youth group on a voluntary basis. Ministers and paid employees such as youth workers should not be dismissed or forced to resign on the basis of suspicion or rumour. There must be no witchhunts. The church needs to observe the principles of natural justice whenever it is believed that a minister has been guilty of sexual abuse but the matter is not resolved satisfactorily through the criminal justice system. To be properly protective of the rights of the minister is not merely a matter of moral obligation. There are laws about wrongful dismissal which would entitle a person unfairly dismissed to be awarded compensation. The church needs not only to have procedures for determining whether a worker should be dismissed, but to follow those procedures in any case where an employee or minister is accused of serious misconduct that might lead to dismissal.

On the other hand, children need to be protected from an unacceptable risk of abuse. Congregations need to be protected from priests who abuse their position of influence. If churches are to grapple with the problem of child sexual abuse effectively, then it is essential that they have appropriate policies and procedures in place which are suitable for the resolution of complaints of sexual abuse against ministers and other paid employees. These issues have to be worked out in advance. By the time a church realises how badly it needs those procedures, it will be too late. These procedures are the subject of the next chapter.

Chapter 11

When Ministers Sin

When a minister is accused of child sexual abuse, and no criminal conviction is recorded, the situation becomes very difficult to deal with. Complaints against ministers come in many forms. A minister may be accused of sexual abuse now or at some time in the past. Complaints that come many years after the events are not uncommon, especially when the victim was a young teenager at the time and at one level responded willingly to the minister's attentions. It is often only in retrospect, as adults, that survivors may come to realise what a gross betrayal of trust was involved and how they were sexually exploited by the minister. It may also be only as adults that victims become aware of the deleterious effects of the abuse or summon up the courage to complain.

In all situations where there is a complaint of sexual abuse against a minister, the complainant should be encouraged to go to the police. If the abuse has happened recently, the church will want to report the matter itself so that the matter can be fully investigated by an independent body, as discussed in the previous chapter. But if the abuse happened many years ago, and the complainant is an adult, it is really up to her or him whether the police should be involved. There is generally no time limit on prosecutions. The Statute of Limitations applies only to civil cases, not criminal cases. Some prosecutions for child sexual assault have been brought many years after the events. However, it is obviously pointless for the church to report the complaint to the police if the victim is not willing to make a statement.

The church may thus be called upon to deal itself with cases of ministers who have been accused of sexual abuse in a variety of situations. There are cases where the complainant is a grown woman and does not want to involve the police, although she is looking to the church to take disciplinary action against the minister for his past behaviour. There are cases in which the offender is convicted and the church needs to determine whether he should be permitted to remain in the ordained ministry. There are other cases in which, following the police investigation, no conviction results but there remain serious concerns about the minister's suitability to remain in pastoral ministry. In all these cases, the church may need to take its own disciplinary action.

The Church as a Professional Organisation

All established denominations have disciplinary processes. Two features tend to be common to them all. The first is that they are rarely used. The second is that the relevant ordinances or resolutions were passed at a time when it was scarcely contemplated that the Church might have to deal with child sexual abuse cases. Consequently, they may not be very suitable for dealing with cases in which evidence must be gathered somehow from children. Because disciplinary procedures are not often used in most churches, or scarcely used at all, there is little institutional memory about how to manage such processes. Indeed, bishops, moderators and other church leaders may feel quite uncomfortable with the idea that they need to take a role either as prosecutor or judge within the formal procedures of the Church.

The rarity of formal disciplinary procedures in churches, and the lack of willingness to invoke such procedures, stands in contrast to the position in other helping professions, such as medicine, where there has long been an awareness that the profession needs to take an active role in ensuring that its members maintain high standards of propriety and professional competence. Disciplinary procedures are often invoked in such professions, and these may involve quite a public process. A register may be kept of the names of those who have been 'struck off', that is, barred from practising.

Churches, in contrast, tend to deal with their problems on the quiet. They force a resignation and tell the minister he will not find another position within the diocese or other such denominational structure. It is unusual, however, for churches to take the further step of examining whether the person should remain as an ordained minister at all.

The position of clergy can be compared and contrasted with that of a doctor in a public hospital. If a doctor was guilty of serious professional misconduct in relation to a patient, we would expect that not only would he be dismissed from his position but that disciplinary procedures would be invoked to ensure that he was struck off and could not find employment in private practice either. In contrast, if a member of the clergy abuses his position of trust, he may well lose his job but he can often remain an ordained minister of the Church. He may even find employment in another part of the country. Word of mouth between bishops and other denominational leaders can only go so far in protecting the public from predatory priests. The status of an ordained minister carries trust and respect, whether or not the person is holding a position as a minister in a congregation. The church that allows an unsatisfactory minister to remain a member of the clergy is implicitly endorsing his ministry.

The quiet resignation can also leave behind a trail of confusion for congregations left uncertain why the minister has resigned, or if the rumours have been spreading, whether they are true. In one church, a minister resigned after a newspaper published a report that he had sexually abused a young teenager in his congregation many years earlier. To his congregation he denied the allegations, although he had apparently made admissions to others in the past. The church rallied around the minister, holding prayer meetings for him and praying that the complainant, now an adult, would repent of telling untruths. This kind of situation cries out for resolution. No prosecution was possible in this case for technical reasons, so there was no independent body which could declare the truth. It was therefore a matter for the denominational hierarchy to resolve. A good disciplinary procedure provides a means by which this kind of situation can be resolved in a way that allows both the complainant and the minister to be heard.

Disciplinary processes in churches fulfil two functions. First, they are a means of dealing with complaints and ensuring that, in the most serious cases of misconduct, a minister will be required to resign from the ministry. The second function is a pastoral one for the victims. It allows them an opportunity to be heard by the Church. It can be very important for victims of abuse by clergy to hear the Church recognise that they are telling the truth, even in cases when the abuse took place many years earlier. The disciplinary process may offer a means by which the victim can find closure of the issue. Otherwise, the abuse may be like a ghost from the past, never seen or acknowledged by others, but haunting the victim for years on end.

Complaints Procedures and Disciplinary Tribunals

There is no one model which represents 'best practice' for complaints procedures and disciplinary structures. Different denominations have different histories and traditions. When the Churches of Christ of New South Wales were seeking to develop their disciplinary processes for the first time, they had to confront the fact that each Church of Christ is an independent congregation tied to others in the denomination by little more than the bonds of fellowship. The way in which they developed their disciplinary process was by transforming the ministers' association from a body that organised an annual conference into a professional association that had the power to discipline its members. The ministers' association has no power over what individual congregations do or whom they employ. However, it is expected that no local church would employ a minister who has been expelled from the ministers' association for serious misconduct. Other denominations, such as the Anglicans, have an established body of ecclesiastical law, which governs the life of the Church, and any revision or renewal of the disciplinary procedures would need to take its place within that ecclesiastical tradition.

There are, however, a number of principles to be considered in devising any procedure for resolving complaints of sexual misconduct by ministers. Such procedures should not deal only with cases of child abuse. There is also the issue of sexual misconduct by ministers in pastoral relations with adults. On any analysis, this is numerically a greater problem than the sexual abuse of children by ministers. The kinds of sexual misconduct that ought to be covered in such procedures include sexual harassment and consensual sexual relations in the course of a pastoral relationship. This is because the minister takes advantage of the dependency and vulnerability of the parishioner, which diminish her capacity to make a proper judgment about the propriety of the sexual liaison. Such cases are quite common in churches. While some boundary violations by ministers may be dealt with by apology and censure, there are some cases in which it emerges that the minister has been engaging for a long time in predatory behaviour towards women in the congregation, having a succession of 'affairs'. Such cases are very serious breaches of pastoral ethics even if the relationships were 'consensual' in the legal sense of that term.[1]

A very serious case of this kind in Australia involved an evangelical minister who appears to have had sexual relations with scores of women over a number of years in pastoral ministry. His victims (or partners) ranged in age from thirteen upwards. Some of these sexual liaisons were clearly criminal but others were not, because the women were over the age of consent. If a disciplinary procedure does not take account of such predatory behaviour with 'consenting' women, as well as the abuse of minors, it will have difficulty removing such a minister. In these kinds of cases, where the minister has charismatic qualities and inspires some loyalty and devotion, it may be a matter of chance whether women who come forward to complain were under or over the age of consent at the time of the sexual liaisons.

Principles for Disciplinary Procedures

The principles for devising complaints procedures and disciplinary processes are that the church needs to welcome complaints, that the procedures should be accessible, that the principles of natural justice (or procedural fairness) should be applied, that the procedure should recognise the variety of interests involved, that it should be clear about the standard of proof to be applied and the rules of evidence to be used in disputed cases, and that the relevant panel should have people with expertise in sexual abuse issues.

Welcome Complaints

The church must welcome, and be seen to welcome, complaints. Complaints will not be 'welcome' in the sense that bishops and moderators will want to hear about abusive priests. Such gross betrayals of trust do not make appealing stories. Churches must be ready to hear them, nonetheless.

The way in which the church responds to complaints will have a considerable bearing on whether disciplinary procedures will be effective. Often, bishops and other leaders will first learn of a problem through a telephone call from the victim or by word of mouth from another minister who has spoken to the victim. If the church's disciplinary procedures are to be invoked, then the complainant needs to come out from the shadows. She may need considerable encouragement to do so. If the bishop makes it clear that he takes such complaints very seriously, and support systems are in place for the complainant, then it is much more likely that she will summon up the courage to tell her story. In some cases in Australia bishops have welcomed complaints in the same way as stiff doors welcome being opened. If the complainants had pushed hard enough, no doubt the bishops would have done something. It is more likely in this situation that the complainant will walk away from the door of the church, wiping the dust from her feet.

Make the Procedures Accessible

Complaints procedures must be accessible and open. 'Bottom drawer' complaints procedures will not be effective. Copies of the complaints procedures could be sent to the churchwardens or church secretary. The names of contact people could be published in diocesan newspapers or other such publications. A complaints procedure will not be accessible or welcoming if all the people nominated to handle complaints are men. Sexual abuse is very difficult to talk about. In order to receive the necessary encouragement to go ahead with a complaint, the complainant needs to have someone with whom she can discuss intimate matters without being further embarrassed by the gender difference.

One way in which a process can be made less intimidating is to have support people appointed for the complainant and the minister against whom the complaint is made. The Uniting Church in Australia, for example, has panels of advisers who can be called upon to support the parties through the process and give them general advice (or a referral to specialist advice).[2] The advisers are specially trained in a two-day workshop about the issues involved in misconduct by ministers. It is expected that the adviser will be of the same sex as the person to be advised.

Apply the Principles of Natural Justice

A disciplinary procedure should comply with the principles of natural justice. There are a number of these. One is that no one about whom there could be a reasonable apprehension of bias should participate as a member of a tribunal.

240

Another related principle is that the person bringing the complaint should not be part of the panel that adjudicates on it.

Three principles of natural justice are particularly relevant to disciplinary procedures concerning sexual abuse. First, the person against whom the complaint is made, the respondent, must be aware of the detailed nature of the complaint against him. This need not be a copy of the written complaint as such. It could be merely a record of the detailed substance of the complaint. It must identify the complainant and the incidents or history of sexual abuse alleged. It is better not to specify where the complainant is currently living, and therefore it may be inappropriate to provide the respondent with a complete copy of the complaint. Second, the respondent will be given an adequate opportunity to respond to the complaints. The third principle is that the tribunal must base its decision on logically probative evidence.

Beyond this, the principles of natural justice do not mandate any particular form of procedure. It is not essential that there should be a quasi-judicial hearing in which the case is dealt with as if it were a criminal trial. It is not necessary for the complainant to be subjected to cross-examination by the respondent or his lawyer, as long as he has an adequate opportunity to be heard. In drawing up these procedures, it is important to have the advice of someone with knowledge and experience of administrative law.

Generally, the disciplinary procedures of professional bodies do involve hearings in which the victim of the alleged abuse or misconduct gives evidence and is available for cross-examination. However, it is important to think through what to do if the complaint is of sexual abuse of an eight-year-old child who is traumatised by the abuse. If there has already been a criminal investigation, the child may have been put through enough, and it would be quite inappropriate to ask her or him to attend a hearing and give live evidence in front of the alleged perpetrator, and even to be cross-examined in person by him. If it were a criminal trial, she would probably be able to use closed circuit television. Church disciplinary procedures ought not to ask children to do what they would not be asked to do in a criminal trial.

In fact, they really shouldn't ask the child to testify at all. The procedures should be so designed that the child does not need to participate. It is unusual for children to have to give evidence outside of the criminal courts. In family law proceedings and care proceedings in child abuse and neglect cases, the relevant evidence from the child is given by others such as social workers, psychologists or counsellors who have interviewed the child. If the church has followed the proper course of leaving the police and social services to investigate the case, the relevant facts should have come to light, and a variety of sources of information will be available to a tribunal. The case could be brought by a complainant on behalf of the church, with the consent of the victim of the alleged abuse or the victim's family, but without needing to involve them further. The tribunal could appoint a committee of investigation to examine the relevant evidence and provide a report to the tribunal. Evidence could be called from the child protection professionals involved in the investigation if they were prepared to co-operate with the church disciplinary procedure. The advantage for the church of having a co-ordinator who liases with the police and social services is that it will be much easier to move from the investigation into the disciplinary process if criminal charges are not laid.

Recognise the Variety of Interests Involved

The fourth principle is that the complaints mechanism and disciplinary procedure must recognise the variety of interests involved. There are three main interests which need to be satisfied through the process. The first is the interest of the complainant who wants to feel that the church has listened to him or her and taken action. This is the pastoral interest. The second interest is that of the respondent, who needs to be treated fairly, and if innocent, vindicated. This is the justice interest. The third is the interest of the church in seeing that its priests and ministers fulfil the commandment of 1 Peter 5, to be good shepherds of God's flock. This is the protective interest, and it requires the church to discipline, and if necessary, remove those who would endanger the welfare of that flock. Other interests should be considered as well, for example the needs of the minister's family, who may be innocents affected by his wrongdoing, and the needs of the congregation, which can be cast into disarray by allegations of abuse against its minister.

The problem with a number of the complaints and disciplinary processes that exist at the moment is that they are designed to meet only two out of those three main interests, and may entirely ignore others. There are two major models of procedure that exist in churches in Britain and Australia today. The first is the adjudication model. This is the traditional model of a disciplinary tribunal, in which evidence is presented and the hearing is conducted along the lines of a trial. This satisfies the respondent's interest in a fair process. It also satisfies the church's interest in having an appropriate disciplinary procedure which allows it to take measures to protect congregations from harm. Depending on how it is run, however, the procedure may be alienating for the complainant. Disciplinary processes tend to be about the defendant, not the complainant. They are about whether he should be found guilty of the charges, and what disciplinary consequences should follow from this. The complainant's status in the proceedings may be little more than as a witness, which means that his or her pastoral needs may be completely ignored.

The second model is a conciliation model. The complainant is encouraged to file a written complaint, and the matter is handled by a sexual abuse complaints committee, which hears the complaint and the minister's response in a confidential process. If the behaviour is admitted, the committee seeks to broker an agreed resolution between the complainant and the respondent. If no agreement can be reached, then the formal disciplinary procedures of the church can still be invoked. Within these, there is a range of options. The procedures of the Uniting Church in Australia, for example, cover all kinds of sexually inappropriate behaviours by ministers in a pastoral relationship. It has a range of outcomes if the complaint is upheld, including warnings to the respondent, written explanations to the complainant (and congregation, if appropriate), apologies to the complainant and congregation, requirements of counselling, resignation from the ministerial position or resignation from ordained ministry.

The problem with the conciliation model is that it seeks to fulfil the respective interests of the complainant and respondent, but it may or may not fulfil the interests of the church in ensuring that congregations are protected from ministers who will abuse their position. For minor sexual boundary violations involving a minister and an adult parishioner, it may be appropriate; but where the complaint is of child sexual abuse then the church has a duty not only to the victim who has been brave enough to come forward, but also to protect other children from abuse. The church authorities cannot just focus on the individual complaint. The problem is not one of conflict resolution between a complainant and a minister, as a private matter. The issue is fitness for ministry, which is a matter for the whole church.

Doing justice by resolving the complaint to the satisfaction of the complainant, and with the acquiescence of the defendant, may be an important part of the process, but the church cannot merely be the mediator. It is the third party in the procedure and its vital role must be to determine the suitability of that person to continue in the ordained ministry.

In some cases, the complainant and the defendant may agree on a resolution of the complaint which is quite unsatisfactory from the church's point of view. In all but the most exceptional cases where a minister has sexually abused a child, nothing less than the resignation of the minister from ordained ministry can satisfy the church's need to give its highest priority to child protection. There remain some cases in which expert evaluation leads to the conclusion that the minister is very unlikely to offend again and could be placed in a position of ministry which does not involve work with children, such as an industrial chaplaincy or work with the elderly. There are gradations of offence even in relation to child sexual abuse.

Even so, all sexual abuse by a minister is of the utmost gravity, and cases in which a person ought to be permitted to remain in ministry would be the exception, not the rule. There is a need for mercy and compassion towards offenders, but that is a separate issue from the question of what is necessary to ensure the protection of children and young people.

There are a number of other problems with the conciliation model, one of which is the nature of the subject-matter. Conciliation and mediation are not means of determining truth. They are methods for conflict resolution. Abusive behaviour is not a matter for negotiation. There can be no reconciliation between right and wrong. There can be no mediation between good and evil. Conciliation cannot function properly unless the abuse is admitted or has otherwise been determined by an investigatory process. Conciliation should focus only on outcomes, not on the truth or otherwise of the complainant's account.

Another issue is that if the process involves a formal mediation, and the church merely provides a neutral mediator, then there must be considerable concerns about the imbalance of power involved between the complainant and the minister. It is axiomatic in mediation practice that mediation is not an appropriate dispute resolution process where there is a serious imbalance of power or where there has been abuse or violence. If, for whatever reason, the complainant is not able to enter into mediation on approximately the same footing as the other party or is likely to be intimidated by him, then mediation is contraindicated. Furthermore, a complainant should not be expected to meet face to face in a mediation process with the man who has abused her without her full and free consent.

Moreover, conciliation may not satisfy the complainant's interest in having her pain recognised formally by the church. This depends, of course, on how the process is structured. If the church is merely a mediator, using its good offices to bring about a resolution of the complaint, then there may be no formal acknowledgment by the church itself that the abuse has occurred.

245

There is a place for the church to adjudicate formally on the validity of the complaint. The complainant needs to be vindicated. What has happened in the shadows needs to be publicly declared in the light of day. There should be no place for confidentiality and secrecy provisions as the price of an agreement. Such provisions are attempts to protect the defendant and the church as an institution. No victim of abuse should have her silence bought, for silence was usually part of the original pattern of abuse. To be bound by a confidentiality clause is to be imprisoned again, rather than liberated from the patterns of abuse.

Whatever the merits of a conciliation process for some kinds of complaints of sexual misconduct towards adults, the process is not well suited to the resolution of child sexual abuse complaints. An investigation and adjudication model, whether or not it includes a formal hearing, is more likely to take account of the different interests involved. In any event, a conciliation model requires that there be a disciplinary process in the background to deal with cases in which the allegations are disputed. However, the conciliation model does allow the complainant to be able to express a view on what actions on the part of the respondent will help her to find closure of the issue. This may be a letter of apology or an assurance that the minister will enter counselling. It is also a forum in which issues of reparation can be discussed without the need to instigate legal proceedings for compensation.

Be Clear about the Standard of Proof and the Rules of Evidence

What standard of proof should be applied in a disciplinary hearing? Does the tribunal need to comply with the strict rules of evidence in criminal trials?

Disciplinary proceedings are civil proceedings. The major issue to be determined is an employment issue. Should this person remain in the employment of the Church? A consequent issue is professional accreditation. Should the person retain the status of being ordained and recognised as a minister, with the endorsement from the Church that accompanies this? The legal requirements of such a process should be those that satisfy the law of unfair dismissal and of professional accreditation. The model should not be a criminal trial, even if criminal offences are among the complaints alleged, for it is not the role of the church to adjudicate on criminal matters. In the course of determining a person's fitness for ministry, the tribunal may well come to conclusions on matters which, if proven beyond reasonable doubt in a criminal trial, would constitute criminal offences. However, its task is neither to convict nor to punish.

In civil proceedings, the normal standard of proof is that the case should be proven on the balance of probabilities. This is subject to an important qualification, that the more serious are the allegations in issue, and the greater are the consequences of an adverse finding, the more certain the court should be that it is satisfied the charges are proven on the balance of probability.[3] Underlying this practice is the notion that the more serious the allegation, the less likely it is that the event occurred.[4]

Views on what the standard of proof ought to be in disciplinary proceedings differ. There have been cases involving the discipline of solicitors and doctors in which it has been said that, if the charges would also found serious criminal charges, then the standard of proof ought to be the criminal standard of proof beyond reasonable doubt.[5] It is not clear whether in England, that would necessarily be applicable to other professions, as there is no case law on other professions. In Australia, it is clearly established that the criminal standard does not need to be applied in disciplinary proceedings involving health professionals.[6] It is sufficient that the case be proven on the balance of probabilities, taking into account the gravity of the allegations and the consequences that would flow from an adverse finding. As a matter of legal principle, this is the better view. Disciplinary proceedings involve serious consequences, but not as serious as in a criminal trial, and the rights of the defendant need to be weighed appropriately in the balance with the need to protect the church community.

In any event, the general legal rules about the standard of proof in disciplinary cases are likely to be subject to whatever rules are laid down specifically in the disciplinary procedures of the organisation. As long as those rules of procedure are stated clearly, and provide the defendant with a process which is absolutely fair to him in all respects, then there is no reason why the tribunal's determination should be challenged successfully in a court. For this reason, the procedures need to stipulate the standard of proof specifically.

More important than the standard of proof, however, is the question of the evidence that is available to the tribunal. As a tribunal of inquiry, it ought to be able to receive all evidence that will cast light on the circumstances of the case without necessarily being restricted by the rules of evidence that apply in a criminal case. The task of evaluating a person's fitness to be employed in Christian ministry necessarily involves a wider body of evidence than would be presented in a criminal trial. Furthermore, a different balance needs to be struck between the rights of the defendant and the interests of the community.

In a criminal trial, the evidence that is admissible is very narrow. The jury is normally not allowed to learn about previous offences, and alleged offences which are unconnected may be tried separately, so that the evidence of one alleged offence does not influence the jury in reaching a conclusion concerning whether the defendant is guilty of the other.

A further feature of the criminal trial is that any evidence which is not strictly relevant to the charges or which is more prejudicial to the defendant than probative of the offence is excluded, and in this way the incident may be shorn of some of its context. Whatever the merits of the strict rules of evidence in the criminal law, the very evidence that is excluded from the criminal trial may well assist a church tribunal or committee of inquiry to decide whether a person is or is not fit to remain a minister

Alice's Story: The Girl Who Promised to Tell the Whole Truth

Alice, her mother and her younger sister were involved in a Bible-believing church in which Fred was an assistant pastor. Fred and his wife were also good friends of the family. At this time, Alice was eleven years old. Alice described Fred as like an uncle to her. He would often take her and her sister out and buy them anything they wanted.

One evening, before going to bed, Alice had shown her mother an article about child sexual abuse in a girls' magazine. They had discussed it together and Alice's mother emphasised that it was wrong for an adult to touch a child in any way that made her feel uncomfortable. After she went to bed, Alice was restless. She kept getting out of bed and coming in to see her mother. Mum was getting a little annoyed. Eventually, Alice came out again crying and asked her mother for a 'special talk'. 'Special talks' were times when Alice's mother knew she had to stop and listen. Alice said to her mother, 'Fred isn't giving me any privacy.'

A little while earlier, she said, Fred had been looking after her and her sister at their house. They had a swimming pool in the back garden, and Alice had got out of the pool and gone into her bedroom to get changed. Fred had followed her into her bedroom. She asked him to go away so that she could get changed out of her swimsuit. He replied, 'It doesn't matter, we are friends and you don't have to be embarrassed in front of me.' Alice's younger sister came in at that point and Fred left. On another occasion Fred had asked Alice in church whether she had a bra on. Alice gave a sarcastic response. Alice also told her mother that one night when she was staying at Fred's house she had woken up to find Fred in bed with her and with his leg over her.

That was all Alice told her mother that evening, but her mother was worried that there might be more. Alice had been brought up knowing she should not allow others to touch her sexually. So Alice's mother rang her sister-in-law, who is a counsellor and who advised the mother to invite Alice into her bed the following morning and to ask her to 'tell the whole story' without asking any questions. Alice's mother did this, and far more detail came out.

This led to a report to the police. In her police statement, Alice told of a number of incidents. The first was the incident after she had got out of the swimming pool. The second was a time when Fred asked Alice and her sister to give him a massage. He paid them for it. They rubbed his back for a while. After this, he came over to Alice and started kissing her on the lips. She asked him to stop. The third incident was the time he asked whether she was wearing a bra.

It was the fourth and fifth incidents that led to criminal charges. In her police statement, she told of two incidents that had occurred while she was staying at Fred's house. Alice's mother had had to go away for a few days, and so she asked Fred and his wife to look after the children. Alice and her sister stayed in the spare bedroom, sleeping on mattresses on the floor. She said that she had woken up about midnight because she heard the noise of someone's footsteps, and she found Fred in bed with her. According to her account, he had his leg on top of her and had pulled the sheets off. She pulled the sheets back on top of her and he took them off again. She said, 'Can you let me get back to sleep?' He told her he was going.

A little while later, she said, he came back in, pulling the sheets off again, and this time, putting his leg over hers. She related how he had pulled her nightie up around her neck and had rubbed her chest with one hand while squeezing her vagina with the other hand. He also put his finger in her vagina a little way, and moved it around. She struggled against him by pushing and elbowing him and eventually he withdrew his finger. She got up to go to the toilet and stayed away for as long as she felt that she could, but he was still there when she returned. She went to her bed, turning her back to him, and he left.

The fifth incident was a few days later. She was in the bathroom in Fred's house and Fred was in the bathroom with her. She asked him to leave so that she could take a bath. He refused, and started to undress her. When she was undressed she got into the bath and he started to wash her. She said that she was old enough and could do it herself. However, he wanted to bathe her and washed her 'all over, everywhere'.

Fred was interviewed by the police and denied the allegations. However, he was eventually charged in relation to the two latter incidents. Fred's account of the bedroom incident was that he had gone in to see Alice because she was having a nightmare. He thought she must have been dreaming when she said she had kicked him. He also acknowledged that he had bathed her, but did so because she was not washing herself properly.

The case went to trial. The trial itself lasted six days. Alice had to endure long periods on the witness stand, with constant interruptions for legal argument. Much of Alice's statement to the police was ruled inadmissible by the judge. She was not allowed to say anything about the first three incidents related above. According to the rules of evidence, material may be excluded if its prejudicial effect is greater than its probative value. If the jury had been told that Fred had asked Alice to massage him, or that he had wanted to watch her getting changed out of her swimming costume, that would not in any way prove that he sexually assaulted her in the middle of the night or that his washing of her private parts in the bathtub was sexually motivated. In this sense, these incidents proved nothing, but they might cast Fred in a bad light in the eyes of the jury and thus the evidence would have been prejudicial to him.

Alice found all this very confusing. She was allowed to take the oath, and promised to tell the truth, the whole truth and nothing but the truth. Yet half of her statement was deemed inadmissible and so, as she saw it, she was not being allowed to tell the whole truth. Quite soon after her evidence began, she began to say the word 'massage'. Before she had completed the word, she was interrupted and the defence counsel successfully petitioned for a mistrial. A new jury was empanelled.

Eventually, Fred was acquitted. Considerable attention was focused at the trial on whether the police statements had been doctored by the detective, by incorporating a passage of what Alice had said to her mother into her direct statement to the police.

If the issue had arisen in a church disciplinary tribunal, the very evidence that was excluded in the criminal trial might be very important in determining whether Fred was a fit and proper person to be a minister. The incidents that were excluded from the evidence in the trial would not have proven the sexual assaults in themselves; but if the tribunal had accepted the truth of those accounts then these incidents would have formed a context in which to evaluate the evidence of the incidents of alleged sexual assault. Furthermore, these incidents, together even with his own explanations of the alleged sexual assaults, might have given rise to questions about Fred's awareness of appropriate boundaries in dealing with children who are old enough to have developed a sense of modesty about their bodies.

The tribunal might or might not have made adverse findings about Fred on the facts of this case. What is important is that, in these kinds of cases, it has access to all the relevant evidence so that it can make a thorough evaluation of it. These matters need to be addressed in drafting the rules of procedure to ensure that the tribunal proceeds by way of inquiry and is able to inform itself of any relevant matters, having regard to, but not being bound by, the strict rules of evidence.

Have Panel Members with Relevant Expertise

The final principle is that the relevant panel that hears disputed cases should have expertise in issues of sexual abuse. In assessing cases in which the evidence is hotly disputed, the ability to bring an experienced eye to that evidence will be of the greatest value. It may help the panel to resolve reasonable doubts in some situations. In others, it may actually help the panel to see flaws in the evidence presented against the minister.

Because church disciplinary procedures have in the past been set up with different kinds of complaints in mind, their composition may be unsuitable for the resolution of a sexual abuse case. The power to co-opt panel members with relevant expertise may help the church to have the flexibility to deal with a variety of different kinds of case.

When the Church Needs to Apologise

Deciding what to do with a minister if there is an adverse finding may be thought to be the final stage of any disciplinary process. Yet there is one further aspect to be considered, and that is what it will mean for the victim to have the church recognise the truth of her story and her courage in bringing it to light. What should the church be saying to the victim?

Disciplinary procedures have the potential to help victims to put the past behind them, by including the possibility that the victim may receive some degree of recognition of her suffering from the highest levels of the church. This may be by a letter of apology from the archbishop, moderator or other such leader.

When something has been cloaked in secrecy for a very long time, and the victim has been bound in shame and guilt about it, there is a therapeutic power in having the church officially and openly recognise the victim's suffering. To apologise is not necessarily to admit that the church itself is legally responsible. The hierarchy may have been completely unaware of the minister's offending behaviour. But for the church to apologise is to recognise that the minister represented God and the church in his pastoral ministry, and the minister's shame is therefore the church's shame.

Robert, who was abused so seriously by the nuns in the orphanage in which he grew up and by the priest who sodomised him sadistically for a couple of years (chapter 6), heard his local Catholic bishop talking on the radio about a priest who had just been jailed for child sexual assault. The bishop said something with which Robert disagreed, and so Robert telephoned him, and told him a little of his story of abuse. The bishop invited Robert to come to see him. Robert replied that he would never go to visit a priest again. The bishop asked if he could visit Robert instead. A few days later he did so, and spent two and a half hours listening to Robert's shocking story of abuse. Subsequently he wrote to Robert in these terms:

> The behaviour of Fr . . . and the Sisters is contrary to everything the Church stands for. I know an apology will not change the past, but I am absolutely ashamed that such behaviour was perpetrated against yourself and others by church personnel. As a Bishop of the Church I declare that there was no excuse for such brutal treatment and I am deeply sorry that it took place . . . When I left you I felt both humbled and ashamed: humbled to have encountered such a good man and ashamed that he had been so cruelly treated.

Nothing that the bishop said could have altered the past. He knew that. But to care for Robert by visiting him and writing that letter meant a great deal to Robert. It was an act of humility and Christian love which is an example to be followed.

Chapter 12

Making Churches Safer for Children

Child sexual abuse in the community is now so widespread that a major effort ought to be made to tackle the problem. For too long, child protection agencies, counsellors, mental health professionals and others have been involved in trying to care for a seemingly endless stream of victims of sexual abuse. It can feel like dealing constantly with the casualties of war without any hope that the war may actually end or at least that the intensity of the fighting may diminish.

In recent years, serious efforts have been made to look at ways in which child abuse might be prevented. Prevention, as the saying goes, is better than cure, and anything that can be done to protect the present generation of children from harm and the misery of child sexual abuse is worth doing. Churches ought to be in the front line of prevention work, not only because they have a God-given mandate to stand against evil, but because they are so vulnerable to the problem of sexual abuse. Churches have an extensive involvement in work with children and young people. There are Sunday schools, youth groups, church-affiliated boys' and girls' associations, holiday clubs, church camps and other such activities. In addition, there are a large number of Christian schools. The church is therefore a community which is likely to attract people with a sexual interest in children.

How then can we make churches safer for children? What can churches do to prevent sexual abuse from happening in its midst? We must acknowledge that we may not be able to prevent abuse entirely. It can happen in any church and in any family. The perpetrators are often so skilled that they will overcome the hurdles we put in their way. Still, we can make it more difficult for them, and, by our vigilance, warn them off.

There is a distinction, however, between healthy prevention and unhealthy prevention. Healthy prevention is born of realism. It looks at putting appropriate programmes and procedures in place as a positive way of dealing with the problem. It is motivated by concern for the welfare of the children. Churches that engage in healthy prevention may find all sorts of collateral benefits in terms of improving the quality of children's ministry.

In contrast, unhealthy prevention is born out of fear, and is negative in its approaches and policies. Unhealthy prevention generally does little to protect children from abuse, but can have harmful effects on the way in which children are cared for.

Healthy Prevention

There are a number of forms of healthy prevention, including education, screening, basic rules about working with children and vigilance about suspicious conduct.

Education

Education of church members can happen at a number of different levels, starting with the general issue about the place of children in our society. Children need to be honoured as present members of the churches, not just because of their potential to be adult Christians in the future. An emphasis on parental responsibilities rather than an authoritarian view of parental rights may also help to create a context in which children are more valued and respected. We also need to talk more honestly about sexuality and the struggles that people have with this area of life. If sexual issues are taboo in the church, it may be the more difficult for children or adults to voice concerns about inappropriate sexual behaviour.

At the next level, church members should be educated about the problem of sexual abuse. Christians need to be aware that it is quite a common experience in childhood and that it can happen in Christian families and churches so that they are not cocooned in a false sense of security. They also need to know about the reporting of child abuse and its recognition as a crime. Parents and care-givers need to realise that children can be educated about sexual abuse without scaring them or worrying them unduly. A number of excellent books, videos and teaching units exist, which can be used by parents or by churches or schools. Different programmes exist for different age groups. In many programmes, the emphasis is on the child's right to feel safe generally, and to learn to distinguish between all kinds of safe and unsafe situations whether the issue is bullying, a household emergency or road safety. In relation to sexual abuse, the emphasis with primary school-aged children is on helping them to distinguish between good touching and bad touching, touching which makes them feel loved and warm inside, and touching which is unpleasant. It encourages them to recognise that their bodies are their own and that they have a right to say 'no' to any touching they don't like. Such programmes may also explain that there is a difference between good secrets and bad secrets, and that bad secrets don't need to be kept. Such programmes also stress the importance of telling someone if something bad is happening. Children can be encouraged to look to adults at church and in school as people they can turn to for help.

These teaching programmes may well help some children who are not sure whether what is happening is right or wrong. Sometimes, parents are not keen to have their children taught these protective behaviours because of the fear that the teaching will destroy their innocence, make them distrustful of loved ones or make them more reticent to have a hug. This depends very much on the way the programme is presented. There is no reason why child protection programmes should have these negative consequences. Parents may also fear that a child will make unfounded allegations against them in relation to something that actually happens in the ordinary run of parenting. Generally such fears are quite misplaced. Children can distinguish between normal touching and touching which makes them feel ashamed or sick inside, and most misunderstandings about an innocent event in the home, occurring while the child is being bathed or having an injury attended to, can be quickly resolved.

Child protection programmes are important because children may not be able to tell their parents about what is happening, even if the relationship is very close. Even if they suffer abuse at the hands of someone outside the immediate family, such as a relative or teacher, there are reasons why a child may not want to talk about it. The child may fear that the parents will be very upset if they find out, and keeping it from them is a way of shielding them. If the perpetrator is a trusted relative or a close friend of the family, the child may be concerned that the parents won't believe the story. It is not difficult, for example, to understand why a child may be reticent to tell Mum about what Grandad is doing. Thus teaching children about protecting themselves may be a way of helping them to deal with situations in which they don't feel able to turn to the parents for help.

One child protection strategy is to encourage children, even from a very early age, to think of five adults to whom they can turn if they feel unsafe or troubled. This can be a mix of people, some inside the family and some outside it. The list needs to be updated as circumstances and relationships change and children may need to be reminded that it exists. It should be emphasised to children that persistence is important. If one adult does not do anything, the child should go to another and another until he or she finds one who will listen and act.

Screening

Healthy prevention also involves screening of all those who volunteer for children's ministry, whether it be in Sunday schools, Christian youth camps or boys' and girls' organisations. The Home Office in England published guidelines for voluntary organisations working with children in 1993,[1] which have assisted the development of child protection policies and procedures in the major denominations. One of the policies adopted is that denominational organisations now encourage local churches to have a procedure for vetting those who apply to engage in ministry where they may have substantial unsupervised contact with children. The applicant is required to make declarations concerning past criminal offences and other matters which might have a bearing on his or her suitability to work with children. Perhaps the most comprehensive of the various forms of procedure, which vary from one denomination to another, is that used by the Church of England. In 1995, the Church of England House of Bishops published its Policy on Child Abuse, which commits the Church to screen all those involved in paid ministry and encourages local parish churches to have similar application procedures and voluntary disclosure forms for volunteers. When a person seeks ordination or paid lay ministry, he or she must complete a form which asks a number of questions. The same form must be completed whenever a minister moves to a new parish or a lay worker takes up a new position. The form requires the person to disclose whether he or she has ever been convicted of a criminal offence, been cautioned by the police or been bound over to keep the peace. It also asks about liabilities for civil wrongs and orders in a court's matrimonial jurisdiction. Finally, it asks: 'Has your conduct ever caused or been likely to cause harm to a child or put a child at risk, or, to your knowledge, has it ever been alleged that your conduct has resulted in any of those things?'

In response to all these questions, the person is required to give details, which can then be evaluated. The voluntary declarations are backed up by screening checks. Some Church of England dioceses, such as Lichfield and Southwell, have their own booklets as well, which give more detail than the national policy and provide information about local social services.[2] Other churches have similar policies and procedures, although they differ in certain respects.

Asking whether people have ever been accused of harming children, as the Anglican questionnaire does, is an important strategy. If the question is answered truthfully, this will pick up a much greater range of people, because only a limited number of cases in which child sexual abuse is discovered lead to criminal convictions.[3] If it becomes known that a person has been accused of sexual misconduct it is important to make further enquiries to ascertain whether the accusations were properly substantiated; many complaints of sexual abuse are not. Mere accusations which were not deemed to have any substance to them should not be a basis on which people should be judged adversely for the rest of their lives.

Of course, questions about previous offences and the causing of harm to a child may not be answered truthfully, but if a person who has been employed to work with children can be demonstrated to have lied during the application process about a material issue, this may obviate charges of unfair dismissal should dismissal become necessary in the light of subsequent information. Even with volunteers, the use of a declaration form puts them on notice that the church is alive to the issue of child abuse.

Voluntary declaration forms need to be backed up as far as possible by police checks and other such mechanisms where they are available. One very helpful resource in England, which might be emulated elsewhere, is the Department of Health's Consultancy Service, which allows local authorities and also private and voluntary organisations to make checks on the suitability of applicants for positions with children. This service records convictions of those who were employed in children's work at the time of their conviction, and also notes the names of people who were dismissed or resigned from such positions as a result of conduct that made them unsuitable to be employed in positions of responsibility with children. While there is no obligation on employers to notify the names of workers who have left for such reasons, they are encouraged to do so if a member of staff has been prosecuted for any offence involving a child, or where a member of staff has resigned or been dismissed in circumstances in which the welfare of a child has been put at risk through physical, sexual or emotional abuse and whether or not there has been a prosecution. This sort of database, which has appropriate safeguards to ensure that people's names are not recorded inappropriately, is a vital resource for the screening of staff working with children and youth.

Another essential component in screening procedures is taking up references. The volunteer application forms in use in many churches require referees to be named, and the churches do take up written references. More useful even than reference checks is making enquiries with the minister of the previous church or churches in which the person has participated. For example, one church employed a young man as a paid youth worker, but dismissed him following complaints of sexual abuse. Within a short while, it was discovered that he was running the youth fellowship in another church belonging to the same denomination and within the same city. A simple enquiry to the minister of the man's former church would have established immediately that he should not be allowed to engage in youth ministry.

The use of volunteer application forms and reference checking need not only be set in the context of screening for potential sex offenders. It can also be a screening process for people who may be unsuitable for all sorts of reasons, including those whose hearts are in the right place but whose gifts might better be used in another kind of ministry. It can also be placed in a positive context, the application form being part of a wider process in which the church ensures that all its volunteers are properly trained, prepared for the commitment, supported and prayed for. This is a feature of a number of the child protection policies of churches in Britain.

Rules about Children's Work

There are also some simple rules which, if adopted in children's activities, might restrict the opportunities for sexually inappropriate behaviour. One is that there should always be at least two adults involved in any children's ministry. This has many benefits beyond ensuring that adults do not have 'free rein' with a group of vulnerable children. Workers learn from each other by watching each other teach or run activities, and their gifts may complement one another. If there is an accident, then one adult can attend to the child who has been hurt, while the other looks after the rest of the group.

There are also rules which can be adopted with minimal inconvenience. For example, the Baptist Union of Great Britain counsels that a worker should not be alone with a child where their activity cannot be seen. In a counselling situation where privacy is necessary, another adult should know that they are talking privately, and where they are. It also advises youth workers, inter alia, not to invade the privacy of children when they are showering or toileting, to avoid rough, physical or sexually provocative games, not to make sexually suggestive comments and to avoid inappropriate and intrusive touching of any form. There are other guidelines as well; for example, not giving lifts to children on their own other than for short journeys, and avoiding sleeping arrangements on trips away which involve adults and children sharing the same sleeping accommodation.[4]

Vigilance

Vigilance about suspicious behaviour by workers is also an important form of prevention. The church member who seems to have very few friends of his own age but loves being with children or young people, the person who seems to have struck up an intimate and rather private relationship with a teenager and who is often alone with him or her, the man who appears to be hanging around the girls' or boys' shower room on church camps – these are all matters for concern. Particular attention needs to be paid to children's comments or complaints about an adult or teenager who makes them feel uncomfortable. They may not be able to articulate quite what it is that makes them uneasy, but children's intuitive sense that a person is strange or unsafe needs to be respected, and the person's behaviour observed more closely.

Unhealthy Prevention

What then is unhealthy prevention? Could any prevention strategies be unhealthy? Quite possibly. There are two forms of unhealthy prevention. The first arises out of a paranoia about sexual abuse and restricts the lives of children because of fear about what might happen to them. The second is not really a form of preventing sexual abuse at all, although it may appear to be. It is prevention driven by a fear that unfounded allegations of abuse may be made against adults. It is thus an adult protection policy, not a child protection policy.

Being Over-protective

Despite everything which has been said in this book about the seriousness of the problem of child sexual abuse, and the possible damage it can do, there is still a need to keep the problem in perspective. A lot of children have very unpleasant experiences in childhood, and some of those involve sexual abuse. Child sexual abuse is a collective term for all kinds of inappropriate and unlawful sexual behaviour towards minors. Some sexual abuse can have the most serious effects, but not all of it does. On a scale of distressing events in childhood, an isolated instance of sexual molestation or attempted molestation may not be nearly as damaging as many other childhood experiences, and need not leave lasting scars. This is not to minimise the seriousness of any form of sexual abuse, but it is important not to be so afraid that it might happen to a child in your care that it colours everything you do. If it does happen, it is also important to realise that it is not something which stigmatises the child. The child does not become 'damaged goods', nor is the victim sentenced to long-term problems as an adult. As with other deeply distressing events in childhood, being able to talk about it at the time and receiving good parental support can make the world of difference.

There has to be a balance between sensible caution and an overprotective approach. Parents who severely limit their children's participation in activities out of fear of what might happen to them when they are out of sight may protect them from harm, but at what cost? The children may miss out on a great variety of enjoyable and beneficial experiences which their friends enjoy and in which there is no obvious risk of harm.

Unhealthy prevention can also be found in churches that impose rules which artificially constrict the ministry of the church towards children. Such rules may be more effective in giving people a sense that they are 'doing something' than in actually preventing abuse. One book on child sexual abuse in churches counsels that at no point should one worker be left alone in the nursery with young children, even for a minute or two, perhaps while another worker goes to get a parent of a distressed child. If a child needs to use the toilet, then an usher should be called to accompany the nursery worker and the child so that the worker is not left alone with the child. Furthermore, says the author, teams of people from the same family, such as husband and wife or father and daughter, should not be allowed to work together without another person in the room.[5]

These restrictions were a response to this church's very bad experience, when a boy in the congregation had sexually abused a number of small children. Nonetheless, such prevention policies are a bit like military commanders preparing for the last war. Had they been in place when that particular perpetrator was looking for targets, these policies might have prevented a few of the incidents of abuse, but they would be useless with another perpetrator who targets a different age group in a different way. Such policies do not really hinder the abuser who grooms children. The offender who is excited by quickly groping the private parts of a young child during a visit to the toilet is only one kind of child molester. Offenders target children in all sorts of ways, and usually with greater subtlety.

Fear of Unfounded Allegations

A second form of unhealthy prevention is where adults refrain from or prohibit innocent activities involving the touching of children because of a fear that they will be accused of child abuse. In laying down guidelines for ministry to children and young people, we do not want to give the message that limitations on adult-child activities exist mainly to protect adults. We should make it clear that our priority is to protect children from sexual abuse, which is a far greater problem than the possibility of unfounded allegations by children against adults, and the rules we adopt should reflect this. At the same time, adults need to take care that their actions towards children are not misinterpreted as sexual in nature, just as they would in their relations with adults of the opposite sex.

Showing affection towards children is a problem area. Many adults, particularly men, express fears about hugging their own children or putting a comforting arm around a little child who is crying. This is a misplaced fear. Showing affection is not molestation. There is a big difference between putting an arm around a little child's shoulder and putting a hand down her pants. Children need to be loved and cared for. Physical contact such as a hug or a kiss on the cheek is a way in which children sometimes show affection towards us, and can be reciprocated in kind if we know them well enough.

This concern about false allegations of abuse poses a real danger that children will miss out on the care that they need, in particular from men. The police will not come knocking at the door because a man cuddles a little child who is distressed. Child sexual abuse is a different league of activity entirely.

Similar fears can arise in the church's ministry to children. One manual on child protection for churches lays down a number of sensible principles for children's ministry.[6] Some of the advice in it, however, might be questioned. The author counsels that no children's worker should kiss or cuddle a child, or 'do anything that is potentially sexual'.[7] Potentially sexual acts are said to include, among other things, wrestling, tickling, frontal hugging and touching anywhere except between the shoulder and elbow. Such activities, 'it says, are easily misunderstood by children who have been exposed to sexual activity'.[8] This may or may not be so, but it is a little difficult to predict what innocent activities of adults might remind a child of the precursors to sexual abuse. We have to ask also whether it is helpful to identify most touching as potentially or actually sexual. Children should learn the difference between good touching and bad touching, but we do not want to give them the message that all but a limited range of touching is bad.

A positive way of expressing the principles about touching is that adults should respect a child's personal autonomy and bodily privacy, just as they would respect those of other adults. This is the heart of the matter. Tickling, for example, may be meant in fun, but the child may experience it as invasive and recoil from it. Similarly, some adults can be very demonstrative in a way that involves a lot of touching, and this may make other people feel uncomfortable. If it makes other adults uncomfortable, it may equally make children so too.

All touching needs to be age-appropriate. What is appropriate in working with the under-fives may be quite inappropriate with teenagers, for all sorts of reasons. The rules in this regard are mostly common sense and are not specific to avoiding problems of sexual abuse. Another important point to bear in mind is that any such affection shown to a child should be for the child's benefit and not to satisfy the adult's emotional need to be loved.

Raising the Status of Children's Ministry

There is a growing awareness of the problem of child abuse in churches. We have recognised the inadequacy of our past practices and procedures, and have been forced to become aware of issues which we scarcely knew existed a generation ago.

However, it is one thing to publish procedures and guidelines. It is another to implement them. Many churches are grateful for anyone who will help out in the Sunday school or volunteer to run the youth group. A considerable sacrifice of time and effort is involved in children's work, although there are also rewards. The people who feel able to continue running children's groups year in and year out are in a minority, and so churches have to deal with a constant turnover of people coming forward as volunteers.

Is it realistic, then, to talk about screening applicants and to insist that two people are involved in running every group? This assumes that the supply of people available is greater than the demand, when the reverse is usually the case. In small and struggling churches, it may be an effort to keep any form of children's ministry going.

But just what kind of price are we willing to pay for having a comprehensive children's programme? Youth work is an area where we may need to pool resources with other churches. In most struggling churches, the problem is not that the kids have nowhere to go. There may be a thriving youth group down the street or in a nearby town. It happens to be in a church of another denomination or in a different parish. If the price we pay to have a youth group is that we will accept anyone who volunteers, whether we know the candidate or not, the question must be asked whether the group should be kept going at all. Not all churches can do everything. Sometimes we may need to acknowledge that the gifting is not there for certain types of ministry or activity.

One of the effects of taking child protection seriously in churches is that children's work is taken seriously. Ministers, elders and other leaders recognise the need to provide oversight for the children's ministry and to encourage the right kind of people to see it as a God-given opportunity and responsibility. This may have many beneficial effects, not only in raising the quality of the children's ministry but also in integrating it better into the life and mission of the congregation.

Healthy prevention of child abuse may seem onerous. But where these policies are integrated into a programme which endeavours to match gifting to ministry and which requires the leadership to provide proper support and oversight, the other beneficial effects may be many. Having a good child protection policy is one way of demonstrating that we believe children matter.

Conclusion: Hope for the Future

It is easy, when examining the problem of child sexual abuse, to be so immersed in the pain of it all that one is left despairing for the future. It is possible to protect children from abuse? Can anyone be trusted?

It is appropriate to end this book on a note of optimism, for there is much to be optimistic about. The current knowledge of child sexual abuse has come too late for those whose stories are told in this book. At that time, little was written or broadcast about the problem. We learnt as youngsters not to get into the cars of strangers, but that is as much as we were taught. We were never terribly sure why we should be wary of strangers. We never knew that they might not be the main problem, that the greater danger lay closer to, or even at, home. Children are more aware now that it is okay to say 'no' to bad touching than they were a generation ago. Adults are more likely to spot suspicious behaviour than they once were.

So many of those whose stories are told in this book suffered in silence for years on end, and when they did disclose the abuse, people found it difficult to understand their pain. People are better at understanding it now, and therapists are better able to help them.

It is probably harder now for a sex offender to get away with abusing a child than at any time in history. The child is more likely to tell, and people are more likely to involve the police. There is a very long way to go, but we have come a long way.

Let us make it harder still for offenders to abuse children. Above all, let the churches not be communities in which they can offend with little risk of discovery. There will need to be a new heaven and a new earth before sorrow and sighing will flee away, but we can diminish this pain now by working to prevent child sexual abuse. And we can care, along with God, about all the little ones who are suffering today.

Notes

Chapter 1

1 R. Sipe, *Sex, Priests and Power* (Cassell, London, 1995).
2 Isaiah 61:1–3. All quotations are from the NIV.

Chapter 2

1 Song of Songs 2: 7.
2 This is my own estimate, based on data from American and Australian surveys.
3 L. De Mause, 'The Evolution of Childhood', *The History of Childhood*, L. De Mause (ed.) (Psychohistory Press, New York, 1974).
4 Didache II, 2 cited in M. Foucault, *Politics, Philosophy, Culture: Interviews and Other Writings, 1977–1984*, L. Kritzman (ed.) (Routledge, New York, 1988), pp. 231–2.
5 P. Trible, *Texts of Terror* (Fortress Press, Philadelphia, 1984), p. 48.
6 S. Radbill, 'Children in a World of Violence', *The Battered Child*, H. Kempe and R. Helfer (eds), (3rd edn, University of Chicago Press, Chicago, 1980).
7 V. Bullough, 'History in Adult Human Sexual Behaviour with Children and Adolescents in Western Societies', *Pedophilia: Biosocial Dimensions*, J. Feierman (ed.), (Springer-Verlag, New York, 1990), pp. 69, 75–6. For legislation, see e.g. the Criminal Law Amendment Act 1885.
8 L. De Mause, 'The Universality of Incest', *Journal of Psychohistory*, vol. 19, 1991, pp. 142–7.
9 J. Leventhal, 'Epidemiology of Child Sexual Abuse', *Understanding and Managing Child Sexual Abuse*, R. K. Oates (ed.), Harcourt, Brace, Jovanovich, Sydney, 1990), p. 18; B. Pilkington and J. Kremer, 'A Review of the Epidemiological Research on Child Sexual Abuse: Community and College Samples', *Child Abuse Review*, vol. 4, 1995, pp. 84–98.
10 D. Finkelhor, *Sexually Victimized Children* (Free Press, New York, 1979).

11 R. and J. Goldman, 'The Prevalence and Nature of Child Sexual Abuse in Australia', *Australian Journal of Sex, Marriage and the Family*, vol. 9, 1988, p. 94.

12 Ibid., p. 98.

13 D. Russell, 'The Incidence and Prevalence of Intrafamilial and Extrafamilial Sexual Abuse of Female Children', *Child Abuse and Neglect*, vol. 7, 1983, pp. 137–46.

14 N. Draijer, *Seksuele Traumatisering in de Jeugd: Lange Termijn Gevolgen Van Seksueel Misbruik Van Meisjes Door Verwanten* (Uitgeverij Sua, Amsterdam, 1990); N. Draijer, 'Long-Term Psychosomatic Consequences of Child Sexual Abuse', *The Free Woman: Women's Health in the 1990s*, E. Van Hall and W. Everaerd (eds), (Pantheon, UK, 1989), pp. 696–709.

15 D. Finkelhor, G. Hotaling, I. Lewis and C. Smith, 'Sexual Abuse in a National Survey of Adult Men and Women: Prevalence, Characteristics and Risk Factors', *Child Abuse and Neglect*, vol. 14, 1990, pp. 19–28.

16 A. W. Baker and S. P. Duncan, 'Child Sexual Abuse: A Study of Prevalence in Great Britain', *Child Abuse and Neglect*, vol. 9, 1985, pp. 457–67.

17 See D. Finkelhor, 'The International Epidemiology of Child Sexual Abuse', *Child Abuse and Neglect*, vol. 18, 1994, pp. 409, 416.

18 D. Russell, 'The Incidence and Prevalence of Intrafamilial and Extrafamilial Sexual Abuse of Female Children', *Child Abuse and Neglect*, vol. 7, 1983, pp. 140–41.

19 D. Russell, 'The Prevalence and Seriousness of Incestuous Abuse: Stepfathers v Biological Fathers', *Child Abuse and Neglect*, vol. 8, 1984, pp. 15–22.

20 K. Faller, 'Sexual Abuse by Paternal Caretakers: A Comparison of Abusers Who Are Biological Fathers in Intact Families, Stepfathers, and Non-Custodial Fathers', *The Incest Perpetrator*, A. Horton, B. Johnson, L. Roundy and D. Williams (eds) (Sage California, 1990), pp. 65–73; L. Margolin, 'Child Abuse by Mothers' Boyfriends: Why the Overrepresentation?' *Child Abuse and Neglect*, 1992, pp. 541–51.

21 D. Finkelhor, *Sexually Victimized Children*; R. and J. Goldman, 'The Prevalence and Nature of Child Sexual Abuse in Australia'.

22 A. W. Baker and S. P. Duncan, 'Child Sexual Abuse'.

23 D. Finkelhor, G. Hotaling, I. Lewis and C. Smith, 'Sexual Abuse in a National Survey of Adult Men and Women'.

24 Ibid., p. 98.

25 E. Burkett and F. Bruni, *A Gospel of Shame* (Viking, New York, 1993).

26 S. Rossetti, 'The Impact of Child Sexual Abuse on Attitudes Toward God and the Catholic Church', *Child Abuse and Neglect*, vol. 19, 1995, pp. 1469–81.

27 T. Haywood, H. Kravitz, L. Grossman, O. Wasyliw and D. Hardy, 'Psychological Aspects of Sexual Functioning Among Cleric and Non-

Cleric Alleged Sex Offenders', *Child Abuse and Neglect*, vol. 20, 1996, pp. 527–36. In the study, they were referred to as 'alleged' child molesters because, although they were in a treatment programme, they did not all admit the offences.

28 The story of this mass emigration of children is told in P. Bean and J. Melville, *Lost Children of the Empire* (Unwin Hyman, London, 1989).

29 B. Coldrey, *The Scheme: The Christian Brothers and Childcare in Western Australia* (Argyle-Pacific, Australia, 1993), pp. 394–9.

Chapter 3

1 J. Conte, 'The Nature of Sexual Offences Against Children', *Clinical Approaches to Sex Offenders and Their Victims*, C. Hollin and K. Howells (eds) (John Wiley, UK, 1991), pp. 1, 25.

2 G. Abel, J. Becker, M. Mittelman, J. Cunningham-Rathner, J. Rouleau and W. Murphy, 'Self-reported Sex Crimes of Nonincarcerated Paraphiliacs', *Journal of Interpersonal Violence*, vol. 2, 1987, pp. 3–25.

3 Ibid., pp. 16–17.

4 Ibid.

5 M. Weinrott and M. Saylor, 'Self-report of Crimes Committed by Sex Offenders', *Journal of Interpersonal Violence*, vol. 6, 1991, pp. 286–300.

6 E. Burkett and F. Bruni, *A Gospel of Shame* (Viking, New York, 1993), ch. 1.

7 K. Faller, 'Sexual Abuse by Paternal Caretakers: A Comparison of Abusers Who Are Biological Fathers in Intact Families, Stepfathers, and Non-Custodial Fathers', *The Incest Perpetrator*, A. Horton, B. Johnson, L. Roundy, and D. Williams (eds) (Sage, California, 1990), pp. 65, 67.

8 G. Abel, J. Becker, J. Cunningham-Rathner, M. Mittelman and J. Rouleau, 'Multiple Paraphilic Diagnoses among Sex Offenders', *Bulletin of the American Academy of Psychiatry and Law*, vol. 16, 1988, pp. 153–68.

9 G. Abel, M. Mittelman and J. Becker, 'Sexual Offenders: Results of Assessment and Recommendations for Treatment', *Clinical Criminology: The Assessment and Treatment of Criminal Behavior*, M. Ben-Aron, S. Huckle and C. Webster (eds) (M & M Graphic, Toronto, 1985), pp. 191–205; K. Freund, 'Courtship Disorder', *Handbook of Sexual Assault: Issues, Theories, and Treatment of the Offender*, W. Marshall, D. Laws and H. Barbaree (eds) (Plenum, New York, 1990), pp. 195–207; M. Weinrott and M. Saylor, 'Self-report of Crimes Committed by Sex Offenders'.

10 R. Sipe, *Sex, Priests and Power* (Cassell, London, 1995), p. 27.

NOTES

11 Calvin College Social Research Center, *A Survey of Abuse in the Christian Reformed Church* (Calvin College, Michigan, 1992).

12 B. Ogilvie and J. Daniluk, 'Common Themes in the Experiences of Mother-Daughter Incest: Survivors: Implications for Counseling', *Journal of Counseling and Development*, vol. 73, 1995, p. 598; D. Finkelhor and D. Russell, 'Women as Perpetrators', *Child Sexual Abuse: New Theory and Research*, D. Finkelhor (ed.) (Free Press, New York, 1984), ch. 11.

13 R. Wyre, Evidence to the Royal Commission on the New South Wales Police Service, (Paedophilia Inquiry), transcript, 26 April 1996.

14 N. Groth and A. Burgess, 'Sexual Trauma in the Life Histories of Rapists and Child Molesters', *Victimology*, vol. 4, 1979, pp. 10–16.

15 Petrovich and Templer (1984) cited in T. Cavanagh-Johnson, 'Female Child Perpetrators – Children Who Molest Other Children'; *Child Abuse and Neglect*, vol. 13, 1989, pp. 571–85.

16 F. Knopp and L. Lackey, *Female Sexual Abusers: A Summary of Data from 44 Treatment Providers* (Safer Society, Vermont, 1987).

17 Anonymous, 'The Greatest Taboo of All', *From Victim to Offender*, F. Briggs (ed.) (Allen and Unwin, Sydney, 1995), pp. 137–51.

18 G. Abel et al., 'Self-reported Sex Crimes of Nonincarcerated Paraphiliacs'.

19 D. Glasgow, L. Horne, R. Calam and A. Cox, 'Evidence, Incidence, Gender and Age in Sexual Abuse of Children Perpetrated by Children', *Child Abuse Review*, vol. 3, 1994, pp. 196–210.

20 T. Cavanagh Johnson, 'Child Perpetrators – Children Who Molest Other Children: Preliminary Findings', *Child Abuse and Neglect*, vol. 12, 1988, pp. 219–29.

21 T. Cavanagh Johnson, 'Female Child Perpetrators – Children Who Molest Other Children', *Child Abuse and Neglect*, vol. 13, 1989, pp. 571–85.

22 Ibid., p. 576.

23 T. Cavanagh-Johnson, 'Children Who Sexually Abuse Other Children: Research and Practice Issues', NSW Child Protection Council, Seminar, June 1996.

24 T. Cavanagh-Johnson, 'Understanding the Sexual Behaviors of Young Children', *SIECUS Report*, August/September 1991, pp. 8–15.

25 K. Wallis, 'Perspectives on Child Molesters', *From Victim to Offender*, F. Briggs (ed.) (Allen and Unwin, Sydney, 1995), pp. 1–17.

26 N. Groth, W. Hobson and T. Gary, 'The Child Molester: Clinical Observations', *Social Work and Child Sexual Abuse*, J. Conte and D. Shore (eds) (Haworth, New York, 1982), pp. 129–44.

27 L. Simon, B. Sales, A. Kazniac and A. Kahn, 'Characteristics of Child Molesters: Implications for the Fixated-Regressed Dichotomy', *Journal of Interpersonal Violence*, vol. 7, 1992, pp. 211–25.

28 J. Conte, 'The Incest Offender: An Overview and Introduction', *The*

Incest Perpetrator: A Family Member No One Wants to Treat, A. Horton, B. Johnson, L. Roundy and D. Williams (eds) (Sage, California, 1990), pp. 19–28.
29 Ibid.
30 M. Weinrott and M. Saylor, 'Self-report of Crimes Committed by Sex Offenders'.
31 A. Salter, *Transforming Trauma* (Sage, California, 1995), pp. 47–8.
32 American Psychiatric Association, *Diagnostic and Statistical Manual of Mental Disorders* (DSM-IV) (4th edn, 1994).
33 K. Freund and M. Kuban, 'Towards a Testable Developmental Model of Pedophilia: The Development of Erotic Age Preference', *Child Abuse and Neglect*, vol. 17, 1993, pp. 315–24.
34 J. Money, 'Pedophilia: A Specific Instance of New Phylism Theory as Applied to Paraphilic Lovemaps', *Pedophilia: Biosocial Dimenensions*, J. Feirman (ed.) (Springer-Verlag, New York, 1990), pp. 445–63.
35 W. Murphy and T. Smith, 'Sex Offenders Against Children: Empirical and Clinical Issues', *The APSAC Handbook of Child Maltreatment*, J. Briere, L. Berliner, J. Bulkley, C. Jenny and T. Reid (eds), Sage, California, 1990), p. 181; R. Garland and M. Dougher, 'The Abused/ Abuser Hypothesis of Child Sexual Abuse: A Critical Review of Theory and Research', *Pedophilia: Biosocial Dimensions*, J. Feirman (ed.) (Springer-Verlag, New York, 1990), pp. 488–509.
36 Anonymous, 'Unholy Orders', *From Victim to Offender*, F. Briggs (ed.) (Allen and Unwin, Sydney, 1995) p. 52.
37 Quoted in A. Salter, *Transforming Trauma* (Sage, California, 1995), p. 12.
38 Anonymous, 'A Priest Child Abuser Speaks', *Slayer of the Soul*, S. Rossetti (ed.) (Twenty-Third Publications, Connecticut, 1990) pp. 102, 108–9.
39 A. Jenkins, *Invitations to Responsibility* (Dulwich Centre, Adelaide, 1990) pp. 196–7.
40 A. Salter, *Transforming Trauma* (Sage, 1995), ch. 2.
41 E. Brongersma, 'A Defence of Sexual Liberty for all Age Groups', *Howard Journal of Criminal Justice*, vol. 27, 1988, p. 35. For responses to such arguments see M. Liddle, 'Child Sexual Abuse and Age of Consent Laws: A Response to Some Libertarian Arguments for Sexual Liberty', *Gender and Crime*, R. E. Dobash, R. P. Dobash and L. Noaks (eds) (University of Wales Press, Cardiff, 1995), pp. 313–39.
42 L. De Mause, 'The Universality of Incest', *Journal of Psychohistory*, vol. 19, 1991, pp. 126–9.
43 P. Sloane and E. Karpinski, 'Effects of Incest on the Participants' *American Journal of Orthopsychiatry*, vol. 12, 1942, pp. 666–73; L. Bender and A. Blau *American Journal of Orthopsychiatry*, vol. 7, 1937, pp. 500–18, cited in S. Rossetti, 'The Impact of Child Sexual Abuse on Attitudes Towards God and the Catholic Church', *Child Abuse and Neglect*, vol. 19, 1995, p. 1469.

44 D. Silva, 'Pedophilia: An Autobiography', *Pedophilia: Biosocial Dimensions*, J. Feirman (ed.) (Springer-Verlag, New York, 1990), p. 487.
45 N. Pollock and J. Hashmall, 'The Excuses of Child Molesters', *Behavioural Sciences and the Law*, vol. 9, 1991, pp. 53–9.

Chapter 4

1 J. Conte, S. Wolf and T. Smith, 'What Sexual Offenders Tell Us about Prevention Strategies', *Child Abuse and Neglect*, vol. 13, 1989, pp. 293–301.
2 Examples taken from E. Jones and P. Parkinson, 'Child Sexual Abuse, Access and the Wishes of Children', *International Journal of Law and the Family*, vol. 9, 1995, pp. 54–85.
3 J. Conte, S. Wolf and T. Smith, 'What Sexual Offenders Tell Us about Prevention Strategies', p. 297.
4 L. Berliner and J. Conte, 'The Process of Victimization: The Victims' Perspective', *Child Abuse and Neglect*, vol. 14, 1990, pp. 29–40.
5 A. Salter, *Transforming Trauma* (Sage, California, 1995), pp. 120–1.
6 L. Laing and A. Kamsler, 'Putting an End to Secrecy: Therapy with Mothers and Children Following Disclosure of Child Sexual Assault', *Ideas for Therapy with Sexual Abuse*, M. Durrant and C. White (eds) (Dulwich Centre Publications, Adelaide, 1990), p. 159.
7 J. Christiansen and R. Blake, 'The Grooming Process in Father-Daughter Incest', *The Incest Perpetrator*, A. Horton, B. Johnson, L. Roundy and D. Williams (eds), (Sage, California, 1990), p. 90.
8 R. Wyre, Evidence to the Royal Commission on the New South Wales Police Service, (Paedophilia Inquiry), transcript, 26 April 1996.
9 Anonymous, 'In Search of Love', *From Victim to Offender*, F. Briggs (ed.) (Allen and Unwin, Sydney, 1995), p. 32.
10 Issues about disclosure are discussed further in chapter 10.

Chapter 5

1 Lord Templeman in *Gillick v West Norfolk and Wisbech AHA* [1986] AC, p. 201.
2 For a discussion of the biological aspects see J. Feierman, 'A Biosocial Overview of Adult Human Sexual Behavior with Children and Adolescents', *Pedophilia: Biosocial Dimensions*, J. Feierman (ed.) (Springer-Verlag, New York, 1990), pp. 8–68.
3 V. Bullough, 'History in Adult Human Sexual Behavior with Children and Adolescents in Western Societies', *Pedophilia*, J. Feierman (ed.), pp. 69–90.

4 T. Sullivan, *Sexual Abuse and the Rights of Children: Reforming Canadian Law* (University of Toronto Press, Toronto, 1992).
5 Ibid., p. 154.
6 S. Rossetti and L. Lothstein, 'Myths of the Child Molester', *Slayer of the Soul*, S. Rossetti (ed.) (Twenty-Third Publications, Connecticut, 1990), pp. 14–16.
7 E. Loftus, 'The Reality of Repressed Memories', *American Psychologist*, vol. 48, 1993, pp. 518–19.
8 *Recovered Memories: The Report of the Working Party of the British Psychological Society* (January 1995), p. 19.
9 D. Lindsay and J. Read, 'Incest Resolution Psychotherapy and Memories of Childhood Sexual Abuse', *Applied Cognitive Psychology*, vol. 8, 1994, p. 294.
10 E. Bass and L. Davis, *The Courage to Heal* (Harper & Row, New York, 1988), p. 22.
11 D. Holmes, 'The Evidence for Repression: An Examination of Sixty Years of Research', *Repression and Dissociation: Implications for Personality, Theory, Psychopathology, and Health*, J. Singer (ed.) (University of Chicago Press, Chicago, 1990), pp. 85–102.
12 L. Meyer Williams, 'Recall of Childhood Trauma: A Prospective Study of Women's Memories of Child Sexual Abuse', *Journal of Consulting and Clinical Psychology*, vol. 62, 1994, pp. 167–76.
13 L. Meyer Williams, 'What Does it Mean to Forget About Child Sexual Abuse? A Reply to Loftus, Garry and Feldman (1994)', *Journal of Consulting and Clinical Psychology*, vol. 62, 1994, pp. 1183, 1184.
14 New International Version.
15 J. Weekes, S. Lynn, J. Green and J. Brentar, 'Pseudomemory in Hypnotized and Task-Motivated Subjects', *Journal of Abnormal Psychology*, vol. 101, 1992, pp. 356–60.
16 E. Loftus and H. Hoffman, 'Misinformation and Memory: The Creation of New Memories', *Journal of Experimental Psychology: General*, vol. 118, 1989, pp. 100–4.
17 U. Neisser and N. Harsch, 'Phantom Flashbulbs: False Recollections of Hearing the News about the Challenger', *Affect and Accuracy in Recall*, E. Winograd and U. Neisser (eds) (Cambridge University Press, New York, 1992), pp. 9–31.
18 For discussion see M. Yapko, *Suggestions of Abuse* (Simon and Schuster, New York, 1994).
19 D. Lindsay and J. Read, 'Incest Resolution Psychotherapy and Memories of Childhood Sexual Abuse', p. 294.
20 M. Harvey and J. Herman, 'Amnesia, Partial Amnesia and Delayed Recall among Adult Survivors of Childhood Trauma', *Consciousness and Cognition*, vol. 3, 1994, pp. 295–306.
21 M. Yapko, *Suggestions of Abuse*.

22 *Recovered Memories: The Report of the Working Party of the British Psychological Society*, pp. 24–5.

23 D. Finkelhor, L. Meyer Williams and N. Burns, *Nursery Crimes: Sexual Abuse in Day Care* (Sage, California, 1988), p. 59.

24 W. Young, R. Sachs, B. Braun and R. Watkins, 'Patients Reporting Ritual Abuse in Childhood: A Clinical Syndrome. Report of 37 Cases', *Child Abuse and Neglect*, vol. 15, 1991, pp. 181–9.

25 For the Oude Pekela case see F. Jonker and P. Jonker-Bakker, 'Experiences with Ritualist Child Sexual Abuse: A Case Study from the Netherlands', *Child Abuse and Neglect*, vol. 15, 1991, pp. 191–6.

26 *Rochdale Borough Council v BW and Others* [1991] FCR 705; *The Report of the Inquiry into the Removal of Children from Orkney in February 1991* (HMSO, Edinburgh, 1992).

27 See for example D. Lotto, 'On Witches and Witch Hunts: Ritual and Satanic Cult Abuse', *Journal of Psychohistory*, vol. 21, 1994, pp. 373–96.

28 The journal in question was *Child Abuse and Neglect* and the articles were those by Young et al. and Jonker and Jonker-Bakker cited above.

29 J. Goodwin, 'Human Vectors of Trauma: Illustrations from the Marquis De Sade', *Rediscovering Childhood Trauma*, J. Goodwin (ed.) (American Psychiatric Press, Washington DC, 1993), pp. 95–110.

30 B. Braun, audiotape, quoted in D. Lotto, 'On Witches and Witch Hunts: Ritual and Satanic Cult Abuse', p. 389.

31 J. Friesen, *Uncovering the Mystery of MPD* (Here's Life Publishers, California, 1991), p. 90.

32 Ibid., pp. 96–7.

33 K. Lanning, 'Ritual Abuse: A Law Enforcement View or Perspective', *Child Abuse and Neglect*, vol. 15, 1991, pp. 171–3; F. Putnam, 'The Satanic Ritual Abuse Controversy', *Child Abuse and Neglect*, vol. 15, 1991, pp. 175–9.

34 K. Lanning, 'Ritual Abuse'.

35 J. Fontaine, *The Extent and Nature of Organised and Ritual Abuse: Research Findings* (HMSO, London, 1994), pp. 23–4.

36 Ibid. p. 24.

37 D. Finkelhor, L. Meyer Williams and N. Burns, *Nursery Crimes*, p. 62.

38 D. Jones, 'Ritualism and Child Sexual Abuse', *Child Abuse and Neglect*, vol. 15, 1991, pp. 163–70.

Chapter 6

1 P. Mullen, J. Martin, J. Anderson, S. Romans and P. Herbison, 'Childhood Sexual Abuse and Mental Health in Adult Life', *British Journal of Psychiatry*, vol. 163, 1993, pp. 721–32.

2 K. Kendall-Tackett, L. Meyer Williams and D. Finkelhor, 'Impact of Sexual Abuse on Children: A Review and Synthesis of Recent Empirical Studies', *Psychological Bulletin*, vol. 113, 1993, pp. 164, 173.
3 A. Browne and D. Finkelhor, 'Initial and Long-term Effects: A Review of the Research,' *A Sourcebook on Child Sexual Abuse*, D. Finkelhor (ed.) (Sage, California, 1986), pp. 143–79.
4 Cathy Ann Matthews, *Breaking Through* (Sydney, Albatross, 1990), p. 114.
5 A. Salter, *Transforming Trauma* (California, Sage, 1995), pp. 175–6.
6 Ibid., p. 118.
7 J. Bradshaw, *Healing the Shame That Binds You* (Health Communications, Florida, 1988).
8 Ibid., p. 10.
9 This account comes from E. Jones and P. Parkinson, 'Child Sexual Abuse, Access and the Wishes of Children', *International Journal of Law and the Family*, vol. 9, 1995, pp. 71–2.
10 A. Salter, *Transforming Trauma*, pp. 123–4.
11 See J. Hanson, *Rape as Bereavement* (Grove, UK, 1992).
12 J. Herman, *Trauma and Recovery* (HarperCollins, London, 1992), p. 34.
13 D. Finkelhor, G. Hotaling, I. Lewis and C. Smith, 'Sexual Abuse and Its Relationship to Later Sexual Satisfaction, Marital Status, Religion and Attitudes', *Journal of Interpersonal Violence*, vol. 4, 1989, pp. 379–99.
14 A. Salter, *Transforming Trauma*, p. 118.
15 M. Silbert, 'Treatment of Prostitute Victims of Sexual Assault', *Victims of Sexual Aggression: Treatment of Children, Women and Men*, I. Stuart and J. Greer (eds) (Van Nostrand Reinhold, New York, 1964), p. 253.
16 D. Finkelhor and A. Browne, 'Sexual Abuse: Initial and Long-term Effects: A Conceptual Framework', *A Sourcebook on Child Sexual Abuse*, D. Finkelhor (ed.) (Sage, California, 1986).
17 S. Sgroi (ed.), *Handbook of Clinical Intervention in Child Sexual Abuse* (Lexington Books, Toronto, 1982), p. 16.
18 D. Finkelhor, L. Meyer Williams and N. Burns, *Sexual Abuse in Day Care*, (Sage, California, 1988).
19 K. Kendall-Tackett, L. Meyer Williams and D. Finkelhor, 'Impact of Sexual Abuse on Children'.
20 Isaiah 53:3.
21 Luke 4:16–21.

Chapter 7

1 D. Finkelhor, G. Hotaling, I. Lewis and C. Smith, 'Sexual Abuse and Its Relationship to Later Sexual Satisfaction, Marital Status, Religion and Attitudes', *Journal of Interpersonal Violence*, vol. 4, 1989, pp. 379–99; D. Kane, S. Cheston and J. Greer, 'Perceptions of God by Survivors of

Childhood Sexual Abuse: An Exploratory Study in an Underresearched Area', *Journal of Psychology and Theology*, vol. 21, 1993, pp. 228–37.

2 J. Herman, *Trauma and Recovery* (Harper Collins, London, 1992), p. 51.

3 J. Feldmeth and M. Finley, *We Weep for Ourselves and Our Children* (Harper, San Francisco, 1990), pp. 99–100.

4 J. Hanson, *Rape as Bereavement* (Grove, UK, 1992), p. 20.

5 For discussion of several distortions of Christian thought see C. Holderhead Heggen, *Sexual Abuse in Christian Homes and Churches* (Herald Press, Pennsylvania, 1993), ch. 5.

6 See for example A. Imbens and I. Jonker, *Christianity and Incest* (Burns and Oates, UK, 1992), p. 190.

7 These are published in various books. See for example M. Pellauer, B. Chester and J. Boyajian (eds) (Harper, San Francisco 1987), pp. 223–47; C. Holderhead Heggen, op. cit., ch. 9.

Chapter 8

1 *King Lear*, IV: vii. The expression is also used in Chaucer's *The Knight's Tale*.

2 D. Allender, *The Wounded Heart* (CWR, UK, 1991), p. 15.

3 P. Bean, *Punishment: A Philosophical and Criminological Inquiry* (Martin Robertson, UK, 1981), p. 99.

4 Pre-trial Diversion of Offenders Programme, Sydney, NSW.

5 P. Horsfield, *Forgiveness and Reconciliation in Situations of Sexual Assault* (Uniting Church in Australia, 1994), p. 4.

6 Ibid., p. 7.

7 Dale Tolliday, Pre-trial Diversion of Offenders Programme, Sydney, personal communication, August 1995.

8 Pre-trial Diversion of Offenders Programme.

9 M. Fortune, paper given at First Australian and New Zealand Conference on Sexual Exploitation by Health Professionals, Psychotherapists and Clergy, Sydney, April 1996.

10 A. Bustanoby, 'When You Can't Forgive', *Carer and Counsellor*, vol. 4, no. 3, 1994, pp. 22–6.

Chapter 9

1 M. Fortune, paper given at First Australian and New Zealand Conference on Sexual Exploitation by Health Professionals, Psychotherapists and Clergy, Sydney, April 1996.

2 *Keppel Bus Co Ltd v Ahmad* [1974] 1 WLR 1082.

3 *Petterson v Royal Oak Hotel Ltd* [1948] NZLR 136. See generally

Winfield and Jolowicz on Tort, W. Rogers (ed.) (14th edn; Sweet & Maxwell, London, 1994), pp. 604–8; F. Rose, 'Liability for an Employee's Assaults' (1977) 40 MLR 420–39.

4 K. Bussey, 'The Competence of Child Witnesses', *The Practice of Child Protection: Australian Approaches*, G. Calvert, A. Ford and P. Parkinson (eds) (Hale and Iremonger, Sydney, 1992), pp.. 69–85.

5 D. Jones and J. McGraw, 'Reliable and Fictitious Accounts of Sexual Abuse of Children', *Journal of Interpersonal Violence*, vol. 2, 1987, p. 27.

6 D. Jones and A. Seig, 'Child Sexual Abuse Allegations in Custody or Visitation Cases: A Report of 20 Cases', *Sexual Abuse Allegations in Custody and Visitation Cases*, B. Nicholson and J. Buckley (eds) (American Bar Association, Washington, 1988), p. 22; P. Parkinson, 'Child Sexual Abuse Allegations in the Family Court', *Australian Journal of Family Law*, vol. 4, 1990, pp. 60–84.

7 K. McFarlane, 'Child Sexual Abuse Allegations in Divorce Proceedings', *Sexual Abuse of Young Children*, K. McFarlane and J. Waterman (eds) (Guildford Press, New York, 1986), p. 121.

8 G. Blush and K. Ross, 'Sexual Allegations in Divorce: The SAID Syndrome', *Conciliation Courts Review*, vol. 25, 1987, p. 7.

9 It used to be the case if the child was too young to take an oath, his or her testimony had to be corroborated by sworn testimony from someone else. In most jurisdictions, this rule of evidence has been abolished, although the judge may still warn the jury about the dangers of convicting on the uncorroborated evidence of a child.

10 *DPP v P* [1991] 2 AC 447.

11 J. Spencer and R. Flin, *The Evidence of Children* (2nd edn; Blackstone, London, 1993), ch. 8.

12 Anglican Diocese of Sydney, Protocol, June 1996.

13 Children (Care and Protection) Act 1987 (NSW) s.22(2) excludes ministers.

14 H. Berman, *Law and Revolution* (Harvard University Press, Massachussetts, 1983), pp. 66, 94–113.

15 P. Parkinson, *Tradition and Change in Australian Law* (Law Book Co., Sydney, 1994), pp. 35, 88–9.

16 B. Coldrey, *The Scheme: The Christian Brothers and Childcare in Western Australia* (Argyle-Pacific, Australia, 1993), p. 396.

17 Ibid., p. 399.

18 L. Buzzard and L. Eck, *Tell it to the Church* (David Cook, Illinois, 1982).

19 For example the Children (Care and Protection) Act 1987 (NSW) s.22.

20 *Gartside v Outram* (1856) 26 LJ Ch 113; *Corrs Pavey Whiting & Byrne v Collector of Customs (Vic)* (1987) 14 FCR 434, Gummow J at 452–6.

21 *Commonwealth v John Fairfax & Sons Ltd* (1980) 147 CLR 39 at 57.

22 *W v Edgell* [1990] 1 All ER 835.

23 *Brown v Brooks*, 18 August 1988, NSW Supreme Court, cited in *Australian Health and Medical Law Reporter* 27–770.

24 Applicable in ACT, NSW, Victoria, Tasmania and the Northern Territory; J. D. Heydon, *Cross on Evidence* (6th Australian edn; Butterworths, Sydney, 1996); S. McNicol, *Law of Privilege* (Law Book Co., Sydney, 1992).

25 *Normanshaw v Normanshaw and Measham* (1893) 69 LT 468; *Wheeler v Marchant* (1881) 17 Ch D 675, Lord Jessel MR at 681.

26 M. Fortune, 'Confidentiality and Mandatory Reporting: A Clergy Dilemma?', M. Pellauer, B. Chester and J. Boyajian, *Sexual Assault and Abuse: A Handbook for Clergy and Religious Professionals* (Harper, San Francisco, 1987), pp. 198–205.

27 Cited in C. Cobley, *Child Abuse and the Law* (Cavendish, London, 1995), p. 112.

28 Ibid., p. 113.

29 This discussion is taken from E. Jones and P. Parkinson, 'Child Sexual Abuse, Access and the Wishes of Children', *International Journal of Law and the Family*, vol. 9, 1995, pp. 54–85.

30 S. Sgroi, 'An Approach to Case Management', *Handbook of Clinical Intervention in Child Sexual Abuse*, S. Sgroi (ed.) (Lexington Books, Toronto, 1982), ch. 3.

31 A. Salter, 'Treating Child Sex Offenders and Victims', paper given at the National Conference on Child Sexual Abuse, Melbourne, March 1994.

32 L. Laing and A. Kamsler, 'Putting an End to Secrecy: Therapy with Mothers and Children Following Disclosure of Child Sexual Assault', *Ideas for Therapy with Sexual Abuse*, M. Durrant and C. White (eds) (Dulwich Centre Publications, Adelaide 1990), p. 159.

Chapter 10

1 T. Cavanagh-Johnson, 'Children Who Sexually Abuse Other Children: Research and Practice Issues', Seminar, NSW Child Protection Council, Sydney, June 1996.

2 T. Sorensen and B. Snow, 'How Children Tell: The Process of Disclosure in Sexual Abuse', *Child Welfare*, vol. lxx, 1991, pp. 3–15.

3 Ibid.

4 Diocese of Southwell, *Children and Young People First* (1996), p. 16.

5 *Furnell v Whangarei High Schools Board* [1973] AC 660; *Lewis v Heffer* [1978] 1 WLR 1061.

6 *Dixon v Commonwealth* (1981) 55 FLR 34.

7 Church of England House of Bishops' Policy on Child Abuse, July 1995, p. 13.

8 For American research see for example, M. Martone, P. Jaudes and M. Cavins, 'Criminal Prosecution of Child Sexual Abuse Cases', *Child Abuse and Neglect*, vol. 20, 1996, pp. 457–64.

9 *S v The Queen* (1989) 168 CLR 266.
10 Mark and Deborah Brennan, *Strange Language* (3rd edn; Riverina Centre, Australia, 1988).
11 *Re G* [1988] FCR 440.
12 *M v M* (1988) 166 CLR 69.
13 *Re H and others (minors) (sexual abuse: standard of proof)* [1996] 1 All ER 1, Lord Nicholls at 19–22.

Chapter 11

1 M. Fortune, *Is Nothing Sacred?* (Harper, San Francisco, 1989); N. and T. Ormerod, *When Ministers Sin* (Millennium Books, Sydney, 1995).
2 Uniting Church in Australia, *Procedures for Use When Complaints of Sexual Abuse are Made Against Ministers* (1994).
3 *Briginshaw v Briginshaw* (1938) 60 CLR 336.
4 *Re H and others (minors) (sexual abuse: standard of proof)* [1996] 1 All ER 1, Lord Nicholls at 18–19.
5 *Re a Solicitor* [1993] QB 69; *Bhandari v Advocates Committee* [1956] 3 All ER 742; *Lanford v General Medical Council* [1990] 1 AC 13 at 19–20. But see *McAllister v General Medical Council* [1993] AC 388 at 399; *R v Hampshire County Council ex p Ellerton* [1985] 1 WLR 749.
6 *Reifek v McElroy* (1965) 112 CLR 517 at 521; *Bannister v Walton* (1993) 30 NSWLR 699, special leave to appeal denied.

Chapter 12

1 *Safe from Harm*, (Home Office, London, 1993).
2 Diocese of Lichfield, *Children: The Churches' Care* (1993); Diocese of Southwell, *Children and Young People First* (1996).
3 See chapter 11.
4 *Safe to Grow* (Baptist Union of Great Britain, 1994), p. 28.
5 B. Anderson, *When Child Abuse Comes to Church* (Bethany House, Minneapolis, 1992), pp. 158–60.
6 D. Goodwin, *Child Abuse in the Church* (Camp David Ministries, New Zealand, 1992).
7 Ibid., p. 31 and appendix: Standard of Conduct for Children and Youth Leaders.
8 Ibid., p. 31.

Further Reading and Resources

There are many excellent books on child sexual abuse. The books below represent a selection of the books written specifically from a Christian perspective, and which, in the main, cover different ground from this book. Some of the books listed also address other issues, such as the abuse of an adult pastoral relationship by clergy.

Child Sexual Abuse and Christian Faith

Bill Anderson, *When Child Abuse Comes to Church* (Bethany House, Minneapolis, 1992).

Hilary Cashman, *Christianity and Child Sexual Abuse* (SPCK, London, 1993).

Peter Gibbs, *Child Sexual Abuse: A Concern for the Church?* (Grove Books, UK, 1992).

David Goodwin, *Child Abuse in the Church* (Camp David Ministries, New Zealand, 1992).

Carolyn Holderread Heggen, *Sexual Abuse in Christian Homes and Churches* (Herald Press, Pennsylvania, 1993).

Alice Huskey, *Stolen Childhood* (IVP, Illinois, 1990).

Annie Imbens and Ineke Jonker, *Christianity and Incest* (Burns & Oates, UK, 1992).

Mary Pellauer, Barbara Chester and Jane Boyajian, *Sexual Assault and Abuse: A Handbook for Clergy and Religious Professionals* (Harper, San Francisco, 1987).

Sexual Abuse by Clergy
Marie Fortune, *Is Nothing Sacred?* (Harper, San Francisco, 1989).
Stanley Grenz and Roy Bell, *Betrayal of Trust* (IVP, Illinois, 1995).
Neil and Thea Ormerod, *When Ministers Sin* (Millennium Books, Sydney, 1995).
Richard Sipe, *Sex, Priests and Power* (Cassell, London, 1995).

Healing from Sexual Abuse
Dan Allender, *The Wounded Heart* (CWR, UK, 1991).
Joanne Feldmeth and Midge Finley, *We Weep for Ourselves and Our Children* (Harper, San Francisco, 1990).
Muriel Green and Anne Townsend, *Hidden Treasure* (Darton, Longman and Todd, London, 1994).
Maxine Hancock and Karen Mains, *Child Sexual Abuse: A Hope for Healing* (Highland, UK, 1987).
Lynn Heitritter and Jeanette Vought, *Helping Victims of Sexual Abuse* (Bethany House, Minneapolis, 1989).
Cathy Anne Matthews, *Breaking Through* (Albatross, Sydney, 1990).
Teo Van Der Weele, *From Shame to Peace* (Monarch, UK, 1995).

Autobiographical
Tracy Hansen, *Seven for a Secret* (Triangle, London, 1991).
Rebecca Newman, *Releasing the Scream* (Hodder & Stoughton, London, 1994).

Where to go for help
If you are seeking advice as a survivor of child sexual abuse, you will find the following organisations helpful:
Christian Survivors of Sexual Abuse, BM - CSSA, London WC1N 3XX, UK (this is the *full* address)
Advocates for Survivors of Child Abuse, PO Box 842, Darlinghurst, NSW 2101, Australia; phone/fax: 02 9331 2487

Index

Rights of children, 228–30
Ritual abuse, 72, 100–108

Screening, 258–61, 267
Secrecy, 27, 176, 193–5
Sexual abuse of children
  as assault, 9
  as sin, 26–8
  definition, 9, 17
  in Scripture, 14–15
  of boys, 3, 21–6
  of girls, 17–21
  prevalence, 16–23
  signs of, 202–204
  types, 10

Silence of victims, 22–3, 25, 58,
  67–70, 206–7, 258
Spiritualising, 196–8
Survivors, 138–9
Suspension, 215–17

Tamar, 14–15, 120
Truthfulness of children, 179–82

Unacceptable risk test, 230–3

Victimisation, 57–70
Victims, selection of, 57–9

Wrongful dismissal, 229, 233, 247